GOING HIGHER
The Story of Man and Altitude

JOHN T. MAHER
1932–1983

Tireless colleague, inspired researcher
Role model and friend to many
He is sorely missed

GOING HIGHER
The Story of Man and Altitude

by
Charles S. Houston, M.D.

Illustrations by
Gary Nelson

Published by
Charles S. Houston, M.D.
Burlington, Vermont

Manufactured in the United States of America
by Queen City Printers Inc., Burlington, Vermont

LCN 83-081995
ISBN 0-9612246-0-6

Cover Photo: Mr. Tsuneo Shigehiro

ABOUT THIS BOOK

If writing costs a great deal of time, effort and discouragement, it also may bring many rewards and much satisfaction and so it has been with this book. For five years I stumbled through several drafts; when one finally seemed adequate it was rejected by many publishers and agents: "Too long"; "Too short"; "Too medical"; "Not scientific enough", they said, or most often "Who will read it?"

In short—failure. The decision to publish it myself was an act of faith—and defiance—which I could ill afford. Thank goodness I did it: the whole experience has been wonderfully refreshing, from working with designers and printers to getting many letters and calls from strangers and friends. As the first edition of 5000 sold out, I began to revise and enlarge, and after a time produced this book, about half new, half old material, considerably expanded and I hope better.

But high altitude and the problems it can cause affect only a tiny number of people, so why bother? Isn't it an insignificant problem compared to automobile accidents, alcohol, environmental posions and the looming nuclear armageddon? Not quite: the number of people engaged in mountaineering, flying, skiing and ballooning, or working in the mountains has been increasing rapidly in the last decade putting more and more people at risk from altitude illness—a preventable problem. Millions of sick or injured patients suffer from conditions that deprive them of a normal supply of oxygen even at sea level.

These all add up to a lot of people who are (or should be) vitally concerned with how their bodies work, and why, like all of us, they are totally dependent on oxygen, and what happens when the supply is threatened. Where can they learn about such things? Though knowledge may be improving, is understanding keeping pace?

The entire world is going through a tremendous social and technological revolution, greater and swifter than any before. So global is its sweep that we find it hard to comprehend or accept. Yet everything we see, hear, and experience is changing.

And the changes are even greater and faster in the less developed world.

We are able to peer into the most intimate crevices of living organisms and to look at the immensity of outer space, though we are unable to comprehend either. We can collect, analyze, transmit, and store tremendous amounts of information with the speed of light, but we know more than we fully understand, and we don't use wisely all we know.

Meanwhile, in every human activity, we see new achievements. Hundreds run a mile in less than four minutes; marathon records fall every year. In the last three decades not only has the highest point on earth been reached, but the feat has been repeated by more than a hundred persons, at least a dozen of them breathing only the air about them.

This book deals with our fascination for uncovering more and more secrets of life and living, such as those which have made possible these scientific and physical feats. We can watch a human ovum grow into a newborn babe; we can predict the wellness and sex of the fetus, anticipate and even occasionally correct its defects. We have "cracked the genetic code" and can manipulate its parts, and we seem close to understanding mysteries like slow viruses, cancer, and environmental poisoning which were either unknown or elusive a decade ago.

Still, our situation is complicated. As science advances with blinding speed, it is surrounded by a confusing cloud of new words, concepts, and capabilities which are difficult for the specialist, and almost impossible for the average person to grasp. If we cannot understand what is happening in science, how can we use it appropriately?

It seems to me that a physician should be involved not only with diagnosis and management of illness, but also in helping people to understand how and why illness begins, and how their bodies function and can be tuned to function better. Better health requires better understanding; prevention depends upon awareness of risks and benefits. Wellness is more than the absence of disease.

So I wrote this book to help the average person understand

the intricate mechanisms of the human body, and how its crucial parts work or fail to work when deprived of essential oxygen. Though I never pretended to be a research scientist, this is a subject I have long been familiar with, on mountains and in laboratories and I longed to explain it clearly to others.

It is not easy to write about modern science in terms the nonscientist will enjoy and understand, nor is it easy to separate what we know for sure from what we think reasonably certain. Scientists far more distinguished than I disagree about some 'facts' and argue over competing theories. Finding understandable words to replace 'medi-speak' is not always easy, and one can oversimplify or overlook important areas. But I thought it better to err than not to try at all.

The history of science so fascinates me that I may have included too much, but I strongly believe that those who are ignorant of the past will be less able to deal with the future. It is both inspiring and humbling to see what those who preceded us were able to do with their limited resources. As Santayana wrote "We must welcome the future, remembering that soon it will be the past, and we must respect the past, knowing that once it was all that was humanly possible." Those who find my enthusiasm for the past uninteresting will find plenty of nourishment in the larger part of the book that deals with the present and future.

This is not a technical book nor does it pretend to be an encyclopedia or text. I chose to examine only the parts of human physiology and anatomy most intimately concerned with oxygen. I also chose to try for clarity at the expense of completeness: many sections in the book could be far longer and more complex—and might then be unintelligible to the people I want most to reach. I have tried to be as scientific as I must, but as simple as I might. Above all I want a book which will be read and enjoyed by many people who may be at risk from lack of oxygen caused by altitude or illness.

I am very very grateful to the many people who gave me suggestions and encouragement. Any remaining mistakes and omissions are solely my own. It has been a pleasure to work with designer Craig Dicken (Battery Graphics), Alan Schillhammer

(Queen City Printers), and illustrator Gary Nelson (University of Vermont). I thank Brian Lawlor and Akio Horiuchi and members of the Mt. Logan High Altitude Physiology Study for letting me use some of their color photographs. And I am most grateful to my wife who has suffered my aberrations, if not gladly at least patiently.

Charles S. Houston, M.D.
Burlington, Vermont
July 1983

ABOUT THIS REVISION

Even before finishing GOING HIGH I realized that new data, new concepts, and new experiences were accumulating so rapidly that some form of update would soon be desirable, even necessary. At the time I thought a simple pamphlet would suffice—but this quickly proved inadequate, and I began to rewrite most of the book, though not without some trepidation.

Quite a few things have been happening which I feel make it desirable to revise what I wrote in 1980. There is a tremendous surge of interest in mountaineering, especially on the highest peaks and without supplementary oxygen and in 'alpine style'. Ballooning (which was all the rage two centuries ago), and soaring have become increasingly popular: a hang-glider soared from the 25,000 foot shoulder of K-2 down to Base camp. Recreational skiing and trekking attract hundreds of thousands—probably millions—to lower but potentially dangerous altitudes.

As a result more people are at risk and even though more of them know something about altitude, too many avoidable illnesses and deaths still occur.

But this is not all. Hypoxia has become fashionable. There is growing interest in the similarities between healthy mountaineers on high mountains, and persons with damaged lungs, paralyzed muscles, failing hearts and other impediments to normal oxygen supply at sea level. In addition, the new technologies make possible scrutiny of processes almost completely inaccessible a few years ago.

Consider the flood of scientific papers, for instance. The Cumulative Medical Index, under the listings "Altitude, high", "Anoxemia" and "Anoxia", showed 209 titles in 1963, 291 in 1973, while in the first six months of 1983 there were 241, which may come to almost 500 for the entire year.

Many of these do not concern man—at least so far as we can see today. The majority are not easily read by the non-scientist and indeed are written in a language foreign to those who might benefit the most. It is difficult enough for the scientist to distinguish "know for sure" from "perhaps", and impossible for the lay person. These considerations led me, not to a supplement, but to a thorough revision, trying to make the most recent advances in science easily available and helpful to the people who may need them.

Revision was almost harder than the original effort. Choosing what to include while trying to be thorough and accurate and still intelligible was very difficult. I see many omissions — as others surely will, but I hope not too many mistakes. It was fun to do, and encouragement from many made it even more so. Though the book may be of most interest to climbers, skiers and trekkers, I hope many others will enjoy and learn from it, as I have in writing it.

Charles S. Houston, M.D.
Burlington, Vermont
July 1983

INDEX OF ILLUSTRATIONS

TABLE OF CONTENTS

Chapter One
MEN AND MOUNTAINS

Dreams of rising far above the earth have been with us for as long as time and there appears no limit to how far from earth man can go—so high in fact that the idea of "height" loses all meaning. We can send probes to outermost space, land men on the moon, or send them to work for months in spaceships hundreds of miles above us. Almost two hundred persons have reached the highest point on earth, at least a dozen of them breathing only air. Free gliders soar to thirty to forty thousand feet, and hundreds of thousands play on high mountains where the air is thin enough to harm them.

But man like other mammals is totally dependent on oxygen for survival and no substitute has been or is likely to be found. If the supply is sharply reduced the delicate machinery of mind and body falters; if interrupted completely for more than six minutes the brain is irreparably damaged and death is near. To reach the highest summits mountaineers must allow time for the body to adjust to less oxygen, but even with superb acclimatization, on the top of Everest man is at his utmost limits, and in the near vacuum of space, travellers must be coccooned in familiar earth-like air. But the high Himalayas and space are not for every one, and even at much lower altitude, illness and sometimes death strike the incautious.

A healthy 38 year old man drove from his home at 5,200 feet to 9,600 feet for a weekend of tennis. On Saturday he was somewhat short of breath but kept up with his peers. That night his shortness of breath grew worse and he coughed a great deal. On Sunday he was able to play only briefly before the shortness of breath alarmed him so much that he drove home, where he still was short of breath. On Monday morning, coughing up frothy bloody sputum, he was admitted to hospital where a diagnosis of high altitude pulmonary edema was made. He recovered within twenty-four hours.

A young teacher drove from sea level to 8,400 feet in forty-eight hours and spent two days there. During the next four days he and his friends, carrying fifty pound packs, skied slowly up to 10,500 feet although he soon developed a headache which grew worse each day. On the fourth day he had trouble breathing and could barely travel. That night his companions noticed a rattling sound when he breathed and he was barely conscious. When a rescue helicopter arrived on the sixth morning he was comatose and on arrival at hospital was found to have severe pulmonary edema (fluid in both lungs), hemorrhages in both eyes, and evidence of brain damage. He regained consciousness slowly and was discharged after five days. Since this incident he has several times climbed slowly to 11,000 feet without difficulty.

A healthy man walked from 5,000 to 16,000 feet in five days. There he became very tired, developed a severe headache, and had difficulty keeping his balance. He became increasingly short of breath. He descended to 14,000 feet with difficulty and rested for three days, but his condition deteriorated and he was air-lifted to hospital where he remained for eleven days under inten-sive treatment. He had brain and pulmonary edema due to altitude and hemorrhages in the retina of each eye. Complica-tions developed and he was not fully recovered when dis-charged.

A 36 year old woman walked from 1,000 to 7,300 feet in one week and during the next twelve days relayed loads up to 17,200 feet where she developed a severe headache, swelling of the face, great pressure in her chest and the feeling that she could not take in enough air. She had no cough. She went down to 14,200 feet, took medication, and improved enough to climb back to 17,200 feet where she spent the next week quietly before going to the 21,000 foot summit.

A middle aged dentist reached 9,600 feet six hours after leav-ing home at sea level. That evening he felt as though he had flu and developed slight fever, nausea and diarrhea. Next morning he was very weak, short of breath and was coughing severely. He was taken down to 8,000 feet but did not improve. Next day he grew worse despite antibiotics prescribed by telephone. He became irrational during the night and died at dawn about sixty hours after leaving sea level. Post-mortem X-ray showed exten-sive pulmonary edema, but a complication (Legionnaire's Disease) was suspected though not provable.

Many hundred otherwise healthy people have problems like these each year while skiing or climbing or hiking above 9-10,000 feet anywhere in the world. Scores die needlessly of such easily preventable illness. Thousands of people trek or climb in Nepal each year and too many of them are sickened enough by altitude to turn back without completing their journey. Yet thousands of climbers have done technically difficult routes and stayed for weeks above 20,000 feet and even much higher without illness. Though far from as strong as at sea level, they have coped with lack of oxygen through the marvellously intricate adaptive processes which — given time — allow mountaineers to function remarkably well on the upper slopes of Everest breathing only the thin air about them.

Lack of oxygen also causes problems for a much larger population than climbers: hundreds of thousands of patients have chronic lung diseases like emphysema which prevent normal oxygenation of the blood and produce several signs and symptoms much like altitude illness. Not a few persons are knocked out and even permanently crippled or killed by accidents which impair their oxygen supply.

A woman unexpectedly developed respiratory arrest during a simple operation. Resuscitation was delayed and full respiration and circulation were not restored for about seven minutes. Though she survived, months later she was still unconscious.

An 18 year old man injured in a car accident was brought to hospital unconscious, barely breathing and blue. Full oxygenation was restored after some difficulty and he improved for a time only to develop evidence of brain swelling and pulmonary edema and die twenty-four hours later.

A heavy smoker gradually developed shortness of breath and cough over a period of many years and became partially disabled. Then he developed pneumonia involving more than half of his lungs. His condition deteriorated rapidly and he became uncooperative and hostile, hallucinating badly, and sinking into a coma before he died.

A housewife, found unconscious from carbon monoxide poisoning, showed evidence of brain damage and had hemorrhages in both eyes. She did not regain consciousness before dying from pulmonary and brain edema.

All these persons had one thing in common: lack of oxygen. For some the problems came from going up only a few thousand feet, while for others the normal supply was drastically reduced and the consequences were much more severe. Different people respond somewhat differently to altitude, and even the same person may react well on one occasion but poorly on another. Some can climb quite high quite fast and get away with it, while others less fortunate are victims even though they climb slowly. The majority who allow ample time to acclimatize can survive and work strenuously at altitudes that cause severe symptoms or even rapid unconsciousness in the unadapted. Patients at sea level can tolerate surprisingly low oxygen levels in their blood if the disease or malfunction comes on slowly, but like the healthy climber, if their oxygen supply is too rapidly decreased, signs and symptoms much like those due to altitude occur.

To fully appreciate why oxygen is essential to the life of mammals and how its lack affects almost every function, it is helpful to look at some fundamental physiology and to follow the stages by which oxygen reaches the living cells. Equally important are the mechanisms by which carbon dioxide — one product of metabolism — is cast out of the body and the subtle integrations by which the body acclimatizes. This review begins with a look at the evolution of our understanding of the physics of the atmosphere and the physiology of our bodies, for the story of man at altitude is interwoven with his exploration of the world about him and the world within.

* * * * * * *

Thousands of years ago when the known world was limited to the horizon a man could see, survival depended on foraging and hunting, and it is not surprising that these early people had little time or reason to explore mountainous country where food and shelter were scarce and weather hostile. Just staying alive was a full time job. Superstition or religion also kept people off the mountains. To the ancient Greeks mountains were home to many gods and decent respect (and perhaps fear) kept them from intruding. Mount Olympus was the majestic home of Zeus, his wife Hera, and their multitude of children, where they feasted on ambrosia between heroic (and often amorous) visits to the mortals below. Long before the Greeks the patriarch

Noah is reputed to have landed on top of 16,400 foot Mount Ararat (the first and only mountaineer to have reached a summit by boat) in circumstances unlikely to recur. Legend describes him as miserably seasick and perhaps suffering from a hangover: whether or not altitude bothered him or his passengers no record remains, but as someone has reminded me, during the flood he was actually at sea level! In the dim past of which we have found traces there were scattered settlements at 12,000 feet on the Andean Altiplano. Fine stone buildings, huge stores of wood and other relics have been identified as high as 20,000 feet on the Andean crest, strongly suggesting that four or five centuries ago Andean man could, and in fact did stay for long periods at altitudes which man does not tolerate for very long today.

One surviving story concerns the philosopher Empedocles a remarkable man who climbed Mt. Aetna to study its volcanic action and also to test his theory that air was compressible—which he showed by experiments with a closed jar, anticipating by two thousand years firm proof of such a revolutionary concept. He was a social reformer and visionary as well as a physiologist who studied the heart and circulation, the inner ear, and advanced a remarkable theory to explain vision. He is said to have leaped or fallen into the seething crater—which allegedly spewed out his brass slippers but kept the philosopher. Did these ancients notice the altitude? Francis Bacon wrote:

"The ancients had already noted that on the summit of Mount Olympus the air was so rare that in order to climb to it one must take with him sponges wet with vinegar and water and place them on the nostrils and mouth since the air, because of its rarity, did not suffice for respiration."

Bacon was quoting Livy who referred to Aristotle but there is no such statement about the rarity of high altitude air in Aristotle's surviving works. Was this perhaps a very early observation that air is 'thinner' at altitude, or did Livy or Bacon mean that it was more dry, or is it all a charming myth? Hippocrates, though he wrote a good deal about "good vapors" and about "pestilential air" and their effect on health, does not mention altitude.

About the same time as Empedocles' leap, Xenophon was

FIGURE I:
WAS NOAH THE FIRST SEA-FARING MOUNTAINEER?

Today Mount Ararat is 16,945 feet, and its lesser neighbor 13,000 feet high but were they so in Biblical days? The story of Noah and his voyage of salvation is woven into our history, but it is far from clear that he landed (if at all) on such a high summit. If he did, he certainly set an enduring altitude record! Presumably the bodies in the foreground of this old print were victims of drowning rather than altitude sickness. Ancient pieces of wood — but no skeletons — have been found imbedded in the permanent ice near the summit of Ararat, but their origin is disputed. Nowhere else in the world can one sail to such an elevation today.

describing the Anabasis of Cyrus, during which he crossed many high mountain passes in Armenia, but he does not mention the effects of altitude, presumably more occupied with hostile Armenians and Kurds and by hunger, thirst, and cold. Eighty years later, Alexander the Great made an even more perilous and longer journey, crossing higher passes, but no records survive to tell what he and his men may have endured from the altitude. In 218 B.C. Hannibal, the formidable Carthaginian general, crossed an alpine pass to overrun northern Italy, which believed itself secure behind the Alps. Just which pass his army with its 400 elephants did cross is uncertain, but all contenders for the honor are higher than 9,000 feet. Livy and Polybius, who described the campaign most vividly, wrote of cold and storm and avalanches which killed many elephants, but they did not mention the thin air at altitude.

Petrarch the great humanist seems to have made the first mountain ascent for pure pleasure, climbing Mount Ventoux (6,273 feet) in 1335 though other travelers preferred to look at mountains from as great a distance as possible and with fear. In 1178 Master John d'Bremble wrote of his crossing of the Great Saint Bernard pass:

"I have been on the Mount of Jove; on the one hand looking up to the heavens of the mountains, on the other shuddering at the hell of the valleys, feeling myself so much nearer heaven, I was sure my prayers would be heard. 'Lord' I said, 'restore me to my brethren that I may tell that they come not to this place of torment . . . where it is so slippery that you cannot stand . . . the death into which there is every facility for falling. . .'"

Peter, King of Aragon and of Sicily and a true mountain climber described his ascent of Pic Canigou (9,815 feet) in the Pyrenees: *"On that mountain no man has ever lived nor has any son of man dared to ascend it, both on account of its excessive height and by reason of the difficulty and toil of the journey."* The King had difficulties. His companions were terrified by the steepness and by thunder and lightning: *"they threw themselves on the ground and lay there as it were lifeless"* and implored the King to turn back. Then the two companions who remained *"began to flag to such an extent that what with their weariness and their dread of the thunder they could scarcely breathe."*

Peter went on alone and *"when he was at the top of the mountain he found a lake there; and when he threw a stone into the lake a horrible dragon of enormous size came out of it and began to fly about in the air and to darken the air with its breath . . ."*

The sixteenth century was filled with such superstition and religion. Dragons were often reported as was the theme of a mountain lake, disturbed, spewing forth either ghosts or dragons. Mount Pilatus (7,000 feet) derives its name from the belief that the body of Pontius Pilate, cast into a small lake near the summit, arose whenever the waters were disturbed and caused terrible storms and floods and even earthquakes. So real were such calamities that the local government in the fourteenth century strictly forbade anyone to even approach the lake; six clerics who did so in 1387 were severely punished. Not until two hundred years later was an official visit permitted, and not for another forty years did someone dare throw stones into the lake: nothing happened!

Long before this the experience of a Chinese mystic was inscribed on stone by one of his followers (Kukai):

"In this very same province is a mountain called Fudaraku, whose peaks soar into the Milky Way, whose snow-covered summit touches the emerald walls of the sky. . . I have asked and been told that no one had ever climbed this mountain before . . . And so (Sramana Shodo) started the ascent of the mountain in the last part of the fourth moon of the first year of the era Jingo–Keiun (767 AD). So deep was the snow and so steep the huge cliffs that he had to rest for some time. After three weeks on the slopes he decided to return home . . . he decided to try once more, but failed to reach the summit . . . Then he tore his robe to pieces, wrapped his feet in the cloth, and with utter commitment searched for the Way . . . he moved across the flashing snows . . . when he had gone half the way up, his body was exhausted, his strength left him. He rested for two days and finally came to see the summit: his ecstasy was like that in a dream, he felt a vertigo like that of an Awakening . . ."

Konrad Gesner, a physician and philosopher, climbed Pilatus in 1585 with official permission, as part of his annual pilgrimages to some mountain. He is the first writer whose works have survived to describe the great pleasures of climbing in his book *On the Admiration of Mountains:*

"I have determined . . . so long as the life divinely granted to me shall continue, each year to ascend a few mountains, or at least one, when the vegetation is flourishing, partly for the sake of suitable bodily exercise and the delight of the spirit. For how great the pleasure, how great think you are the joys of spirit touched as is fit it should be in wondering at the mighty mass of mountains while gazing upon their immensity and as it were in lifting one's head among the clouds . . . I say therefore that he is an enemy of nature whosoever has not deemed lofty mountains to be worthy of great contemplation. . . . And so of all the elements in the variety of nature the supreme wonder resides in the mountains. In these it is possible to see 'the burden of the mighty earth' just as if nature were vaunting herself and making trial of her strength by lifting to such height so great a weight."

Though a physician he makes no mention of the unpleasant effects to be so vividly described by mountaineers still to come, and which, in fact during his lifetime, were being noted and would soon be described in another country and another tongue, by Jose de Acosta. This intrepid Jesuit travelled throughout Peru, after the Conquistadores, and his account *The Natural and Moral History of the Indies,* written and published in 1590, some forty years after his travels, contains a graphic description of altitude illness:

"There is in Peru, a high mountaine which they call Pariacaca, and having heard speake of the alteration it bred, I went as well prepared as I could according to the instructions which was given me by such as they call Vaguianos or expert men but not withstanding all my provision, when I came to mount the degrees, as they call them, which is the top of this mountaine I was suddenly surprised with so mortall and strange a pang, that I was ready to fall from top to the ground: and though we were many in company yet everyone made haste (without tarrying for his companion), to free himself speedily from this ill passage. . . . I was surprised with such pangs of straining and casting as I thought to cast up my heart too; for having cast up meate fleugme, and choller, both yellow and greene; in the end I cast up blood with the straining of my

*stomacke. To conclude, if this had continued, I should un-
doubtedly have died. . . . Some in the passage demanded con-
fession thinking verily to die . . . others left the ladders and
went to the ground, being overcome with casting and going to
the stoole: it was told to me that some have lost their lives there
with this accident.*

*I beheld one that did beate himself against the earth, crying
out for the rage and griefe which this passage of Pariacaca
hadde caused. But commonly it dooth no important harme,
onely this, paine and troublesome distate while it endures: and
not onely the passage of Pariacaca hath this propertie, but also
all this ridge of the mountaine which runnes above 500 leagues
long, and in which place soever you passe you shall find strange
in temperatures, yet more in some parts than in other and rather
to those which mount from the sea and from the plaines . . .*

*For my part I holde this place to be one of the highest peaks
of land in the worlde; for we mount a wonderful space. And in
my opinion, the mountaine Nevade of Spaine, the Pirenees, and
the Alpes of Italie, are as ordinarie houses, in regarde of hie
Towers. I therefore perswade myselfe that the element of the air
is there so subtile and delicate, as it is not proportionable with
the breathing of man, which requires a more gross and
temperate aire, and I beleeve it is the cause that doth so much
alter the stomacke, & trouble all the disposition."*

Dan Gilbert has examined maps of the Andes dating back to
Acosta and concludes that Pariacaca was a well-travelled pass,
almost 15,000 feet high, on the road from Lima to Jauja, near a
mountain of the same name. From comparing several different
translations of Acosta's book, he believes that Acosta also
described the relative immunity to altitude shown by natives
who came more slowly up the longer, more gradually rising
eastern slopes, thereby taking time to acclimatize.

Acosta is the only participant in these adventures whose
description of altitude sickness has survived, if any others were
written. Cortes and Pizzaro sent many of their men to craters on
top of the Central American volcanoes to bring back sulfur to
make gunpowder, but they left no record of their reaction to the
altitude. They may have attributed any symptoms to the
volcanic fumes, but more likely they were partially acclimatized

from their long stay in the high valleys and their slow rate of climb.

In the Andes altitude sickness was familiar and called *puna* (literally meaning high dry desert), *mareo* (sea sickness), or *veta,* but whether all these names were of local origin or made up by the invaders is not clear. In Bolivia and Chile altitude sickness was called *soroche,* the Spanish word for antimony — and emanations from that ore were blamed for the symptoms. In other areas rhubarb plants, primroses, heather or mosses were alleged to produce pestilential vapors that made men sick. There was general agreement that some places were worse than others — a belief that persists today!

The Incas recognized that climate affected health, as shown by the elaborate laws established by the Great Inca regarding migration of his subjects. Apparently he knew that persons who lived by the seashore died in great numbers if transported to work in the mines at 12,000 feet or higher, but whether this was due to disease, cold, malnutrition or altitude is unclear. Indeed the combination must have been overwhelming for those accustomed to the comparatively soft life along the fruitful coast. Mountain residents were also forbidden to move to the seductive coastal areas, perhaps because they would be exposed there to a bewildering variety of unfamiliar tropical diseases.

* * * * * * * * *

As the fifteenth century ended and the glorious years of the Renaissance began, men were venturing farther across the oceans and higher onto the mountains and writing about the phenomena they observed. Acosta's long detailed description of mountain sickness was followed in the next century by an explosion of scientific curiosity and by exciting discoveries in physics, chemistry, anatomy, and physiology. At the same time the great navigators crossed the oceans and more travellers penetrated high mountain ranges, crossed the deserts, and reported their sensations along with their discoveries. The Renaissance was a crowded, fertile, and exciting period of exploration — exploration of the physical universe and of the human body, and of their interrelationships.

Chapter Two
TOWARD UNDERSTANDING THE
PHYSICAL UNIVERSE

The principles of Aristotle influenced the beliefs of Europe for fifteen hundred years and were fundamental to the Church, which also believed in a static universe responsive to external perfection. But Aristotle's science, though logical and consistent, was flawed because based on too little experimental evidence. Many of his principles withered as actual measurements showed them to be inadequate or false. Looking toward the heavens Aristotle could not conceive that space could be empty, because it would then have no dimensions. Light could not penetrate a space that did not exist and therefore the stars could not be visible if a vacuum intervened between them and earth. At the same time he also argued that *". . . in its own place every body has weight except fire, even air. It is proof of this that an inflated bladder weighs more than an empty one."* Theologians, while agreeing with Aristotle that a vacuum did not exist, declared that it was certainly possible because if God wished to create one he could surely do so.

Then like flowers at the end of a long winter, the arts and sciences burst into bloom as the Renaissance succeeded the Dark Ages. Suddenly, almost abruptly, established doctrines were challenged and new ideas, freed from the shackles of the past opened new vistas in physics, chemistry, medicine. It would almost seem that some ferment must have been loosed to catalyze so many fresh ideas in so many brilliant minds in so short a span.

Considering the difficulties of travel it is remarkable how rapidly ideas spread across Europe, enabling a Dutchman, for example, to repeat and build upon the observations of a Paduan. Looking back on those inspiring times it is clear that the great philosopher scientists taught and learned from one another — and occasionally developed the same academic rivalries that scholars do today.

Not surprisingly the nature of the universe, particularly the nature of the atmosphere, attracted great attention. Air and life and fire have been associated throughout recorded history and the concept of 'vital spirit' or 'breath of life' goes back at least 4000 years. The ancient Egyptians used a blowpipe to increase the heat of their furnaces; the Romans tested the safety of air at the bottom of a well by lowering into it a lighted candle, and Cicero appreciated the nourishment which the lungs drew from inspired air. Nevertheless recognition that air has clearly definable physical properties was slow in coming, cramped by doctrinaire positions taken by many of the famous. One early dissenter was a Dutch philosopher, Isaac Beeckman who wrote in his medical doctoral thesis in 1618. *"It happens that air, in the manner of water, presses upon things and compresses them according to the depth of the super-incumbent air . . ."* He soon came into conflict with the famous French mathematician and religious philosopher Rene Descartes who denied the possibility of a vacuum, while the great Italian scientist Galileo Galilei averred that air had no weight but was ambiguous about the existence of a vacuum! Beeckman was defiant: *". . . for I admit nothing in philosophy, unless it is represented to the imagination as being perceptible to the senses."* The controversy could not be settled by argument. As Beeckman said, experiments had to be done and data collected to prove one side or the other right.

During the first years of the seventeenth century some of the tools became available to make such studies. The microscope, the telescope, the clock and the barometer and thermometer were all conceived and built in the space of a few decades. Of these the barometer was most crucial to studies of the atmosphere, and with the vacuum pump built in 1647 by Otto von Guericke, put an end to the debate over the vacuum. Torricelli is usually credited with having conceived the barometer, but a self-effacing young Italian, Gaspar Berti seems to have been the first to build a working model sometime around 1641. His friend and contemporary Emmanuel Maignan described how a long leaden tube was carefully filled with water, sealed at one end, and lifted upright against the wall of his house and how the water column then fell, leaving a space into which, when the upper tap was opened, *"the air rushed with a loud noise, filling the space previously abandoned by the water."*

*FIGURE 2: VON GUERICKE DEMONSTRATES THE WEIGHT
OF THE ATMOSPHERE*

Controversy over the existence of a vacuum, suppressed for some time
by the traditions of the Church, was resolved early in the seventeenth
century by several different approaches. One of these was Otto von
Guericke's use of the vacuum pump (which he had perfected) for an ingenious public demonstration. Carefully fashioned hemispheres of
heavy copper were tightly fitted together and the air pumped out of the
resulting sphere known as the "Magdeburg sphere" for the town where
this was first done. Teams of horses attached to strong rings on each
hemisphere could not separate them, although they were not bolted but
pressed together by atmospheric pressure. Later demonstrations used
teams of strong men and pulley systems for the same purpose during the
years when Berti and others confirmed existence of a vacuum by
demonstrating that the weight of the 'super-incumbent air' would raise
liquid to a fixed height in a sealed tube.

More experiments followed — some using red wine in place of water — and Torricelli soon saw that using mercury would greatly reduce the height of the clumsy long leaden tube which led him to make the first true barometer, though there is some dispute over details. Interestingly enough, Robert Hooke, writing in 1659 makes no mention of Berti and gives Torricelli credit for making the first barometer in 1643.

Priority in science is a will o' the wisp; few great ideas have sprung *de novo* from any one person, but each man climbs on the shoulders of his predecessors. Torricelli did more to advance the measurement of atmospheric pressure than did his contemporaries: let him have the credit — a unit of measurement named in his honor, the torr, which is the pressure exerted by a column of mercury one millimeter high. To Berti may go the honor of proving that a vacuum could exist — although one little-known part of his experiment almost persuaded him to the contrary!

Word of these experiments spread rapidly through Europe. In the fall of 1646 a physicist named Pierre Petit visited Blaise Pascal, one of the most distinguished French scientists, and together they repeated the Berti-Torricelli experiment. Pascal saw that there could be several explanations for the observed phenomena and determined to examine the questions further. Sometime later, in a letter (whose date has been the subject of heated controversy ever since), Pascal wrote to his brother-in-law Florin Perier:

"I have imagined one decisive experiment that alone will fully enlighten us, if it can be executed with precision. It would mean repeating the experiments on vacuum several times in one day, in the same tube, with the same quicksilver, both at the foot and at the top of a mountain of at least 5-600 'toises,'* in order to establish whether the height of the quicksilver suspended in the tube is different or the same in the two situations. You no doubt already see that this experiment would decide the question, and that, if the height of the quicksilver is less at the top than at the bottom of the mountain (as I have reason to believe to be the case, even though all those that have thought about this are contrary to this opinion), it will necessarily follow

---

* *A "toise" is 6.9 feet*

FIGURE 3: THE FIRST BAROMETER

Emmanuel Maignan, a close friend and associate of Gaspar Berti left a detailed description of how Berti first demonstrated the effect of atmospheric pressure on a column of water: *"This distinguished Gaspar . . . erected a rather long leaden tube (AB) on the wall of his house and made it secure . . . The upper end (A) of the tube was opposite one of the windows . . . while the lower end (B) was not far from the ground and was provided with a brass tap or cock (R), this being within the cask (EF) filled with water for the purpose. To the upper end (A) was fitted . . . a glass vessel rather large but very solid, and having two necks and mouths, the wider one below into which the end of the tube was inserted at (A) as into a box; the narrower above at (C) made so it would fit the stem of the threaded brass screw (D) . . .*

"This being made ready, the tap (R) closed and the cask (EF) filled with water . . . the entire tube as well as the glass vessel was filled from above through the opening (C). Then the opening (C) was closed with the screw (D) in order to seal the entire apparatus . . .

"At length when the tap (R) was opened the water flowed (contrary to the hope of many) out of the pipe into the cask (EF) to an easily observable height, but not all of it flowed out and it soon stood quite still . . . although the tap (R) had been open all the time. Then, when this tap (R) had been carefully closed again, the screw (D) was taken out above. And as soon as it was taken out behold! the air rushed in with a loud noise, filling the space previously abandoned by the water . . ."

Later, using a sounding line, Berti determined that the water had stood in the tube 18 cubits above the level of water in the cask, which Maignan remembered because it was the height that Galileo had observed was the most which water could rise in a suction pump or siphon.

At least ten years before this epochal demonstration, in 1630, Baliani, concluding like Beeckman that it was the existence of a vacuum which prevented water being sucked or siphoned above a certain height, had written a long letter to Galileo pointing this out and at least seeming to suggest the experiment done by Berti.

Within a few years many others had repeated this experiment, and Torricelli was using honey, salt water, wine, and finally mercury to develop what has become our modern barometer.

that the weight and pressure of the air are the sole cause of this suspension of the quicksilver, and not the horror of the vacuum, since it is quite obvious that there is much more weighing on the foot of the mountain than on its summit; whereas one could not say that nature abhors a vacuum at the foot of a mountain more than at the top."

Several years earlier Giovanni Baliani had written Galileo two long letters stating his belief that air had weight, and that *"the higher we go into the air, the less heavy it is."* He did nothing to prove this, or if he did, no record has survived, and Galileo ignored the letters. Then on September 18, 1648 came another great moment in the development of science when Florin Perier determined to test Pascal's idea and to measure the weight of air on the summit of a small mountain called Puy-de-Dome (3,500 feet). At five that morning he assembled six highly trustworthy local dignitaries in the garden of the monastery in Clermont. There *"he took two similar glass tubes, hermetically sealed at one end, and repeated the Torricellian experiment."* He filled both tubes with mercury, and then dexterously dipped each in the same vessel containing sixteen pounds of redistilled mercury, and observed that *"the mercury level fell to the same height — twenty-six inches, three and one-half lines,* in each,"* leaving what we now know to be a near vacuum in the (sealed) upper end. To eliminate all doubt he repeated the observation three times, and then, *"leaving one tube set up at the monastery in charge of one of the monks who was to observe it frequently throughout the day,"* his distinguished party carried the other tube and the mercury up to the summit of Puy-de-Dome, where he repeated the experiment: *"The mercury stood at only twenty-three inches two lines . . . Thus between the heights of quicksilver in these two experiments there was a difference of three inches and one and one-half lines; which ravished us all with admiration and astonishment and surprised us so much for our own satisfaction we wished to repeat it."* The party though excited, was perhaps still skeptical and they made the experiment five times, each time getting identical results. Half-way

---

* On most barometers of the day, an inch was divided into twelve parts or lines; three and one-half lines would thus be about one-third of an inch.

down the mountain using the same method, they found the level of mercury to be twenty-five inches. When they were assured back at the monastery that the height of mercury in that tube had been constant throughout the day, they knew they had for the first time demonstrated that the weight of air—the barometric pressure—decreases as altitude increases. This experiment, so simple to our modern eyes, was a great triumph for Pascal, by then sickly and turning from science to religion.

By 1660 Robert Boyle had repeated Berti's experiment (also using a long water-filled tube attached to his house, if the illustration in his book is accurate) and made many types of mercury barometers. He showed that barometric pressure decreased with increasing height, and seems to have been the first to use changes in barometric pressure to predict changes in weather. An extraordinary series of experiments confirmed an observation made by Beeckmann that the volume of a gas decreased as the pressure on it was increased—a law which bears Boyle's name today although his assistant and later colleague Robert Hooke did most of the experiments and first elucidated the 'law'.

Many others were conducting similar studies throughout Europe, and it became clear very rapidly that air had weight and was compressible and thus the atmospheric weight or pressure was less the higher one went. Boyle read Acosta's writings and his curiosity was piqued. He made inquiries of a number of travellers who had crossed high passes and of others who lived among mountains: all agreed that breathing was more difficult at altitude, and Boyle concluded that this was due to thin air, as Acosta had speculated.

These great scientist-philosophers of the seventeenth century still believed the Aristotelian doctrine that the universe was made of four elements—fire, water, earth, and air—even though Paracelsus had somewhat earlier begun questioning this concept as he generated a new kind of "air" (hydrogen) from iron filings and acid and showed that it burned violently. Paracelsus conceived of a kind of spirit which he called *"the archaeus"* that drew particles of matter together. By then a number of basic elements like sulfur, mercury and iron were already known though not yet seen as building blocks for other substances. The Belgian Johann Baptista van Helmont (who died after thirteen years of torture by the Inquisition because of his beliefs) used a new word "gas" to describe a state of matter separate from solids and liquids, probably drawing from the German "geist" or "spirit." Van Helmont described several new gases and proposed a theory of combustion that later led to the phlogiston theory which influenced studies of the atmosphere for more than a century.

Robert Hooke after serving Boyle for several years, was appointed curator of the newly formed Royal Society and soon was charged with bringing to the meetings a number of new experiments each week. Boyle was one of the more active contributors, and during an incredibly productive five year period Hooke and Boyle produced some of the most ingenious and important studies of the composition of air that had yet been made. One of the more famous caused a great deal of confusion: when a mouse and a lighted candle were placed under a bell jar, the candle went out long before the mouse died, which led to the concept that life and combustion might be different. Though Hooke opposed this view he received little support. The Society observed all sorts of experiments: mice, snakes, shellfish, birds, flowers, plants and insects were all studied under the bell jar, or in flasks evacuated by the "New Pneumatical Engine" built by Hooke but based on the vacuum pump first made by Guericke around 1647.

Hooke was asked by the Society to make a chamber large enough to contain a man which could have the air sucked out of it. In due course he entertained the Society at his rooms where he entered the large wooden tub while about a tenth of the air was pumped out by his pneumatic engine. He noticed no ill effects other than slight pain in his ears as the pressure changed. Since this experiment came soon after Von Guericke's famous hemisphere experiment it is probably the first time a "decompression chamber" was used by man.

Boyle had some insightful concepts:

". . . the atmospherical air consists of three different kinds of corpuscles . . . first, these numberless particles . . . in the form of vapors . . . the second more subtle consists of those exceedingly minute atoms the magnetical effluvia of the earth . . .

the third sort is its characteristic and essential property, I mean permanently elastic parts."

He outlined a program of studies which might well have led to a true understanding of combustion had he been able to complete them but he turned to other interests. Another brilliant contemporary took up the work. John Mayow, who had become first a lawyer, then a physician, was attracted by a new theory, probably first proposed by the Dane Ole Borch (also called Olas Borrichius), that air contained a special life-giving substance much as van Helmont had postulated. In 1678 Borch actually generated this substance that we now know to be oxygen, by the decomposition of potassium nitrate, but failed to appreciate the significance of his discovery.

Advances in instrumentation had been keeping pace with theories and expanded opportunities for experimental proofs. One of these was the improvement in glass making—a process known for several thousand years but only in this period brought to a specialized skill kept secret by the Venetians at Murano. Reliable laboratory glassware permitted more accurate volumetric measurements, and the concurrent evolution of very sensitive analytical balances made possible precise measurement of weight lost or gained by combustion, for example. Technology was ready for the next great leap ahead.

John Mayow used these advances to make his major contributions. He soon appreciated that the atmosphere consisted of at least two kinds of gases: *". . . nitro-aerial particles are necessary for the support of life and . . . combustion; while the other, remaining after this constituent has been removed, is incapable of supporting either life or combustion."* His theories were backed by careful experiments. In 1674 he wrote: *"I take it for granted that the air contains certain particles termed by us elsewhere nitro-aerial which are absolutely indispensable for the production of fire . . ."*

He showed this by burning a candle under a bell jar sealed with water and watching the water level rise as the candle burned out just as van Helmont had done many years earlier. He carried this experiment one exciting step forward:

"Let a small bell jar in which a little animal say a mouse has been put be accurately applied to a tightly stretched skin to form

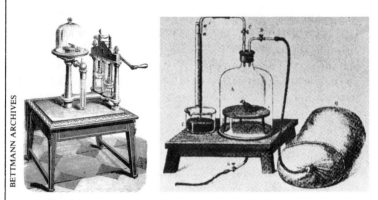

FIGURE 4: LIFE IN A VACUUM: BENEFITS OF OXYGEN

John Mayow tried to determine the composition of air by watching the extinction of a candle (or the death of a small bird or mouse) within a sealed bell jar, concluding in 1674 that some element in air was essential for 'combustion.' Later a vacuum pump was used to prove that low pressures too were incompatible with life in experiments such as that shown above (left). Pressure was measured by the changes in mercury level in the U-shaped glass gage. Soon larger containers were used, eventually evolving into the steel 'bell' used by Bert. The modern counterpart is a huge 'room' sometimes accommodating 15–25 persons, and capable of reaching 50,000 feet or more in simulated low pressure. Just a hundred years after Mayow, Lavoisier repeated his work, adding oxygen to the bell jar and showing that a mouse or bird lived longer in the enriched gas, confirming Mayow's belief that some "vital spirit" in air was necessary for life. Lavoisier named the new gas "oxygine," and Priestley, who had publicly reported similar work shortly before Lavoisier, breathed some of the gas himself, writing that he fancied he perceived a peculiar lightness to his breathing. These studies laid the foundation for Paul Bert's important studies. He was able to make bags of leather to contain oxygen and showed that this sustained life in animals kept under evacuated bell jars (above right), and also prevented or relieved his own symptoms in the decompression chamber.

a seal. When things have been arranged in this manner, it will in a short time be seen that the jar is firmly fixed to the skin, and the skin also at the place where it lies under the jar is forced upwards into the cavity of the glass just as if the jar had been applied with a flame enclosed in it. And this will take place while the animal is still breathing. From this it is clear that the elastic power of the air enclosed in the aforesaid jar has been diminished by the breathing of the animal so that it is no longer able to resist the pressure of the surrounding air." After many experiments, Mayow was satisfied: *"And in fact I have ascertained from experiments with various animals that the air (in the sealed jar) is reduced in volume by about one-fourteenth by the breathing of the animal."* And further: *"From what has been said it is quite certain that animals in breathing draw from the air certain vital spirits. . . That nitro-aerial spirit is by means of respiration transmitted into the mass of the blood and the fermentation and heating of the blood are produced by it."*

Not for another hundred years would so clear a statement of the essential role of oxygen in supporting life be formulated. Some feel that Mayow deserves credit for identifying the importance of oxygen to life and combustion—a concept that would not come for another century, but to history he remains one of the background contributors.

Today we are so accustomed to the headlong pace of science, and the apparently endless flow of new ideas and inventions tumbling over one another faster than we can absorb or use them, that the developments of the first century of the Renaissance might seem slow and obvious. But consider what took place from 1550 to 1650: The Aristotelian theory was refuted and the existence of a vacuum proven. That the atmosphere which envelops earth had weight and was compressible was not only proven, but changes in atmospheric pressure with altitude were measured. And the *"spiritus mundi"* or aether on which life depends had been recognized to be a mixture of gases, one of which was essential to life and combustion. Many of the scientist-philosophers turned experimenters and began to prove in the laboratory what their predecessors had merely hypothesized. Torricelli and Berti, Pascal and Perier, Borch and van Helmont, and Boyle and Mayow had built a set of giant

FIGURE 5:

ROBERT HOOKE'S 'DECOMPRESSION CHAMBER' – 1671

As soon as Robert Boyle heard of von Guericke's vacuum pump, he and his then assistant Robert Hooke made their own *"New Pneumatical Engine"* and examined the effects of a partial vacuum on all sorts of animals, minerals and vegetables. In December 1670 after many reports to the Royal Society, Hooke proposed *"a new way of making a vessel for extracting the air, so large, that a man might fit in it, and so contrived, as to rarefy the air to a certain degree . . ."* He was instructed to proceed and on February 2, 1671 *"being asked, whether the air-vessel for a man to fit in was yet ready, answered that it was . . . Being asked, how it was contrived, he said, that it consisted of two tuns, one included in the other; the one to hold a man, the other filled with water to cover the former, thereby to keep it staunch; with tops to put on with cement; or to take off; one of them having a gage, to see to what degree the air is rarefied; as also a cock to be turned by the person who sits in the vessel . . ."*

A month later he reported *". . . that he himself had been in it, and by the contrivance of bellows and valves blown out of it one-tenth part of the air (which he found by a gage suspended within the vessel) and had felt no inconvenience but that of some pain in his ears at the breaking out of the air included in them, and the like pain upon the readmission of the air pressing the air inward."*

Hook'e courageous experiment is undoubtedly the first time a man was 'taken up' in a decompression chamber and with all his other studies of air and pressure, should give him a prominent place in altitude physiology. The illustration is as close as my illustrator and I could come from the above description included in a History of the Royal Society, reprinted in 1967 in Brussels. Curiously I could find no mention of this experiment in Hooke's book *"Curious Philosophical Observations and Experiments"* where he describes many experiments with increased and decreased atmospheric pressure, or in Boyle's works.

steps toward understanding of the world they lived in. For each of these there were many others whose names are today almost unknown (Baliani for example) who also contributed, sometimes long before those who are now so famous.

Near the end of the seventeenth century a chemist, J. J. Becher, encouraged one of his students Georg Ernst Stahl to study Borch's concept of a special life-supporting substance in air. Stahl soon postulated that all substances which could be burned were compounds, one part of which was an odorless invisible gas which he christened "phlogiston" or "fire-substance." He theorized that when something burned, this principle was released and the substance became 'dephlogisticated'. But the delicate scales by then available showed that some substances gained rather than lost weight by combustion. Stahl tried to explain this by theorizing that phlogiston had a property the opposite of weight, that is the quality of levity so that as this negative weight escaped, the compound became heavier. Though there were demonstrable flaws in this theory, it prevailed for over a century and engaged the minds of some of the most brilliant scientists of the time.

One of these, Joseph Black, became Professor of Chemistry at Edinburgh in the mid eighteenth century and was thought the most eloquent teacher of his time. Students copied his lectures word for word and he read his classes the identical lectures for twenty-five years. In one he demonstrated a new gas, *"fixed air,"* which we know as carbon dioxide. He described this as: *"A sort of air quite distinct from common air, though it is commonly mixed with it in small quantity."* He showed that this different gas was heavier than air and could be poured from one container to another, that it was formed by burning, that it was present in the exhaled air, and was a major constituent of *"choke damp,"* the bane of miners. His was the first series of clear and well-planned experiments where everything was carefully measured and nothing was taken on trust. Daniel Rutherford and later Henry Cavendish continued his studies, and Cavendish supported the phlogiston theory for several years after all others had abandoned it, arguing that hydrogen, which he showed to be lighter than air in 1766, was phlogiston. Much effort in the first half of the eighteenth century went to the studies of his curious concept, but it was scarcely wasted.

Oxygen is so central to life and to any discussion of altitude illness that the tangled and controversial story of its birth (or perhaps its delivery) deserves a little more than passing mention, even though the "facts" seem to depend somewhat on the nationality or the biases of the reporter. The gas was actually made in the late seventeenth century by Olas Borrichius (otherwise known as Ole Borch) but he did not realize what he had done and did not pursue the finding. Then between 1770 and 1773 a Swedish pharmacist, Carl Wilhelm Scheele, after an extraordinary and systematic series of experiments, not only generated oxygen from saltpeter, but even though young had the courage to point out shortcomings in the popular phlogiston theory of combustion, which of course did not endear him to his elders. He called his new gas "vitriol air" but soon changed this to "fire air" when he realized it was essential for combustion. Though primarily a chemist, he was also much interested in physiology and botany, and made many significant experiments in these fields as well.

In France, during this same time, Antoine Laurent Lavoisier was doing similar experiments. Unlike his British rival Priestley, Lavoisier came from a well-to-do family and after an excellent education devoted himself to science from an early age. By 1771, though only 28 years old, he made experiments he considered important enough to prompt this letter to the French Academy:

As this discovery appears to me to be one of the most interesting which has been made since the time of Stahl, I thought it expedient to secure myself the property by depositing the present note in the hands of the Secretary of the Academy, to remain secret until the period when I shall publish my experiments."

On September 30, 1774 Scheele wrote Lavoisier to thank him for a book and in the letter (only recently uncovered), described how oxygen might be made. Lavoisier was interested and, as his laboratory notes show, used Scheele's instructions to supplement experiments he had been conducting for several years. It seems likely he was also spurred by the fact that a summary of Scheele's experiment had been published early in 1772,

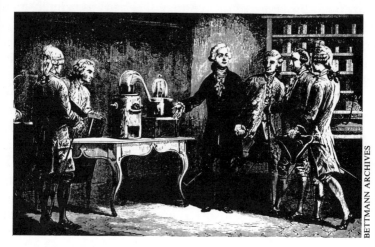

BETTMANN ARCHIVES

FIGURE 6: LAVOISIER IN HIS LABORATORY

Antoine Laurent Lavoisier was a brilliant chemist and although he did not originate the experiments which led to the isolation of oxygen, he shares with Priestly credit for most of the final work. Here he is demonstrating the distillation of mercury to his colleagues. In order to obtain the hydrogen which he needed for the newly developed Charlieres balloons, he decomposed water into hydrogen and oxygen by percolating water through rings in a large gun barrel heated to incandescence! Ingenious though this method was, it proved impracticable for the generation of the large volumes needed, and balloonists soon turned to chemical sources. Lavoisier's laboratory was a gathering place for many distinguished scientists, and his textbook of chemistry remained a classic for many years.

though Scheele's book, delayed by the procrastination of a colleague, did not appear until August 1777, three years after the generally accepted "birthday" of oxygen. Lavoisier also knew that another inquisitive and imaginative scientist was also on the trail.

Joseph Priestley was a theologian whose interest in chemistry was apparently stimulated by Boerhaave's textbook in 1755 and led to his teaching the subject a few years later. This interest in chemistry, particularly in gases, lasted the rest of his life, and his efforts climaxed in the fall of 1774.

On Saturday, November 19th he set up his crucial experiment, but on Sunday, pre-occupied with his duties as a minister, he did not work in his laboratory. On Monday, November 21, 1774, he placed some mercuris calcinatus (red lead or mercuric oxide) in a closed glass vessel and heated it, obtaining about an ounce of vapor which he carefully transferred to another container. Then:

"In this air as I had expected, a candle burned with a valid flame. . . In ignorance of the real nature of this kind of air I continued from this time to the first of March following. I procured a mouse and put it into a glass vessel containing two ounce measures of the air obtained from mercuris calcinatus. Had it been common air, a full grown mouse such as this was would have lived in it about a quarter of an hour. In this air however my mouse lived a full half hour."

Priestley was well aware of the limitations of animal experiments, apparently, and he proceeded cautiously:

"I did not certainly conclude that this air was any better, because though one mouse would live only a quarter of an hour in a given quantity of air, I knew it was not impossible but that another mouse might have lived in it half an hour." So he *"procured another mouse, and putting it into less than two ounce measures of air extracted from mercuris calcinatus. . . I found it lived three-quarters of an hour. Being now fully satisfied of the superior goodness of this kind of air I proceeded to measure that degree of purity with as much accuracy as I could. . ."*

This he did quite ingeniously by mixing what he called *"dephlogisticated air"* with *"nitrous air"* which was nothing more than room air in his laboratory. He titrated the capacity of his new air to support life and combustion by testing different mixtures and then, bravely and prophetically:

"My reader will not wonder, that, after having ascertained the superior goodness of dephlogisticated air by mice living in it, and the other tests above mentioned, I should have the curiosity to taste it myself. I have gratified that curiosity, by breathing it, drawing it through a glass-syphon, and, by this means, I reduced a large jar full of it to the standard of common air. The feeling of it to my lungs was not sensibly different from that of common air; but I fancied that my breast felt peculiarly light and easy for some time afterwards. Who can tell but that, in time, this pure air may become a fashionable article in luxury. Hitherto only two mice and myself have had the privilege of breathing it."

Scheele in Sweden was writing at about the same time:

". . . our atmosphere ought not to be considered as a simple fluid substance, for, when freed from all heterogeneous admixture, it is found . . . to consist of two very different kinds of air; the one is called <u>corrupted air</u>, because it is very dangerous and fatal, as well as to living animals as vegetables; it constitutes the greatest part of our atmosphere. The other is called <u>pure air, fire air</u>. This kind of air is <u>salutary, supports respiration</u>, and consequently the circulation; without it we could form no distinct idea, either of fire, or how it is kindled. It constitutes but the smallest part of the whole atmosphere. Now as we know this air is of the most immediate necessity for the support of our health . . ."

The experiments which he carried out during 1778 and 1779 led him to conclude:

"Our atmosphere, therefore, contains always, though with some little difference, nearly the same quantity of pure or fire air, 27%, which is a very remarkable fact; and to assign the cause of it seems difficult, as a quantity of pure air, in supporting fire, daily enters into a new union; and a considerable quantity of it is likewise corrupted, or changed into aerial acid, as well by plants as by respiration; another fresh proof of the great care of our Creator for all that lives."

Although Lavoisier had been working toward oxygen for a long time, one cannot help suspecting that he was hurried by the letter from Scheele and by a meeting with Priestley—both of which showed that others were nearing the same prize he sought.

At any rate, Lavoisier described his experiments in a paper read to the French Academy on April 26, 1775, five weeks after Priestley's report, and in 1789 published in his great textbook of chemistry, among many other studies, details of the experiment which had led him to oxygen:

"I introduced four ounces of pure mercury into the (container) and, by means of a siphon exhausted the air so as to raise the quicksilver level, and I carefully marked the height at which it stood by pasting on a slip of paper . . . I lighted a fire in the furnace which I kept almost continually burning twelve days so as to keep the quicksilver always very near the boiling point. Nothing remarkable took place during the first day; the mercury, though not boiling, was continually evaporating. . . At the end of twelve days . . . I extinguished the fire and allowed the vessel to cool . . . the remaining air . . . had lost about one-sixth of its bulk and was no longer fit either for respiration or for combustion. Animals being introduced into it were suffocated in a few seconds and when a taper was plunged into it, it was extinguished as if it had been immersed in water."

Both Priestley and Lavoisier were giants in their time and their places in history are assured on many counts. They were also competitors in a great race and to some degree antagonists. Priestley clung to the phlogiston theory to the end of his life although he insisted he would abandon it were he convinced that it was wrong. Lavoisier too was reluctant to abandon phlogiston until his demonstration that water was made up of hydrogen and oxygen; he was then convinced that his "oxygine" was a separate element, essential to life and combustion.

Both were versatile scientists and social reformers. Priestley supported the French Revolution, while Lavoisier was put to death in 1794 by a revolutionary tribunal. Though the comment "The Republic has no need for chemists" attributed to the judge who condemned him is apocryphal, a witness to the execution said more tellingly: "It took only an instant to cut off that head and a hundred years may not produce another like it."

By the end of the century it was clear that a portion of the ambient air supported life and combustion while the remainder was inert. The phlogiston theory was effectively eliminated by Lavoisier's demonstrations and by Priestley—though he never fully renounced it. Several questions arose: Was this vital air, this "oxygine" present in all air everywhere? Was it constant in amount or did it differ from place to place? And most important—bearing in mind the candle and mouse experiment that had puzzled the Royal Society a century before—if "burning" and "living" were similarly dependent on oxygen, why did not the generated heat burn up the living tissues? It would be almost another century before this question was answered.

The experiments of Scheele, Lavoisier and Priestley were repeated in many parts of Europe, and on the summits of low mountains with the same results—about one fifth of the air was oxygen. John Dalton, an imaginative scientist who revived the ancient atomic theory of Democritus, after ingenious studies and hypotheses advanced the law which now bears his name: *"The total pressure exerted by a mixture of gases is equal to the sum of the pressures of the different gases making up the mixture, each gas acting separately and independently of the others."* This "law of partial pressures" governs all of our theories and observations relating to respiration and was a major contribution to scientific progress. How simple this sounds today and how obvious, yet what immense imagination and painstaking experimentation was necessary to reach these conclusions. Advances came with a rush and in clusters, rather than as a steady flow. The names of the giants survive, but one wonders how many others had flashes of inspiration and made new discoveries only to be, through some quirk of time or publicity, *"unwept, unhonored, and unsung."*

Meanwhile the oceans and continents were being explored as well. Konrad Gesner and Professor Marti made their annual pilgrimages onto the mountains for pleasure. Domp Julian de Beaupre, in the same year that Columbus sailed to the New World, was ordered by the King of Spain (apparently on whim) to climb a formidable rock pinnacle—Mont Aiguille (7,000 ft) —the first major rock climb. That there were many other mountain travellers and explorers then is suggested by the popularity of a remarkable book published in 1574, by Josias Simler. Titled *"De Alpibus Commentarius"* it could be described as the first Baedeker guide, cataloging just about all one would want to know about mountain journeys. Simler described the dangers of avalanches and rockfalls, storms and the hazards of travelling on snow-covered glaciers. He included remarkable descriptions of the various aids to climbing used in his time and much like those of today—crampons, ice axes, and ladders. He advised the use of ropes on glaciers and described what we now call hypothermia, an insidious sleep brought on by cold and often leading to death. Commercial travellers must have found invaluable his advice about the food and lodging to be found in remote villages. Simler makes no mention of mountain sickness . . . nor of dragons.

Konrad Gesner, one of the earliest to proclaim his love of mountains, published seventy-two books in his lifetime and had no less than eighteen in manuscript when he died at the age of forty-nine during the great plague of 1565. One of his most ambitious efforts was an inventory of all the known animals—including descriptions of 250 varieties of dragons. An even more comprehensive work was undertaken by Aldrovandi but only four volumes were published between 1559 and his death in 1605; nine more appeared in the next fifty years. Aldrovandi too took dragons seriously, and indeed they were taken for granted even as late as 1712 when a distinguished Swiss professor, Johann Jakob Scheuchzer, made a systematic catalogue of them, apparently led to the study through his passion for paleontology, a field which he is said to have originated. Scheuchzer was born in 1672, wrote an immense number of scientific works and travelled extensively throughout the Alps. For several years he took sworn depositions from *"persons of good character and repute"* who had seen or, in some cases, even been attacked by dragons in mountainous areas. He described and painted these beasts very carefully: they came in several sizes; some had wings but no feet while others had feet but no wings and some had long tails. Some breathed fire and smoke, and some were very small—not much larger than a dog. Were these eye-witness accounts like those many thousand

*FIGURE 7: THERE WERE (ALLEGEDLY) DRAGONS
ON THE MOUNTAINS*

Scheuchzer patiently collected many affidavits from persons who had actually seen—or even claimed to have been attacked by—dragons in the Alps and made many drawings of them. Probably fear of dragons as well as other superstitions did keep many people from climbing in the sixteenth and seventeenth centuries, but there was also cold and storm to deter them. Are these stories and pictures any more unbelievable than our contemporaries' reports of the Loch Ness monster, or UFOs, or visitors from outer space?

"reliable" sightings of unidentified flying objects which have made UFO part of our language? What did these persons of good repute and character actually see?

Did the fear of dragons keep men from the mountains? Perhaps attractions like rock crystals, topaz and amethyst or game like chamois overcame anxiety over dragons, because some did climb and explore, and of course certain passes like the Great St. Bernard had been used for many generations. Nevertheless fear of the unknown — including dragons — was more common than altitude illness.

A sleepy little hamlet in the French Alps was the scene of the first major mountaineering efforts. In 1741 Windham and Pococke with nine British companions visited the valley below Mont Blanc and published a small booklet describing its splendors. Tourists were soon attracted by that magnificent snow-covered mountain, the highest in Europe, among them an artist named Marc-Theodore Bourrit who made many paintings of the valley and the lovely mountain. He later made four attempts to climb it, once coming within a few hundred feet of the 15,400 foot summit before turning back because of illness (from altitude?). Bourrit was an artist and amateur climber, not a scientist like the man whose name is most often and widely associated with Mont Blanc — Horace-Benedict de Saussure.

De Saussure first visited Chamonix in 1760 at the age of twenty, just two years before being appointed Professor of Philosophy at Geneva National Academy. He was the first of the great scientist-mountaineers drawn to high peaks by both these loves. In 1760 he offered a substantial reward to the first person to reach the summit, and two years later the first serious attempt was made by a local named Pierre Simon. Eight more attempts were made before a Chamonix doctor, Francois Paccard, and a local guide Jacques Balmat reached the summit on August 8th, 1786. They were carefully watched from the valley through telescopes but it was impossible to tell which of the two first stepped on the actual top, which led to an ugly controversy for many years. They made no mention of altitude illness. During the next forty years, according to Auldjo, who in 1828 published one of the most beautiful histories of Mont Blanc, there were fourteen successful ascents, less than take place in one week today, and a larger but unrecorded number of failures. De Saussure made the third ascent in 1787, after his two previous attempts, one with Bourrit, had failed. He spent four hours on top, later writing a vivid description of his misery from the altitude:

"I myself who am so accustomed to the air of the mountains, who feel better in this air than in that of the plain, was completely exhausted. . ." And when he tried to conduct his various experiments: *". . . I was constantly forced to interrupt my work and devote myself entirely to breathing . . . the kind of fatigue which results from the rarity of the air is absolutely unconquerable; when it is at its height, the most terrible danger would not make you take a single step further."*

De Saussure made observations of pulse and respiration on many summits and compared these readings with those made in the valleys. His travels and experiments were published between 1786 and 1796 in four volumes titled *"Voyages dans les Alpes."* On one trip he journeyed up the great glacier above Chamonix, known as the Mer de Glace, to the Col du Géant, an 11,000 foot pass leading to Italy and stayed there for several days. This was particularly daring because contemporaries believed that even a single night at so great a height would be fatal. Instead he enjoyed himself greatly, and carried on his experiments for two days, being forced to leave only when it was found that his guides had ransacked the supplies and left him without wine.

For several decades climbers attempted Mont Blanc with some success, and the mountain became world-famous in 1852 due to a young physician Albert Smith who reached the top in 1851, and gave a well-advertised public lecture in March of the following year profusely *"illustrated by a brilliant series of Dioramic Views painted expressly from the original sketches . . ."* Smith was such an instant success he left medicine for show business, giving nightly accounts of his ascent for six years. His detailed description was reasonably accurate on facts, and the paintings were dramatic. Although trained as a physician, Smith did not contribute to the science of altitude except indirectly. His companions on the climb described him as:

". . . utterly exhausted. He passed two nights (during the climb) almost without sleep and this, with lack of appetite,

FIGURE 8: DE SAUSSURE ON MONT BLANC:
THE FIRST SCIENTIST-CLIMBER

De Saussure loved Mont Blanc for its beauty and for the challenge it offered to the daring; his first attempts on the summit failed, but on August 3rd, 1787, with a large party of guides led by Balmat (who had made the first ascent in 1786 and the second earlier in 1787) he reached the summit. His guides (pictured here in a contemporary painting) were burdened with scientific equipment even on this pioneering venture, for De Saussure was primarily a man of science, and he made many observations of the weather, temperature, snow conditions and especially of the physiological reactions of himself and companions (including his valet who had never before been on a mountain). He continued these studies for several years on other peaks in the range of Mont Blanc, and his records are the first major scientific contribution to the study of high altitude.

dispirited him. He was walking fast asleep with his eyes open, with strange illusions that people he knew in London were following and calling after him."

Was he perhaps suffering from brain edema, a form of altitude illness? A cup of champagne on the summit revived him.

Smith undoubtedly stimulated hundreds of tourists to visit the Alps, particularly Mont Blanc, but a small group of true mountaineers were already making spectacular climbs throughout the Alps. They founded the Alpine Club, still today the doyen of mountaineering excellence, whose annual journal carries the subtitle "A Record of Mountain Adventure and Scientific Observation." Though few of the early articles mention mountain sickness, a member named Joanne wrote in the Journal in 1872:

"The lightness and great rarity of air in the Alps . . . cause at certain altitudes very noticeable physiological phenomena such as . . . nausea, drowsiness, panting, headache, fatigue, etc.; some of these symptoms even compel certain individuals to turn back as soon as they have reached 3,000 meters."

Paul Bert, generally regarded as the father of high altitude physiology, commented in 1877:

". . . If these symptoms are so frequent . . . why not mention them in accounts which are often so prolix and loaded with uninteresting details. We must confess their importance and severity have been so exaggerated that travellers affected only by panting and palpitations are willing to deny even the reality of an illness they read so much in advance . . . most of the tourists whose narratives fill the Alpine Journal have hardly any scientific interest in their ascents; they climb for the sake of climbing . . . they are almost afraid of being ridiculed for mountain sickness as they are for seasickness."

On the other hand there was a time when failure to record the agonies of mountain sickness cast some doubt on the validity of the summit claim.

During this golden age of alpine climbing (1850–1875) virtually all of the alpine peaks were climbed and on many the usual route led to the opening up of more difficult alternatives. Most climbers were from the leisured or professional class in

England: geologists, physicians or university faculty. Though they climbed for adventure and excitement, the scientifically minded described their symptoms at altitude, while others evolved theories to define the motion of glaciers and formation of mountains. Before long mountain climbers were travelling all over the world in search of new peaks to conquer and their observations contributed greatly to what scientists like Angelo Mosso and Paul Bert would soon learn about high altitude physiology.

Chapter Three
EXPLORATION OF THE HEAVENS BEGINS

Just how high into the mountains did it extend, this "vital air"? Did the atmosphere end abruptly, as many people believed the oceans to end before the great scientists proved the world was round? Or did it become thinner and thinner the higher one went above the earth? Cold, storm, mountaineering difficulties, and superstition limited observations to comparatively low mountains; some way would have to be found to go much higher.

Men must have dreamed of flying from the earliest times, as they watched the effortless soaring of hawks and eagles and longed to be high above the earth, free in the endless oceans of the sky. In 3,000 B.C. a Chinese Emperor Shun is said to have been taught to fly by two daughters of another Emperor, but the secret must have been well kept. One of the kings of ancient Persia, as legend has it, harnessed wild eagles to his throne, stimulating their flight by holding fish before them. He travelled far and wide before the eagles tired, dropping him in China. There are many variations of the story of how Daedalus, architect of the Labyrinth which housed the Minotaur, escaped from Crete by fashioning wings of wax in which were set real feathers. His son Icarus, intoxicated with freedom, flew too near the sun which melted the wax, plunging him into the sea, while the more conservative Daedalus landed safely.

But the first authentic aeronautical engineer of whom we have knowledge was Leonardo da Vinci, whose insatiable curiosity and immense genius led him into so many fields of art and science in the fifteenth century. He designed and built a helicopter and a parachute, but most of his passion for flight was directed toward copying birds' wings and his notebooks contain sketches of different kinds of 'ornithopters'—though none flew. He is said to have understood and designed a hot air balloon. His notebooks were hidden after his death and lost for two centuries, until Napoleon found and had them published. By that time others had far out-stripped Leonardo's efforts.

An imaginative step upward was taken by a distinguished

Jesuit scientist and professor of mathematics, Francesco de Lana-Terzi who, learning of the observations of Torricelli, designed an aerial ship to be lifted by four large globes made of thinnest copper and evacuated like the famous Magdeburg Spheres of von Guericke. Being thus lighter than air, Lana-Terzi theorized they would have considerable lifting power. Alas, the thin-skinned spheres were crushed by atmospheric pressure while being evacuated, and the project failed. Later the Jesuit prophetically saw a greater obstacle: *"God would surely never allow such a machine to be successful, since it would cause much disturbance among the civil and political governments of mankind."*

An outstanding pioneer in practical aeronautics, Laurenco de Guzmao, in 1686, petitioned the King of Portugal for a patent on a flying machine named the *Passarola*. Though he tried to launch a model of the strange craft, nothing came of it, and he turned to hot air balloons and became the first to use this method of levitation. On August 8, 1709 he demonstrated the 'flight' of a small globe filled with hot air from the *"combustion of various quintessences"* and flew it in one of the larger rooms of the King of Portugal's palace. The little model rose to the ceiling, bounced against the wall and fell, setting fire to the draperies in the process. His majesty *"was good enough not to take it ill."* Guzmao sank into obscurity afterwards—there was talk of sorcery. He went to Spain and died at Toledo in 1724.

Attention then turned to wings, though only briefly, sometimes in the form of gliders, sometimes mechanically operated. In 1755, stimulated no doubt by recent demonstrations that air grew thinner and lighter the higher one went, a Dominican friar named Joseph Galien published specifications for a giant airship, ten times as large as Noah's Ark, which would be filled with thin high-altitude air, but not much progress seems to have been made! Then chemist Joseph Black heard of Henry Cavendish's production of hydrogen and recognized that this gas, so much lighter than air, if suitably enclosed could lift weights. He planned to fill the birth sacs of sheep with hydrogen to demonstrate its lift to his students, but he was diverted and left the actual experiments to an Italian, Tiberias Cavallo, who tried various types of bladders of cloth and paper, none of which were sufficiently tight to contain the hydrogen. Cavallo abandoned the attempt in 1782, after blowing soap bubbles with hydrogen and writing:

"In short, soap-balls inflated with inflammable air were the only things of this sort that would ascend into the atmosphere; but as they are very brittle and altogether untractable, they do not seem applicable to any philosophical purpose."

Joseph Montgolfier and his brother Etienne are the most famous of the early pioneers in ballooning. They studied the 1776 edition of Priestley's *Experiments and Observations on Different Kinds of Air* and also began to speculate about the nature of the atmosphere. Joseph, as history has it, was watching bits of paper rising from the fire in his fireplace when he was suddenly struck by the nature of the force that took the light bits—along with smoke—up the chimney. If paper and smoke could rise, why could he not capture the 'gas' that propelled them? Why should he not *"enclose a cloud in a bag and let the latter be lifted up by the buoyancy of the former"*? At first he and Etienne believed that 'burned' air was lighter in accordance with the phlogiston theory; smoke was 'burned air' and thus had 'levity'. Only later did they realize that it was heat which provided the lift.

In November 1782 a small hot air balloon of taffeta was allowed to float to the ceiling of a room, and shortly afterwards in the open a 750 cubic foot balloon rose over 600 feet. In these early designs a grill was hung below the narrow open throat of the balloon; on it smouldered a pile of moldy hay (wisdom of the day indicating this was the best fuel) so that the hot smoke rose into the balloon providing the lift. After many private experiments, on June 5, 1783, they held a public demonstration before a large and enthusiastic crowd. Their linen balloon was thirty-eight feet in diameter and after being filled with smoke (and of course hot air) slowly rose out of sight, carrying 500 pounds, later landing a mile and a half away. Though the brothers still attributed the lift to some substance formed by burning a special kind of hay, Cavallo did understand that hot air was lighter than cold and thus would rise.

There was so much enthusiasm for these early flights that public subscriptions were raised to make more and larger balloons and in September 1783 a huge balloon was demonstrated

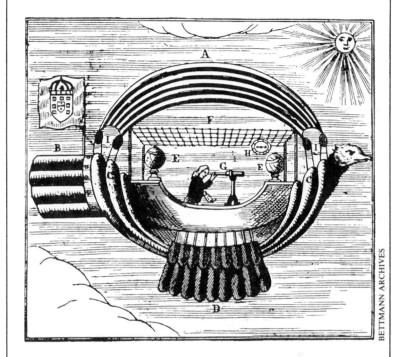

BETTMANN ARCHIVES

FIGURE 9: WOULD THIS 'FIRST AIRSHIP' REALLY FLY?

Laurenco de Guzmao demonstrated the lifting power of hot air by flying tiny balloons for the King of Portugal in 1709. But before then he (and doubtless many others long forgotten) dreamed of ships which would "sail the purple twilight" as they did the ocean. Of these the best known is his *Passarola* which, to the best of our knowledge never existed save on paper. Unable to find for his larger balloons fabric capable of containing a large volume of hot air for long, Guzmao abandoned his dream, leaving to the Montgolfier brothers the fame of first flight. More than a hundred years before Guzmao, Leonardo Da Vinci had designed and built models of heavier-than-air machines, but his notebooks were hidden for centuries. Not until the invention of an engine more powerful than man, could flight in such a machine become reality.

before King Louis the 16th, his Queen, and innumerable people of every rank and age. To dramatize the safety of the flight, live animals were taken up in the basket, rising over 1,500 feet to the surprise and excitement of the crowd. Though the sheep kicked the rooster, neither was harmed by altitude.

Obviously a man would be next to go — but who? Hearing that a criminal condemned to death had been chosen, an apothecary, Pilâtre de Rozier insisted that such an honor should not go to the dregs of society and persuaded the Montgolfiers to give him the place. On October 15, 1783 de Rozier entered the basket, the fire was stirred and the balloon rose easily to the end of its tether before being pulled back to earth. A few weeks later a balloon carrying de Rozier and a certain Marquis d'Arlandes was allowed to rise free. The two were carried up more than 3,000 feet, landing safely a half hour later several miles away. The first men had been airborne!

While all of this was going on, a prominent physicist, Jacques Charles, was developing another form of lift. He had no idea of what force lifted the Montgolfier balloons, but from their dimensions he calculated that the lift could not be as great as that of the new gas which Henry Cavendish made by treating iron filings with sulfuric acid and called *"inflammable gas,"* just as Black and Cavallo had earlier suggested. Charles engaged two brothers, Nicolas and Charles Robert, to make a small globe of silk varnished with rubber. On August 23, 1783 this trial balloon was ready but it took three days to generate enough hydrogen to fill it. Finally before an immense crowd on August 27th a gun was fired and the balloon rose easily, disappeared into a low cloud and two hours later landed fifteen miles away, thoroughly startling the people of a tiny village despite a public warning previously issued by the government. The great lifting power of hydrogen had been proven.

Three months later Jacques Charles and Nicolas Robert inflated another balloon, this one twenty-seven feet in diameter, with hydrogen, and (again before a huge crowd) climbed into the basket and took off, waving small flags to show that they were well. They flew much higher, landing twenty-seven miles away, where Nicolas Robert got out while Jacques Charles rose again, more rapidly this time, later writing:

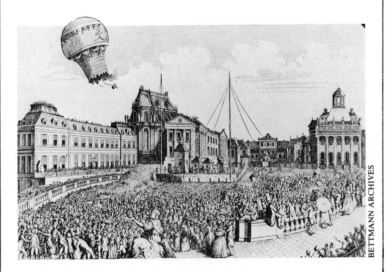

BETTMANN ARCHIVES

FIGURE 10: THE FIRST FREE BALLOON FLIGHT — 1783

As Gibbs-Smith wrote: *"It came as a great surprise that floating, rather than flapping, flight should first take human beings into the air, especially after the expenditure of so much time and energy by the 'tower jumpers' and the breaking of so many bones."* Guzmao had shown that hot air had lifting power, and Black had realized the possibilities of using Cavendish's newly discovered hydrogen in 1767 but did not pursue the matter as Cavallo did a few years later. So it was left to the Montgolfier brothers to first make real man's dream of flight. Their first effort was made indoors in 1782. Their second, more ambitious flight *"filled the assembled multitude with silent astonishment which ended with loud unfettered acclamations."* They did not know exactly why their balloon rose, supposing it to be due to a special light vapor formed from mouldy hay. The Montgolfier brothers lit a fuse which set off an explosion of interest in "aerostation" though they themselves soon abandoned ballooning.

"In twenty minutes I was 10,000 feet high, out of sight of terrestrial objects. . . I passed from the warmth of spring to the cold of winter, a sharp dry cold but not too much to be borne. . .

In the midst of my delight I felt a violent pain in my right ear and jaw which I ascribed to the dilatation of the air in the cellular construction of these organs. . ."

Jacques Charles was a scientist; we know him best for his gas law which states that if the pressure on a confined gas is constant, its volume is directly proportional to its temperature.

Ballooning became the current fashion and all sorts of stunts were tried: A certain Mr. Testu-Brissey made an ascent riding on a horse; an opera singer floated above Paris singing arias, and Dr. Leullier-Ducag advocated balloon flights to treat pestilential or nervous fevers, scurvy, hysteria, chlorosis and melancholy because the air was purer at great heights. A more serious excursion was the crossing of the English Channel by Jean Pierre Blanchard and an American physician Dr. John Jeffries who collected samples of air during the flight, and showed that the composition of all samples, even from different altitudes was the same. De Rozier, rising to the competition, developed a balloon which combined the lift of heated air and hydrogen despite the warnings of Jacques Charles that hydrogen was highly flammable. De Rozier took off, and the predictable explosion took place, killing him and his passenger.

Soon the balloonists were competing to make the longest or the highest flights and as they went higher into the thin cold air, the effects of altitude became more and more serious. Blanchard, whose Channel crossing had brought him notoriety, claimed to have gone up to 32,000 feet where he *"grew languid (and) felt a numbness, prelude to a dangerous sleep. . ."* His claim was disputed and of course could not be proven and he died poor and obscure. Others also claimed altitude records, most credibly a prominent physicist Gay-Lussac who noted at 22,000 feet that his:

"respiration was noticeably hampered; but I was still far from experiencing such severe discomfort as to wish to descend. My pulse and respiratory rate were much accelerated; and so, breathing very frequently in a very dry air I was not surprised to find my throat so dry that it was painful to swallow bread. . .

BETTMANN ARCHIVES

FIGURE 11: BALLOONS CREATED SPECIAL PROBLEMS

Though the new sport of ballooning rapidly became popular, communications were not good enough in the early days to inform rural folks of the arrival of such apparently supernatural objects, and the first balloon landings (top) often met hostile receptions. A young girl, almost struck by a chair apparently falling from a clear sky, enjoyed a brief period of reverential notoriety. Soon a cartoonist suggested (bottom) that balloon flights be preceded by announcers on land and in the air to quiet the fears of the populace. A century or so later a man waving a red flag would be required to precede the first automobiles!

These are all the inconveniences I experienced."

The altitude which could be reached by Montgolfier hot air balloons was limited as was the duration of flight, by the amount of fuel (usually straw) which could be carried and also by the decreased combustion in rarefied air, so these enjoyed limited popularity as hydrogen became more available. Even the Charlière hydrogen balloons had limitations: ascent and descent were constantly affected by air temperature, progress was deranged by wind, and since no replacement hydrogen could be carried, once it had been vented through the special escape valve, further ascent was possible only by dropping off weights— usually sand—which experienced astronauts threw out in small handfuls with the cunning of a miser. After his famous Channel crossing, Jeffries reported that only discarding five or six pounds of urine had saved him and Blanchard from a dunking!

Though balloons were internationally popular for a few decades, by the end of the century attention turned to heavier-than-air machines. George Cayley published important articles on the history and principles of aerial navigation and Walker wrote a *Treatise on the Art of Flying by Mechanical Means* in 1810 which is remarkable in its perceptions. But without a lightweight engine such machines were not practicable and interest turned back to ballooning.

An English meteorologist Henry Coxwell and James Glaisher were carried very high, possibly to over 29,000 feet, in a hydrogen balloon in 1862 and escaped death from hypoxia only because Coxwell, in his last conscious moments was able to pull the release valve with his teeth, releasing hydrogen and allowing the balloon to descend. Glaisher became something of an authority on the effects of high altitude and after a great many ascents felt that he had developed a tolerance:

"At length I became so acclimatized to the effects of a more rarefied atmosphere, that I could breathe at an elevation of four miles at least above the earth without inconvenience, and I have no doubt that this faculty of acclimatization might be so developed as to have a very important bearing upon the philosophical uses of balloon ascents."

Today there is no firm evidence that repeated ascents improve acclimatization; in fact in the U.S. air forces quite the opposite was held to be true. However, Soviet and Japanese climbers train by spending an hour or two each day at slightly higher altitudes in a decompression chamber. They believe that some unusually fast and high climbs have been facilitated by this preparation. In Seattle today one may see masked runners carrying back-packs with cylinders of a compressed low oxygen gas mixture which they breathe while running. This bizarre spectacle is attributable to the belief with no data to prove it, that training at simulated altitude enhances performance at sea level — and stimulates acclimatization for desired Himalayan performance. Who knows?

It was now almost a century since the vital properties of oxygen had been described, and even longer since Mayow and others had shown that small animals died when deprived of it in a closed vessel. The decrease in barometric pressure at altitude had been demonstrated along with the attendant decrease in oxygen pressure. Yet the early balloonists had not fully grasped that the dangers of altitude were due to lack of oxygen and could be prevented by breathing that gas. It remained for an extraordinary man, often called the father of altitude physiology, to show how the catastrophes could be prevented.

Paul Bert was born in Burgundy less than a hundred miles from Paris, and first studied engineering, later changing to law, which he found too boring so he entered medicine, graduating at the age of thirty, though he never practiced medicine. Instead he studied under the great physiologist Claude Bernard and found his true love in experimental physiology including transplant surgery. For almost twenty years he studied the effects of reduced and increased pressure on small animals and later on man using steel cylinders (or bells) especially designed for his laboratory. His experiments clearly showed that breathing air under reduced pressure — as at altitude — was dangerous because of oxygen lack, and that breathing oxygen even under considerably reduced pressure, restored normal function. Bert turned to the study of blood, and was able to define the first crude curves showing the relationships between hemoglobin and oxygen under different pressures, laying the foundations for much later work in oxygen transport.

Bert collected accounts from travellers as well as scientists from all over the world and in addition to his studies in decompression chambers, became interested in the opportunities that balloons offered for studying altitude. In March 1874 two aspiring astronauts, Joseph Crocé-Spinelli and Theodor Sivel came to Bert's laboratory *"with the purpose of studying upon themselves the disagreeable effects of decompression and the favorable influence of superoxygenated air"* in preparation for an attempt to set a new altitude record. During the hour they spent in the chamber the pressure was reduced to that equivalent to 24,000 feet, and they experienced dimming of vision, dulling of mind, and difficulty with calculations, all promptly relieved by a few inhalations of oxygen which they breathed whenever the symptoms became severe. Crocé-Spinelli had already been up to 15,000 feet in a balloon without noticing any unpleasant effects and may have been a bit blasé about the risks. Bert, in contrast, was very much concerned and wanted to demonstrate conclusively how effectively oxygen could protect the balloonists. On March 28th he had himself decompressed in the chamber to 21,000 feet breathing oxygen without interruption from 16,000 feet up. From the hour and a half experiment he concluded *"that continuous inhalations of oxygen, after having checked painful symptoms, will prevent them from reappearing, though the barometric pressure continues to fall."*

On March 22, 1874 Crocé-Spinelli and Sivel ascended to approximately 24,000 feet (7,300 m) in a great balloon "The Polar Star" and wrote:

"We felt in our flight impressions similar to those which we had experienced in the decompression bells of M. Bert in which several days before we were taken to a pressure of 304 mm* (23,000 feet). . . In the bell, the pure oxygen which we were breathing caused dizzy spells like those of drunkenness, whereas on the contrary we were very comfortable with the two mixtures, one of 40% oxygen and 60% nitrogen, and the other of 70% oxygen and 30% nitrogen which M. Bert had furnished for our ascent. . ."

---

* Scientists were beginning to define altitude by the barometric pressure, usually measured in the height of the column of mercury in a barometer, normal sea level pressure sustaining the column at 760 mm.

FIGURE 12: PAUL BERT'S DECOMPRESSION CHAMBER

Paul Bert used this steel 'bell' or decompression chamber, given him by his generous sponsor Dr. Jourdannet, for studying the effects of high altitude in the laboratory. He was able to evacuate the chamber to simulate any desired altitude, and in it one person at a time could experience lack of oxygen while protected by outside observers. This was before the days of pressurized gas cylinders, but by keeping a leather sac filled with oxygen in an adjoining chamber (connected by a small pipe to the subject's chamber), Bert could supply oxygen or allow the subject to breathe the thinner air. This showed dramatically how beneficial oxygen was at altitude, after showing how much the mind and body deteriorated while breathing only air. The lesson undoubtedly saved many lives, though the *Zenith's* crew did not take enough oxygen to prevent the death of two of the three. Bert also used the 'bell' to study the effects of increased pressure, as for example on divers.

After these experiments Bert and the balloonists were fully convinced of:

". . . the favorable effects of inhalation of oxygen. Return of strength and appetite, decrease of headache, restoration of clear vision, calmness of mind, all the phenomena already observed in the cylinders of the laboratory . . . we produced with a certainty . . . that was very striking. . ."

Consequently they arranged to carry oxygen in three large leather bags on their record-breaking flight. Bert was in Paris on the day planned for the attempt. Crocé-Spinelli had written to him that they would have approximately 150 liters of oxygen in the three skin bags. Bert was alarmed. He wrote back immediately:

"In the lofty elevations where this artificial respiration will be indispensable to you, for three men you should count on a consumption of at least 20 liters per minute; see how soon your supply will be exhausted."

But the letter arrived too late. The story of the flight of the balloon *Zenith* on April 15, 1875 is dramatic, but it is only one of the many tragedies which occurred as daring men used balloons and later heavier-than-air machines to reach great altitudes without thorough understanding of the risks of oxygen lack. Bert quotes the vivid account, given immediately after the flight, by the sole survivor, Gaston Tissandier, in which he describes in detail the symptoms of hypoxia which overcame him somewhere above 25,000 feet and would have killed him as well as his two companions had he not somehow gathered strength and will to vent some hydrogen and cause the *Zenith* to descend:

"The last very clear memory that remains to me of the ascent goes back to a moment a little before this . . . soon I was keeping absolutely motionless, without suspecting that perhaps I had already lost use of my movements. . . Towards 7,500 m the numbness one experiences is extraordinary. The body and mind weaken little by little, gradually, unconsciously and without one's knowledge. One does not suffer at all, quite the contrary. One experiences an inner joy, as if it were an effect of the inundating flood of light. One becomes indifferent; one no longer thinks of the perilous situation or the danger; one rises and is happy to rise. . . I soon felt so weak that I could not even turn my head to

look at my companions. . . I wanted to seize the oxygen tube but could not raise my arm. My mind, however, was still very lucid. I was still looking at the barometer, my eyes were fixed on the needle which soon reached the pressure number of 290, then 280, beyond which it passed. . . I wanted to cry out 'We are at 8,000 meters,' but my tongue was paralyzed. Suddenly I closed my eyes and fell inert, entirely losing consciousness."

This tragedy, though neither the first nor the last in the history of ballooning, became a major milestone along the path to understanding how lack of oxygen saps the mind and body. Bert's enthusiasm for altitude research seems to have been damped by the accident and he became more active in politics and was sent to become Resident General in Indo-China, to resolve the endless turmoil there. He died within five months of dysentery, leaving as a lasting monument his great book *La Pression Barometrique.* Though little known for several decades, Mr. and Mrs. Fred Hitchcock's translation in 1943 made it available to many just when its lessons were most helpful to aviation at great altitudes in WW II. Bert was encouraged throughout his life by a wealthy friend and co-worker, Dr. Denis Jourdannet, who was especially interested in the effects of altitude on the health of the highland people of Mexico where he travelled extensively, publishing several books on atmospheric pressure and oxygen transport by red blood cells. Jourdannet was generous, supplying Bert with expensive equipment, and lending him the steel decompression chambers in which so much of his altitude work was done.

Bert was strongly influenced by another physician, also ahead of his time: Dr. Conrad Meyer-Ahrens of Leipzig who had, in 1854, published a book containing a summary of his conclusions from many travellers' tales and many experiments:

"The principal symptoms (of altitude illness) or at least those which occur oftenest in man are: discomfort, distaste for food, especially distaste for wine (however, the contrary has sometimes been noted), intense thirst (especially for water, which quenches the thirst best), nausea, vomiting; accelerated and panting respiration; dyspnea, acceleration of the pulse, throbbing of the large arteries and the temples; violent palpitations, oppression, anxiety, asphyxia; vertigo, headache, tendency to syncope, unconquerable desire for sleep, though the sleep does not refresh

but is disturbed by anguish; finally, astonishing and very strange muscular fatigue. These symptoms do not always appear all together. . . Others are observed, although less frequently, such as pulmonary, renal, and intestinal hemorrhages (in animals also); vomiting of blood; oozing of blood from the mucous membrane of the lips and the skin (due merely to the desiccation of these membranes), blunting of sensory perceptions and the intelligence, impatience, irritability, . . . finally, buzzing in the ears. . . All that we have just said about the etiology of mountain sickness shows (1) that it appears at varying altitudes; (2) that meteorological conditions, temporary or general personal characteristics, and the speed of walking vary the altitude at which one is attacked and the severity and number of the symptoms. . . In my opinion, the principal role belongs to the decrease of the absolute quantity of oxygen in the rarefied air, the rapidity of evaporation and the intense action of light, direct or reflected from snow, whereas the direct action of the decreased pressure should be placed in the second rank. I find the immediate causes of mountain sickness in the changes made in the composition and formation of the blood by the decrease in oxygen and the exaggerated evaporation, changes to which are added others due to the action of light on the cerebral function, an action which affects the preparation of the blood liquid."

We cannot improve much on this today!

Balloons were widely used for recreation, excitement, and (in our Civil War and the Franco-Prussian war of 1870) for important military missions, as well as for research, but as the century ended it was clear that heavier-than-air machines would soon fly, and the Age of Aviation soon began. The first tentatives scarcely threatened lack of oxygen, but the advent of the First World War confirmed that high flying aircraft would become decisive factors in warfare. Within a few short years engines and airframes were able to go higher than could pilots unaided by oxygen and fighting took place higher and higher, with all its terror just as Lana-Terzi and da Vinci had predicted. Altitude physiology received a tremendous stimulus from war high in the atmosphere and by the nineteen twenties sophisticated studies were again being done on high mountains, because aircraft went up too fast and for too short a time for the kind of work which needed to be done.

In both world wars high altitude killed many aircrewmen due to failure of equipment or bravado or ignorance, or when equipment was damaged in combat. But hypoxia in aviation is quite different from that on mountains or in most illnesses: it is more abrupt in onset, more severe, and the outcome more dangerous. The story of oxygen in aviation is a dramatic one but not relevant to this book, which deals with more gradual, subtler, and far more common problems.

As the nineteenth century ended most scientists were in agreement that the basic cause of altitude illness was lack of oxygen due to decreased barometric pressure. One exception was a distinguished mountaineering physiologist, Angelo Mosso who extended his laboratory studies to the summit of Monte Rosa (15,025 ft) on the Swiss-Italian frontier, where Queen Margherita sponsored and dedicated in person a small stone laboratory. Not many queens would have made the long and not always easy climb, even unimpeded by the long skirts and numerous ladies-in-waiting mandated by those times.

Mosso published his observations in a fascinating book *Life of Man on the High Alps* in 1896 which was translated into English two years later. He concluded that lack of oxygen could not adequately explain all that happened at altitude, and coined the word "acapnia," meaning lack of carbon dioxide, which he thought would cause the symptoms. There was — and still is — some truth in this because the strong stimulus to breathe more than normally does wash out carbon dioxide from lungs and blood at altitude, and the result is a drift toward the alkaline side, which does cause problems. But Mosso's ideas did not gain much acceptance, and Bert, and later Haldane and Barcroft conclusively showed that lack of oxygen was the primary (but as we will see later) not the sole cause of altitude problems.

Mosso has left us several major contributions, however. First he observed irregular breathing at altitude during sleep, attributing this correctly to derangement of the normal stimuli to breathing and suggesting that this was why mountain sickness was worse at night or early in the morning. He also wondered what was happening in the brain to cause the headache so characteristic of mountain sickness and was able to find two youths who had holes in their skulls as a result of accidents. The first (Cesar

Lasagno) was taken in Mosso's decompression chamber to about 17,000 feet where there was *"some diminution in the tonicity of the blood vessels of the brain"* but no evidence of congestion or anemia. The second boy (Emmanuele Favre) was given a mixture of 10% oxygen in nitrogen to breathe, equivalent to breathing air at 18,000 feet. He had some minor symptoms which Mosso attributed to *"a disturbance in nutrition of the brain"* rather than to *"paralysis of the blood vessels."* Mosso did not observe any swelling, but did conclude, correctly, that altitude headache was somehow related to circulation.

His third contribution was to record for the first time details of the death of a young physician high on Mont Blanc, the first record we have of high altitude pulmonary edema.

As our century began, balloons had taken men more than five miles above the earth, briefly and occasionally tragically. Adventurous mountaineers had reached 21,000 feet, but many had been miserably sick and some had died. The use of decompression chambers had shown that decreased pressure led to all the signs and symptoms seen at altitude—and when these were prevented or relieved by breathing oxygen, it seemed obvious that lack of oxygen due to the decreased barometric pressure was the basic cause of altitude sickness. Other causes—some outlandish, but some at least partly correct had been proposed. As the twentieth century began, powered aircraft brought great opportunities as well as risks and grave threats to mankind (as Lana–Terzi had predicted three centuries earlier). Who at that time would have believed men would be able to sample air using helium balloons thirty miles above earth, walk on the moon, and control rockets sent millions of miles into space? Mt. Everest had been discovered and its height measured, but no one then believed it could be climbed, let alone without oxygen.

Chapter Four
ON MOVING AIR IN THE BODY

Of all the stuffs essential to life, oxygen alone can neither be stored nor manufactured in the body: the supply must be replenished almost as fast as it is used. This hand-to-mouth existence is especially characteristic of birds and mammals and an absolute constraint on where they go and what they do. As Mayow showed with his mouse under a bell jar, the processes of life depend upon a *"vital spirit . . . that is by means of respiration transmitted into the mass of the blood and the fermentation and the heating of the blood are produced by it."* Scheele, Priestley and Lavoisier repeated such studies many times, concluding that animals needed this vital spirit (oxygen) to 'burn' foodstuffs to fuel every activity much as a candle needs oxygen to burn, creating light and heat. Everything we do—thinking and dreaming, running or mountain climbing, eating, resting, getting angry or making love, even lying in a trance requires oxygen to create the energy which pumps the blood, moves the muscles, excretes wastes and makes the body function.

True—some functions can go on for a short time without oxygen (an-aerobically) but they rapidly build up an 'oxygen debt' which must soon be repaid by a greater than average oxygen consumption. True too that a special form of blood pigment (myoglobin) can hold or store small amounts of oxygen for short periods in large muscles, but for all practical purposes the body is dependent on an uninterrupted supply of oxygen—more during activity and less at rest. Without an adequate supply, functions falter, fail and soon cease completely.

Diving mammals, just as dependent on oxygen as is man, appear to store oxygen during prolonged dives, but in reality they simply shut off blood flow (and thus oxygen use) to non-essential organs and become "heart-lung-brain preparations." Of course as they swim, their muscles demand fuel, so that the more strenuous they are under water, the less time they can spend without surfacing to breathe.

Other apparent exceptions are high-flying birds like the barheaded goose or the Andean condor that are able to fly from

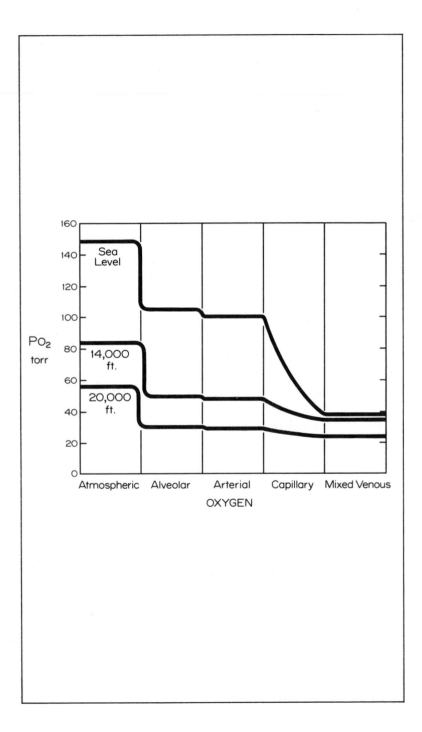

FIGURE 13: THE OXYGEN CASCADE

At each stage in its passage from outside air to tissues, oxygen loses some pressure. This series of drops is known as the oxygen cascade. At each stage some measures will minimize the drop, thereby raising the oxygen available to tissues, but at each stage there are diseases or abnormalities which can increase the drop, thereby decreasing the tissue oxygenation.

Between outside air and alveolar air, oxygen pressure falls sharply because mixing is incomplete. Over-breathing improves mixing and decreases this drop.

Between alveolar air and lung capillary blood (which will be arterial blood as it leaves the lung) there is a small oxygen pressure drop due to resistance of the alveolar-capillary membranes. This may increase sharply due to chronic disease like fibrosis, or acute disease like early pulmonary edema. This A-a gradient can be quite important in oxygen delivery.

Little if any oxygen pressure is lost during transit of blood from lungs to tissue capillaries.

As oxygen diffuses from capillary into individual cells, more pressure is lost due to membrane resistance and to the distance between capillary and cell. By opening up new capillaries, this capillary-cell gradient can be decreased, whereas accumulation of water in the tissues, or sluggish blood flow will increase the gradient, aggravating tissue oxygen lack.

Mixed venous blood is the blood entering the right side of the heart from all veins of the body and is an indicator of both the body's need for oxygen and its utilization of oxygen. Mixed venous oxygen falls as exertion increases; mixed venous is lower at altitude than at sea level. It can be used as a better indicator of tissue oxygenation than arterial blood oxygen.

sea level to over 30,000 feet in a very short time and to stay there, apparently unimpaired for long periods. But for land-bound air-breathing animals, an almost uninterrupted supply of air containing adequate oxygen is absolutely essential.

The process of respiration can for convenience be divided into breathing, transporting and using oxygen, and discharging carbon dioxide. Breathing in and breathing out are functions of lung, chest and diaphragm; transportation a function of heart, blood and blood vessels; utilization is carried on by tiny parts of each living cell. All must function well if the organism is to function well.

The chest cavity is separated from the abdominal cavity by a great platelike muscle, the diaphragm; the chest contains heart and vessels (slung in a thin tough sac) and the lungs, which open to the outside air through bronchial tubes, trachea, mouth and nose. Expansion of the chest is accomplished by small muscles between the ribs, and by flattening of the diaphragm which is normally domed. As the rib cage expands, the chest cavity enlarges like a bellows, allowing atmospheric pressure to push the outside air in. When the chest contracts the diaphragm relaxes and staler air is driven out.

One cannot improve on the description of breathing in and out written by John Mayow in 1674, on the verge of discovering oxygen a century before Priestley and Lavoisier:

"With respect then to the entrance of the air into the lungs, I think it is to be maintained that it is caused . . . by the pressure of the atmosphere. For as the air, on account of the weight of the superincumbent atmosphere . . . rushes into all empty places . . . it follows that the air passes through the nostrils and the trachea up to the bronchia. . . When the inner sides of the thorax . . . are drawn outwards by muscles . . . and the space in the thorax is enlarged, the air which is nearest the bronchio inlets . . . rushes under the full pressure of the atmosphere into the cavities of the lungs. . . From this we conclude that the lungs are distended by the air rushing in, and that they do not expand of themselves, as some have supposed. . ."

The upper airways — mouth and nose and trachea — provide air conditioning. Their membrane linings are kept moist by diffusion of water from a dense network of small blood vessels just beneath the surface which also warms the in-rushing air. A thin film of mucus lines the airways, capturing small particles much as fly-paper catches flies. The trachea and larger bronchial tubes are also lined with cells that have hair-like appendages — cilia — which constantly sweep the film of mucus and its wastes upward to the mouth to be swallowed or spit out. By the time outside air has moved only a short distance it is saturated with water, warmed, and cleansed of all but the smallest particles. Even when the rush of air is ten or twenty times greater than normal during strenuous exertion, air conditioning is complete. This means that the body loses a great deal of water and heat when we breathe the cold dry air of altitude; this is not recaptured during expiration and so breathing dry air results in loss of a great volume of body water, terribly important to mountain climbers.

Cold air must be warmed to body temperature as it is breathed in, and consequently heat is lost with each exhalation. When breathing is very rapid, obviously more heat will be lost. Sir Brian Matthews pointed out years ago that evaporation of water from the mucous membranes that line the nose, mouth and the bronchial tree also soaks up heat, and calculated that near the top of Everest a man may lose more heat evaporating moisture to saturate the bone-dry air than he can replace by 'burning' his food and by working.

The trachea divides into major bronchi which in turn divide into smaller and smaller bronchi and these into bronchioles. Each of these small tubes ends in a cluster of tiny air sacs 0.25 mm in diameter, called alveoli (from the Latin for 'concave vessel'), which is where exchange of oxygen and carbon dioxide takes place between inspired air and blood. In the normal human lung each of the 300 million alveoli is enmeshed in a network of small capillary blood vessels, terminations of the branching vessels which carry blood from all over the body, through the heart and into the lungs. After passing the alveoli these capillaries join again, like brooks into streams and rivers, to form the large vessels which return blood filled with oxygen and depleted of carbon dioxide to the heart and thence to all parts of the body.

A crucial step in respiration occurs during the brief moments when blood is in these capillaries for it is only there that oxygen and carbon dioxide can pass between alveoli and blood. The

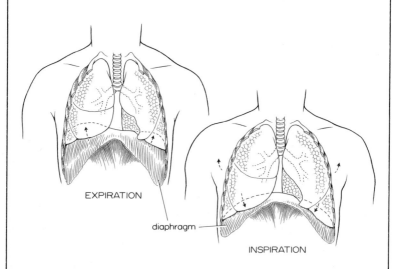

EXPIRATION

diaphragm

INSPIRATION

FIGURE 14: HOW AIR ENTERS AND LEAVES THE LUNGS

Inspiration is an active process, requiring muscular work: the dome-shaped diaphragm contracts and flattens, increasing the vertical dimensions of the chest cavity, and the small muscles between the ribs also contract, pulling the ribs outward and upward, thus increasing the dimensions fore and aft. As a result, just as Mayow perceived, air is pushed into the increased space by outside atmospheric pressure. Expiration, by contrast, is more passive: the diaphragm relaxes and returns to its upward dome-shape. The intercostal muscles also relax and the rib cage becomes smaller. Air then is under more pressure than outside the chest and flows out. One result of living for generations at altitude is enlargment of the chest (Chapter Eight).

pulmonary capillaries are only slightly larger (and many are slightly smaller) than the diameter of a red blood cell. The tiny disc-shaped red cells are twisted and distorted (and might easily become stuck) as they pass through capillaries which are thin walled, fragile and elastic, each serving several different alveoli. At altitude, and during exertion more capillaries open, allowing a larger flow of blood to come in contact with the alveoli.

The passage of a gas (in this case oxygen or carbon dioxide) through a semi-permeable membrane (the alveolar wall) depends on several factors: the difference in pressure of the gas between the two sides of the membrane, the area and thickness of the membrane, and a 'diffusion coefficient' peculiar to the gas, being among the more important. Division of the lung into millions of tiny air sacs provides a diffusing area of about 750 square feet — about 100 times as large as the area of a single sac the size of the entire chest cavity. The difference between oxygen pressure in the alveolus and in the blood entering the lung capillary, depleted of oxygen, is rather large, so oxygen diffuses swiftly into blood, and the pressure of oxygen in blood leaving the alveolus approaches that in the alveolus. The difference between the two is called the alveolar-arterial or (A-a) gradient and is normally only a few torr.

So large is this total area available for diffusion, and so rapid is passage of oxygen across the membrane, that blood rushing through the capillary network around the alveoli picks up all the oxygen it is capable of carrying at that particular alveolar pressure.

But let the surface area be decreased by a disease like pneumonia or by a collapsed lung, or by destruction of the walls of many alveoli (emphysema) and the A-a gradient for the whole lung area will be larger. If the membrane is only a little thicker, as is the case when fluid collects between capillary and alveolus, or when fibrosis scars the membrane, the A-a gradient becomes larger too. At great altitude, where alveolar pressure is low, passage is slower, though the A-a gradient is usually the same or even slightly less than at sea level — in healthy lungs without any accumulation of fluid. The time it takes for blood to pass through the short stretch of alveolar capillary is rarely a limiting factor except perhaps on top of Everest, where the heart rate is

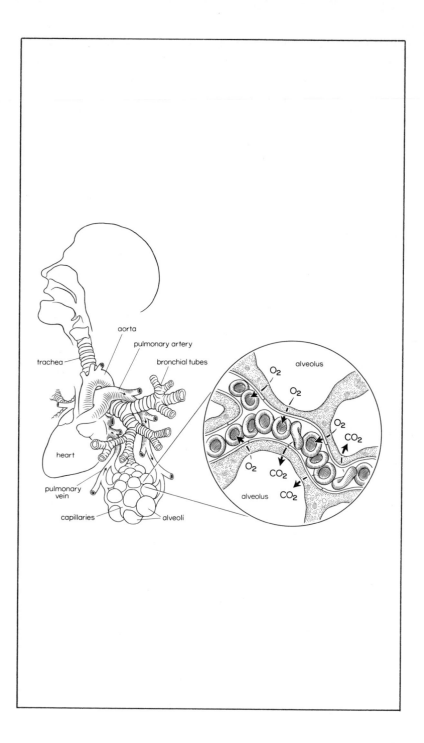

FIGURE 15: THE LUNG CAPILLARIES AND ALVEOLI

The heart and its great vessels (aorta, pulmonary artery, and great veins) are so intimately intertwined with the airways (trachea and bronchial tubes) that they are difficult to show except in a fore-shortened illustration such as this. The bronchial tubes branch into ever smaller passages, each terminating in a cluster of air sacs (alveoli) much like a bunch of grapes. With each breath air moves in and out of this intricate system, partially replacing 'stale' air in the alveoli with fresher air from outside. Each alveolus (smaller than a pinhead) is surrounded by a network of capillary blood vessels, barely large enough to allow red cells to pass, and each capillary serves several alveoli. Oxygen diffuses from the alveolus (where its pressure is higher) through the alveolar wall, through a narrow space (interstitial space) and through the capillary wall into the red blood cells. Blood arriving in the lungs contains more carbon dioxide than is in the alveoli, so carbon dioxide flows from capillary to alveolus and actually expedites passage of oxygen in the opposite direction. The whole transaction takes only a fraction of a second, but by the time each bit of blood has passed through alveolar capillaries it has taken on a full load of oxygen and released most of its carbon dioxide. High altitude, where oxygen pressure is lower in the atmosphere and hence in the alveolus, decreases the flow of oxygen into blood but does not affect the release of carbon dioxide. Diseases which impair ventilation or which thicken or change the alveolar walls, also impair oxygen flow, but affect carbon dioxide flow as well.

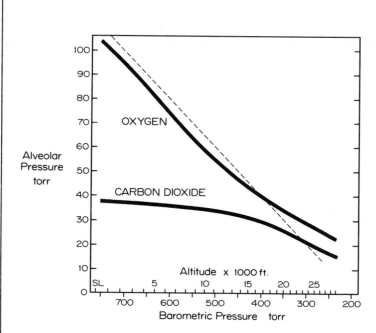

FIGURE 16:
CHANGES IN ALVEOLAR GASES AT INCREASING ALTITUDE

With increasing altitude, the pressure of oxygen in alveolar air decreases, as does that of carbon dioxide. However, around 8,000 feet ventilation increases enough to cause considerable improvement in the mixing of incoming air with that deep in the lungs. As a result oxygen pressure falls less steeply, but carbon dioxide more steeply as the individual goes still higher. The broken line shows how atmospheric pressure (scaled along bottom of lower axis) falls as altitude (scaled along the upper side of the lower axis) increases. Note that the fall in oxygen parallels the fall in pressure only up to 12-15,000 feet, where greater increase in breathing sustains oxygen while 'washing out' carbon dioxide more rapidly than at lower altitude. By deliberately forcing hyperventilation, alveolar oxygen can be kept higher, but carbon dioxide lowered perhaps to dangerous levels, at any altitude. The standard altitude/pressure curve is usually drawn with equal intervals along each axis and is a curve of decreasing slope. Here since the scales are different, the dashed line is straight.

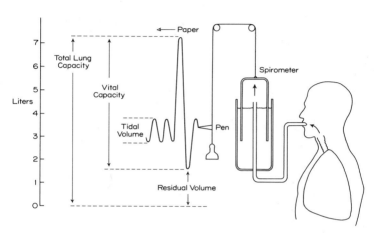

FIGURE 17:
HOW DIFFERENT LEVELS OF VENTILATION ARE DEFINED

After taking in the deepest possible breath, the subject exhales into a bell jar over water (spirometer). Rise and fall of the spirometer are recorded on paper on a revolving drum. Even after the fullest expiration some residual air remains in the lung. Residual air plus the maximum volume which can be exhaled after the maximum inhalation is called total lung capacity. Total lung capacity minus the residual air is the vital capacity, or useful breathing capacity. In normal breathing at rest, inspiration and expiration move a much smaller volume known as the tidal air. This simple set of measurements is made more informative by measuring the number of seconds it takes to move air, thus obtaining the timed vital capacity. A decrease in vital capacity may be one of the earliest signs of beginning altitude sickness (pulmonary edema); changes in several of these measurements occur in different lung diseases and at altitude.

rapid and the alveolar oxygen pressure very low. Under normal sea level conditions, oxygen diffuses through the alveolar walls in less than 0.4 seconds, while a red cell takes from 0.6 to 0.8 seconds to traverse an alveolar capillary.

The normal A-a gradient in youth is only 2-5 torr, but it increases to 10-15 torr or more in old age. During exertion it usually decreases, while at altitude it may increase or decrease. From our point of view the most important influence on the A-a gradient is the accumulation of fluid in the alveolar walls or in the alveoli themselves.

The trachea, bronchi and alveoli are dead-end passages, and air moves in and out rather than through as it does in some animals. This ebb and flow is called the "tidal air" and is of course increased with deeper or faster breathing. The greater the tidal air, the better the mixing of purer outside air with stale air deep in the lungs. So anything which decreases respiration interferes with tidal air and is likely to decrease oxygen in the alveoli. A good example is the slow shallow breathing characteristic of sleep in some persons which may — especially at high altitude — decrease oxygen in the blood quite significantly. Conversely, over-breathing increases alveolar oxygen, and many climbers practice deliberate over-breathing (sometimes called 'grunt breathing') which was developed as an emergency procedure during World War Two for aviators who lost their oxygen supply at altitude.

But just as the partial pressure of oxygen in the alveoli is increased by deeper breathing, so too is the partial pressure of carbon dioxide decreased. Carbon dioxide is constantly formed in tissues as part of combustion, in greater amounts during work. It diffuses rapidly from tissues into blood where it is carried partly in solution, but mostly in a loose equilibrium as carbonate-bicarbonate. This is a most fortunate arrangement because carbon dioxide diffuses twenty times as rapidly as does oxygen and would tend to rush out of the blood into the lungs too rapidly were it not slowed a little by this loose chemical combination.

Carbon dioxide is the principal regulator of the acidity of the blood, and a very precise one it is, since its level can change in a second or two depending on the level of breathing and the amount of work being done. Over-breathing deliberately may lower carbon dioxide enough to make the blood too alkaline and cause a condition known as hyperventilation syndrome which leads to painful cramps and various unpleasant and alarming symptoms. The climber or flyer who deliberately controls his breathing at altitude must walk between the Scylla of oxygen lack if he breathes too little, and the Charybdis of carbon dioxide lack if he breathes too much; it is a tricky path.

Twenty or thirty years ago several groups identified another factor which would decrease oxygenation of blood leaving the lungs and thus contribute to increasing the overall A-a oxygen gradient. This is the presence in blood leaving the lungs of some blood which has not passed near a functioning alveolus. Such 'shunted blood', which would contain the same amount of oxygen as venous blood from all parts of the body, may by-pass the alveoli through normal anatomical channels, or may be unable to receive oxygen because the alveoli it passes are collapsed or choked with fluid as in pneumonia or pulmonary edema and thus not aerated. In some types of congenital heart disease some blood actually goes from one side of the heart to the other without entering the lungs at all and is thus unoxygenated. Shunts like this are not major contributors to the A-a gradient under most circumstances but become very important in certain diseases, especially at high altitude.

Once oxygen is in the lung capillaries it enters the red cells swiftly and combines with hemoglobin to be carried to all parts of the body without losing appreciable pressure on the way. In the tissue capillaries, the higher PO_2 in the arterial end of the capillary causes oxygen to 'flow downhill' as it were, diffusing through the capillary wall, through the loose (interstitial) space between cells, through the thin cell wall into the watery fluid called cytoplasm that fills each cell, and finally into the minute granules — the mitochondria (from the Latin for 'thread-grains') where the real action is. The flow of oxygen is matched by the flow — in the opposite direction — of carbon dioxide, from cells where it is formed, through various barriers into the venous end of capillaries and thence to the alveoli and out.

Understanding the oxygen cascade enables us to understand better why and how high altitude causes lack of oxygen where it is most needed — in the cells: (1) by a decrease in the partial pressure of oxygen caused by decrease in the atmospheric pressure as shown by Perier on the Puy-de-Dome, (2) when fluid accumulates between alveolus and capillary by impeding diffusion of oxygen, and rarely, (3) by a similar impedance to diffusion when tissues accumulate excess fluid as well. The cascade diagram shows where illness or injury are most likely to result in oxygen deficiency. The cascade also hints where changes, either deliberate, or spontaneous, will improve oxygen flow to the ultimate consumer — the cells.

What makes our breathing fast or slow, deep or shallow? Very seldom do we think about breathing because it is mostly dictated by stimuli which we are unaware of. We know, for example, that strenuous exertion, sudden excitement, fear, passion, or stepping under a cold shower make us breathe faster or deeper or both, but we don't control this deliberately. When we are resting or sleeping, breathing is slower and more shallow, again controlled for us. How does this happen — and where? More interestingly — can this control be modified to suit our needs or wishes?

It seems reasonable to imagine that lack of oxygen in the blood (or even the alveolar air) would initiate instructions to breathe more air, and in fact hypoxia does stimulate breathing. It also seems reasonable that if carbon dioxide accumulated to a dangerous degree, breathing would be increased to wash it out, and in fact accumulation of carbon dioxide is a more powerful stimulant to respiration than is lack of oxygen. When you hold your breath it is build-up of carbon dioxide rather than fall in oxygen which forces you to breathe again and it is difficult or impossible to hold your breath long enough to become very hypoxic.

Both lack of oxygen and increase in carbon dioxide act on a collection of sensitive cells in the mid-brain (nervous tissue at the base of the skull). Like the thermostat in your house, which turns on the furnace when the temperature is too cold or the air-conditioner when it is too hot, this respiratory center is part of a feed-back loop which controls with exquisite sensitivity one aspect of our internal environment.

Other changes affect breathing too. If the blood becomes too acid from strenuous exertion or from too many waste products (most of which are acid) breathing is increased. A much less frequent situation occurs when the blood becomes too alkaline — and breathing is slowed. Other subtle influences affect us: passion makes us pant, fear "catches your breath," as that cold shower certainly does. These stimuli go through the autonomic (automatic) nervous system which regulates most of the functions we are unaware of like digestion, urine secretion, blood pressure and heart rate and many others.

Other centers also influence breathing but they are less important. What is unclear at altitude is how the control is accomplished—is it through the gin-clear spinal fluid that bathes the brain, or is it via the flowing blood—or a combination of both?

Obviously this is a greatly over-simplified description of a delicate and complex system that regulates our vital functions with great sensitivity and almost completely without our being aware of it. The control of respiration has been hotly debated for years but is too complex to discuss here.

What is important is that we can artificially stimulate 'natural' ventilation to improve oxygen supply at altitude, and it does seem to help. And as we will discuss in Chapter Seven, we can to some extent correct some of the aberrations in breathing which occur at altitude, when the respiratory center seems almost to be confused whether to respond to lack of oxygen by more breathing or to lack of carbon dioxide by breathing less.

Chapter Five
THE CIRCULATION OF THE BLOOD

Breathing moves air in and out of the body, and physical laws dictate the passage of oxygen from lungs to blood, but the blood must be adequate to carry its load and must move at a speed and volume appropriate to what the tissues need for all to function harmoniously. To understand how altitude affects us we need to know something about the heart, blood and blood vessels and how and why they function or fail.

The heart is the most immediately indispensable organ of the body in the sense that man can live for months (cynics say for years) with little or no apparent brain activity, and for days or weeks without kidneys or liver, but death occurs in less than ten minutes if heart or respirations stop. We define the circulatory system as including the heart and blood vessels of different kinds and size and myriad destinations which carry blood from heart to lungs, from lungs to heart, from heart to every distant nook and cranny of the body and back to the heart. The motions of the blood move food and water and vital oxygen, carry away wastes of all sorts, and cool or heat the various parts of the body as needed. Circulation is almost completely controlled by the autonomic* nervous system; we are usually unaware of the ceaseless changes and adjustments responsive to many feedback systems which ensure *the constancy of the internal environment (which) is the condition of the active life*" as Claude Bernard so aptly put it.

Poets and lovers to the contrary notwithstanding, the heart serves no other purpose than to pump blood hour after hour, year after year, responsive to many stimuli, but inherently able to maintain and adjust its pace without outside intervention. For the heart is self-governing: in the thin-walled auricles (antechambers to the muscular ventricles which do the work) a tiny group of nerve cells initiates the electrical impulses which spread to the ventricles, driving them to contract at a rate set by this pacemaker.

---

* "Autonomic" comes from the Greek "self regulating"; most of the bodily activities not subject to wilful control have their activities regulated by this special nerve network.

This autonomy enables the heart to continue beating so long as its needs for oxygen, heat, moisture and nourishment are met, even if removed from the body. It will beat indefinitely in the body, spurred by its own internal circuitry, even when all nerve connections to the rest of the body are severed. But it will beat at its own unchanging intrinsic rate, and such independence would not permit a very active life with changing demands now for more, now for less blood. How could the output be slowed during sleep — or speeded to meet the challenge of sudden exertion? The variety and freedom of life depend upon a network of stimuli, some along the nerves, some along the blood, to direct the heart to pump harder or faster, or more gently.

The stimulus to fight or flee, the throes of passion or fear, meditation and biofeedback — and lack of oxygen — all direct the work of the heart. These stimuli pass through the hypothalamus, a kind of control center in the brain which receives and evaluates nervous and hormonal signals from all parts of the body and switches them to other brain centers which in turn dispatch messages to the appropriate destinations for action.

Lack of oxygen is one of these stimuli: when detected by specialized chemo-receptors (tiny collections of nerve cells not unlike the thermostat in our house), messages are sent to increase breathing, as we saw, and to increase the rate of the heart as well as the output per stroke. As a result the heart pumps more blood each minute, thus conveying more oxygen to tissues. This response lasts for hours to days, but as other adjustments take over, output falls to or below normal, only slowly returning to the sea level value.

Other sensors perceive blood pressure and signal appropriate changes locally or throughout the body — but hypoxia does not stimulate these pressure receptors and therefore blood pressure is seldom affected by altitude. Other 'emergency gate' controls shunt blood from one organ to another in times of stress, for example shunting blood away from stomach and intestines to muscles when an emergency calls for intense effort. This is what enables diving mammals to stay under water long after their inhaled oxygen is exhausted, as we will see in Chapter Nine.

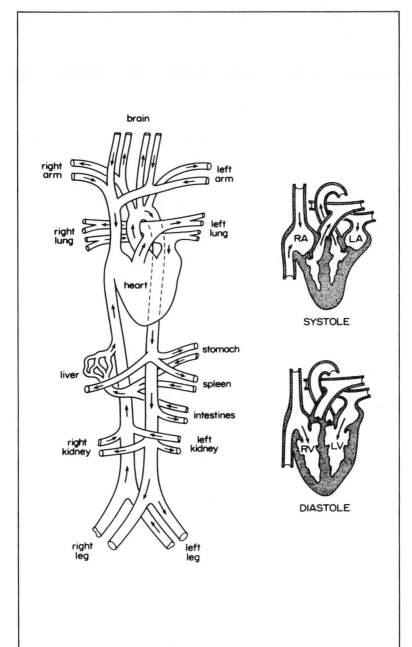

SYSTOLE

DIASTOLE

FIGURE 18: THE HEART AND CIRCULATION

During systole (contraction), blood is forced out of the muscular left ventricle (LV) through the arched aorta into a system of arteries which feed all parts of the body. At the same time blood is pumped from the right ventricle (RV) through the smaller pulmonary artery into the lungs. During systole the smaller thin-walled auricles (LA and RA) relax and are filled with venous blood returning (to the left auricle) saturated with oxygen from the lungs, and (to the right auricle) blood from all parts of the body containing carbon dioxide but depleted of oxygen. Then the ventricles in turn relax (diastole), valves between auricles and ventricles flop open allowing blood to flow from each auricle into its adjacent ventricle. After the ventricles fill the cycle repeats. The left ventricle is a thick-walled muscular chamber, capable of raising the blood pressure in aorta and arteries to 100-250 torr, while the less muscular right ventricle generates 15-40 torr in the pulmonary arteries. The auricles are weaker, generating only enough force to empty completely as the ventricles relax.

Galen understood most of this though he believed that blood passed between the ventricles through minute pores in the wall between them, and that the lungs were 'dead-end' as it were, serving only to cool the blood. Ibn-al-Nafis, Colombo, Servetus, and many others added bits and pieces to this knowledge until Harvey was able to put them all together in his explanation of "The Motions of the Heart and Blood" which is how we understand the circulation today.

Chemical sensors detect changes in acidity and act — cooperatively with the respiratory system and the kidneys — to restore normalcy. You are too hot? Receptors signal the brain for greater blood flow to the skin, and for greater evaporation of water as sweat to cool the body. Too cold? Skin circulation is reduced — perhaps shut down almost completely, to save heat for the crucial core. The runner knows that his legs need, and will automatically be sent much more blood than at rest — perhaps at the expense of the stomach — so running after a full meal may cause indigestion or stomach cramps. Cramps signal lack of blood carrying both oxygen and food to muscles and, just as importantly, carrying wastes away. The angina of heart disease is a 'cramp of the heart' crying out for more blood; intermittent claudication (cramps in the legs which occur when persons with narrowed blood vessels walk too fast or far) means that the muscular demands for oxygen and food are greater than the supply. Sensitive receptors in the tissues respond to oxygen lack by signalling for more blood flow, more breathing. Other receptors, responding to an excess of carbon dioxide send similar signals. The flowing blood is a common carrier for oxygen and nutrients and hormone messengers, as well as wastes and carbon dioxide which must be taken away from the cells.

As mentioned above, lack of oxygen usually does not affect the blood pressure, but the blood flow to the lungs (pulmonary circulation) is different. Hypoxia causes an immediate increase in the pressure in the pulmonary artery, and the rise is at first directly proportional to the altitude or degree of hypoxia. This pulmonary hypertension is almost universal, coming on rapidly, but subsiding to normal just as fast with descent or breathing adequate oxygen. We don't really understand this increase in pulmonary artery pressure: is it beneficial? Does it represent a strong and useful compensation to oxygen lack? Or is it a failure to adjust, a breakdown in the system? For most people the pressure 'levels off' at about two or three times the normal 10-14 torr but in some the pressure may go high enough to cause — if prolonged — strain of the right heart and eventually heart failure.

Probably man has always been curious about what made his heart tick, and some writings have survived for two thousand years to show the extent of that curiosity—and the limits of knowledge.

In the western world, one of the first to recognize the pumping function of the heart and the role of the blood vessels was the versatile philosopher Empedocles who likened the circulation to the ebb and flow of the tide, a concept accepted by Aristotle soon afterwards. Aristotle taught that there were two different bloods: a "spiritual" blood, purified by passage through the lungs, and a "venous" blood, not so purified. He believed that the two mixed only to a limited extent, and then only by passage through almost invisible pores or holes between the two chambers of the heart. These beliefs were adopted by Galen five centuries later, became the official doctrine of the church, and prevailed for a thousand years.

Not surprisingly the great Leonardo turned his mechanical genius toward the human body, meticulously detailing the leverages of muscles and, perhaps for the first time, recognizing (in 1500) that the heart was only a pump whose function was to move blood—a liquid which behaves like other liquids.

Another early pioneer was the Spanish scholar Michael Servetus who trained first as a lawyer, then became deeply engrossed in religion, and not till 1537—at what was for those times the ripe age of twenty-six—took up medicine. As was common for scholars then, Servetus was interested in all natural processes and in their relationship to the divinity. He fell into conflict with the Church however, became a fugitive, and ultimately, pursued by the Inquisition (as were Galileo and van Helmont), was apprehended while at church in Geneva, and speedily burned at the stake. Unorthodoxy, even in the name of science, was poorly accepted in those times. Servetus' great works (anonymously published in 1553, the year he was executed) were burned with him; three copies are known to have been saved, and from these it is clear that he understood very well the circulation of blood through the lungs, and dared to refute the great Galen (one of the 'crimes' which led to his execution).

Two centuries earlier a Persian physician Ibn-al-Nafis had also challenged Galen's pore theory. Though for religious reasons he performed no dissections, he theorized that blood leaving the right ventricle passed through the lungs and back to the left side of the heart and thence to the body, and that Galen's "pores" between the two ventricles did not exist, further postulating that the true purpose of the lungs was to aerate blood. He developed this theory five centuries before oxygen was discovered, but his manuscripts were lost until 1924, though there is some evidence to suggest that Servetus had heard of his ideas. Renaldo Colombo, who was developing the same theories as Servetus and about the same time, seems also to have known Ibn-al-Nafis' work. Colombo's important book *"De Re Anatomica"* was published in 1559, but as early as 1546 he was teaching a theory of blood circulation remarkably close to what we know today. Shortly after Colombo's book appeared, an Italian, Andrea Cesalpino, published a small treatise in which he stated that blood flowed from the right ventricle through the lungs to the left ventricle, and that valves in the vessels imposed uni-directional flow. Unfortunately in his final book, published in 1606, he mistakenly described blood as flowing out from the heart not only in the arteries but through the veins as well. These speculations and observations laid the groundwork for the right man to assemble facts correctly and define how the heart and circulatory system function.

William Harvey was one of the parents of the scientific method and a pioneer in the young study of physiology. From Cambridge he went to Padua, then one of the great centers of medicine, where Vesalius first laid the foundations of the relationships between medicine, anatomy and surgery. Galileo was also there and as Professor of Physics and of Mathematics undoubtedly influenced young Harvey's thoughts. Padua must have been an exciting place to study then, since it was well endowed and surprisingly free from bigotry considering that the shadow of the Inquisition still lay across Europe. Harvey built freely on the work of Vesalius, postulating—though he could not see—the capillaries which permitted the flow of arterial blood through capillaries into veins in lung and all other tissues. He returned to London, entered private practice and continued his dissections and lectures at the College of Physicians. Of his works by far the most important is his *"De Motu Cordis,"* written in 1628 as a message to King Charles:

"May I now be permitted to summarize my view about the circuit of the blood, and to make it generally known! Since calculations and visual demonstrations have confirmed all of my suppositions, to wit, that the blood is passed through the lungs and the heart by the pulsation of the ventricles, is forcibly ejected to all parts of the body, therein steals into the veins and the porosities of the flesh, flows back everywhere through those very veins from the circumference to the centre, from small veins into larger ones, and thence comes at last into the vena cava and to the auricle of the heart; all this, too, in such amount and with so large a flux and reflux . . . I am obliged to conclude that in animals the blood is driven round a circuit with an unceasing, circular sort of movement, that this is an activity or function of the heart which it carries out by virtue of its pulsation, and that in sum it constitutes the sole reason for that heart's pulsatile movement."

Harvey based his conclusions on the simple observation that both the valves within the heart and those in the veins would permit the blood to flow in only one direction. In his manuscript notes which have survived since 1616 he calculated that the heart pumped in one hour blood weighing more than three times the weight of the whole body. His beautifully written *"De Motu Cordis"* may seem obvious today but was one of the great advances in anatomy and physiology.

How did Harvey synthesize so brilliantly when so many of his equally brilliant predecessors and contemporaries failed? One of his outstanding contemporaries, Robert Boyle explained:

"And I remember that when I asked our Famous Harvey in the only discourse I had with him (which was but a while before he dyed) What were the things that induced him to think of a circulation of the blood. He answered me that when he took notice of the Valves in the Veins of so many Parts of the Body, several were so Plac'd that they gave free passage of the Blood Towards the Heart, but opposed the passage of Venal Blood to the Contrary Way he was invited to imagine that so Provident a Cause as Nature had not Placed so many Valves without Design."

Four years after Harvey's death, Malpighi of Pisa, using the microscope which had by then appeared on the scientific scene (whether first from Leeuwenhoeck or Jannsen or from Galileo, is relatively unimportant) was able to see the capillaries, thus providing final proof of Harvey's theory.

The feverish growth of knowledge and the flowering of so many new ideas and the invention of such important new instruments, despite the heavy hand of dogma and the terror of the Inquisition is a never dull source of wonder and inspiration. Though the exact composition of air and the essential role of oxygen had not been fully defined, the work of Borch, Mayow, Boyle and Hooke and many others unsung today made possible the final contributions of Lavoisier and Priestley. Empedocles, Erasistratus and Aristotle prepared the way for Galen who was supplanted by Ibn al Nafis and climactically by Harvey. After Swammerdam and Leeuwenhoeck described red blood cells the way was open for Lower to establish that the major role of the lungs was to aerate blood and that something in air turned dark venous blood to bright red.

Chapter Six
HEMOGLOBIN

The mechanical processes of breathing in and out and of driving blood throughout the body would be incomplete without a highly perfected way of carrying oxygen to and carbon dioxide from the minute engines in the cells which make all functions run. This transport is provided by a simple yet marvellously intricate carrier, the red blood cell, which is packed with a complex molecule — hemoglobin. Since our survival, especially at high altitude, depends on how hemoglobin carries oxygen, we need to look closely at this carrier system.

Throughout history, blood has been associated with life, even more so than air perhaps because it is more easily spilled, and the Old Testament is particularly bloody. Back in the fifth century BC Empedocles wrote that *"the blood is the life"* and Aristotle believed that the soul depended upon the composition of blood. Their contemporary, Anaxagoras was more specific: *"The blood is formed by a multitude of droplets, united among them."* But not until 1674 were the red blood cells of man described. Then Anton van Leeuwenhoeck, told the Royal Society:

"I have diverse times endeavored to see and to know what parts the blood consists of and at length I have observed, taking some blood out of my hand, that it consists of small round globules driven through a cristaline humidity of water; yet whether all bloods be such I doubte."

Leeuwenhoeck was a skilled lens-grinder: he made many elegant microscopes, often leaving specimens permanently on stage and making others. He estimated the size of red blood cells as he estimated the size of his "little animals" by comparing them with grains of sand, and came astonishingly close to the 7.5 micra which we know today to be their average diameter.

Several years before this, Richard Lower, one of the brilliant members of the Royal Society observed that blood changed from a dark red to a brighter carmine when it was agitated with air. His contemporary, Robert Hooke, in one of his most famous demonstrations to the Royal Society, showed that an

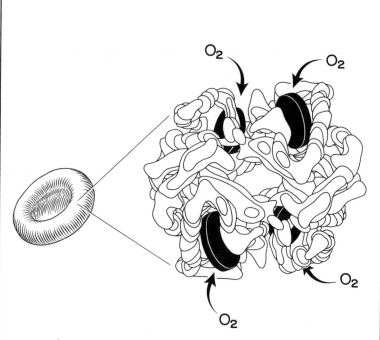

FIGURE 19: THE RED BLOOD CELL AND HEMOGLOBIN

The red blood cells, shaped like doughnuts with the hole not completely punched out, are packed with hemoglobin, a large and complex molecule containing four molecules of iron-containing heme shown here in solid black. As oxygen enters the red cell by diffusion from the air sacs in the lungs, it combines with heme loosely enough for oxygen to be easily released as blood enters tissue capillary blood vessels surrounded by fluid and cells where oxygen pressure is low but carbon dioxide pressure high. Entry of carbon dioxide into the red cell helps to release oxygen. The contour-like lines in this illustration represent other components of hemoglobin which make it uniquely able to attract and release oxygen and to a lesser extent carbon dioxide under usual environmental conditions. Abnormal or mutant hemoglobins have slightly different arrangements of these molecules. Though they contain the same amount and form of heme, their association with oxygen and the shape they give to red cells are less favorable for man's normal life.

experimental animal could be kept alive, even when the chest was opened, if the lungs were rhythmically inflated. Lower then confirmed that blood changed from dark to bright red while passing through the lungs, but since oxygen had not yet been identified, the connection between breathing and oxygen transport by the red stuff in blood was not made for many years.

Menghini in 1747 burned blood and showed that its ash could be attracted by a magnet, preliminary work which led Justus von Liebig a century later to theorize that red cells contained an iron compound that carried oxygen, not in simple solution but in some chemical combination. Lothar Meyer soon proved this to be true, and Felix Hoppe-Seyler crystallized this iron-containing substance in 1865.

By then a good deal was known about oxygen and Paul Bert — a close friend of Hoppe-Seyler — began to explore the conditions under which the red substance combined with oxygen. He exposed blood to different percentages of oxygen at normal pressure and to air under increased and decreased pressure, then extracted the oxygen with a vacuum pump. From these experiments he was able to define the relationship between the partial pressure of oxygen and the amount taken up by blood, and to sketch a predecessor of the oxyhemoglobin dissociation curve we know today. Since Bert's time refinements in analytical techniques have permitted very accurate measurement of oxygen-hemoglobin combinations under different conditions of pressure, temperature and acidity. Such data are plotted to give several differently shaped curves defining how hemoglobin acquires and releases oxygen in different parts of the body and under a variety of circumstances. What is this red stuff and how do its characteristics fit its functions?

Hemoglobin is a rather large molecule, with a molecular weight of 68,000, composed of a pigment (porphyrin) which occurs throughout nature, a species specific protein (globin), and a metal (iron) which is unique to mammals. Chlorophyll, the plants' equivalent, contains magnesium rather than iron but is otherwise similar to hemoglobin.

One molecule of hemoglobin contains four porphyrin-iron groups called heme, each of which contains one atom of iron in reduced or ferrous form. The four heme groups combined with ninety-six globin groups make up the loose and occasionally distorted hemoglobin molecule. The four iron atoms carry oxygen, not as one might expect by being oxidized from ferrous to ferric form, but in a much looser combination. The iron atoms have a large appetite and will bind other substances besides oxygen, for example carbon monoxide, which is held more avidly than oxygen; the resulting carboxy-hemoglobin causes the bright cherry-red coloring typical of carbon monoxide poisoning. The iron atoms also take up nitrite, forming methemoglobin which gives a bluish color to lips and nails not unlike the cyanosis due to reduced or non-oxygenated hemoglobin seen at high altitude. Both carbon monoxide and nitrite poisoning interfere with normal oxygen transport and thus cause oxygen lack, with many of the signs and symptoms seen at high altitude. Either or both aggravate oxygen lack at altitude, hence the risks of smoking or burning fuel in a tightly closed tent on a mountain.

Thousands of different forms of hemoglobin are possible, and all animals use some kind of respiratory pigment to carry oxygen in whatever form of blood they have; some of these contain copper or magnesium rather than iron, seemingly determined by the needs of each particular species. Man, like all mammals, relies on an iron-based pigment, but not all are alike: several hundred mutant or variant forms have been identified in humans, and far more varieties in other mammals.

Wintrobe has estimated that about half of one percent of Europeans have one or another of these abnormal hemoglobins. Though most are laboratory curiosities, a few are of practical importance at altitude. One of these (S-hemoglobin) manifests itself as chronic anemia in about 0.3% of Americans while an additional 8-10% have the "sickle trait" but are not anemic. Those with "sickle trait" tend to form clumps of cells when their blood oxygen is decreased and these clumps may precipitate what is called a "sickling crisis." There are several forms of crisis, and persons with sickle anemia or trait are at some risk when their blood oxygen is decreased by illness or by a trip to the mountains.

The sickling trait is usually associated with Negro ancestry, but it has been found in some other races whose black ancestry may not be traceable. The mutant S-hemoglobin has a slightly different molecular configuration than common hemoglobin, and it exerts different stresses within the red blood cell, some of which are distorted into sickle or half-moon shapes instead of the flattened doughnut usually found. The stresses within the cell increase when S-hemoglobin is less saturated with oxygen and more bizarre shapes form, apparently interfering with the rolling tumbling passage of rounder cells through capillaries. As a result they clump in muscles or spleen or liver blocking small or even large vessels and causing the sickling crisis.

Although sickle crisis has caused sudden death in Negroes doing strenuous work soon after being taken from sea level to 4,000 feet, this is extremely rare. But persons have had a sickle crisis on going from 5,000 to 8,000 feet, and Githens found that 20% of persons with sickle cell anemia and 28% of persons with two other forms of S-hemoglobin developed symptoms attributable to sickling when they travelled above 6,000 feet. Yet another mutant (Hemoglobin C) is associated with anemia and those red cells also clump abnormally when exposed to low oxygen. Patients with C-hemoglobin are less often diagnosed than those with the S form and consequently might be at greater risk in the mountains or even in aircraft.

Although S-hemoglobin can on occasion cause serious illness, ironically the sickle-shaped red cell is also a protection because it is more resistant to the entry of malarial parasites, and thus persons with sickle hemoglobin have been more resistant to that often fatal and widely prevalent disease and, as "the fittest" more have survived over the centuries past.

What this adds up to, given our current knowledge of this complicated subject, is that persons with Negro ancestry who plan to climb above 10-12,000 feet should be carefully screened beforehand by an expert in blood disorders, but from what we know today the risks are neither great nor do cases occur very often. Just how common are mild episodes of sickling at lower altitude on mountains or in aircraft is hard to say at this time.

Actually, all of us have had three mutant forms of hemoglobin at one time or another. The blood of the embryo contains a primitive form — P-hemoglobin, which is soon converted to the fetal or F form which has an affinity for hemoglobin much stronger than that of normal (A) adult hemoglobin, a characteristic which contributes to the ability of the unborn infant to flourish in an environment containing less oxygen than is found in air on the summit of Mt. Everest. F-hemoglobin changes to the A form soon after birth.

In recent years, genetic engineers have learned that sickle cell anemia and sickle cell trait are due to specific mutations in one of the globin genes which is not present in fetal hemoglobin. Reasoning from this that changing adult to fetal hemoglobin might be an effective treatment for sickle cell anemia and another similar problem, a drug was found which could reactivate the fetal genes and thus dramatically reverse serious sickle cell anemia. Other research showed that baboons, whose hemoglobin is similar to our adult form, start making the fetal form when they lose blood — or when they are short of oxygen.

These two startling studies suggest that we might be able to change adult to fetal type hemoglobin and thus help patients who are struggling with lack of oxygen. Or — in fact — it may be that persons who are already short of oxygen — as at high altitude — may be making fetal hemoglobin. Could those persons be the super climbers who do so well at altitude — while those who continue to make the same old adult hemoglobin do not? Undoubtedly this needs study because the implications for climbers — and for hypoxic patients are great.

Two other potential problems could result, in theory at least, from mutant hemoglobins. Some mutant forms are known to take up oxygen normally, but to cling to it tenaciously as oxygen partial pressure falls. Thus the fully saturated hemoglobin would not release oxygen in the tissue capillaries except at very low pressure. Other mutants are sluggish in accepting oxygen and cannot carry a full load and, though release in the tissues is normal, tissue oxygen lack also results. So far few problems have been traced to such abnormalities.

If the blood of a healthy normal person is exposed to an excess of oxygen, each gram of hemoglobin will bind 1.34 ml* of

---

* ml = mililiter or one gram of water

oxygen. Since there are fifteen gm** of hemoglobin in each hundred ml of blood, a total of about twenty ml of oxygen is carried by each hundred ml of blood — if fully saturated. We call this the oxygen carrying capacity of blood which, under usual conditions, is twenty volumes percent; it is a measure of the number of molecules of oxygen combined with hemoglobin when the latter is fully saturated. Changes in acidity, temperature and carbon dioxide pressure alter carrying capacity.

If the available oxygen is decreased, carrying capacity does not change, but the amount of oxygen carried (oxygen content) does decrease because the blood is less fully saturated, so at altitude arterial oxygen saturation and content are less than at sea level but can be brought to normal by breathing more oxygen. Both oxygen capacity and content can be increased by increasing the total amount of hemoglobin in blood, even though the capacity of each gram of hemoglobin is unchanged. Nature does this as a part of the adaptive process. Within a day of arrival at altitude, the circulating hemoglobin increases from the usual fifteen or sixteen gm due to release of 'stored' blood. Later, during the next few weeks of residence at altitude, new hemoglobin is made, increasing the amount to eighteen or twenty gm per hundred ml or even more.

This increase in carrying capacity was for a long time considered one of the most effective changes of acclimatization, and up to a point this is true. Today we know that when the amount of hemoglobin exceeds eighteen or nineteen gm per hundred ml of blood, the red cells tend to stack like dishes instead of tumbling through the blood vessels end over end. Stacked together their diffusing surface is decreased and they not only can carry less oxygen but tend to clump and obstruct vessels more easily; this thicker blood is more viscous and tends to flow more sluggishly. All in all too much hemoglobin is an unfavorable response to oxygen lack. Some limited experiments on very high mountains suggest that replacing one or two pints of blood with plasma (the liquid portion of blood) may actually improve performance in the acclimatized climber but this needs

---

** gm = gram, about 1/30th of an ounce

much more study before it is proven to be of value.

The pickup and release of oxygen are functions just as vital as breathing in and out and like breathing are affected by many factors. Paul Bert drew the first rough curve relating the pressure of oxygen to the percentage of hemoglobin which was combined with oxygen (the percentage saturation), and demonstrated that when the pressure of oxygen to which blood is exposed falls, the saturation decreases. Since Bert's time the shape of this curve — called the oxy-hemoglobin dissociation curve — has been greatly refined and we recognize today that it is S-shaped and uniquely suited to its functions.

The significance of the S-shape is best understood by reference to Figure 20. Hemoglobin is almost completely saturated when the partial pressure of oxygen is high and still is more than 96% saturated when the oxygen pressure has fallen by 20 torr. Translated into practical terms, this means that there is very little change in the oxygen carriage by blood up to 5-6,000 feet. At the same time, when oxygen pressure is quite low — in the 30 to 50 torr range — even a small decrease results in a sharp fall in saturation. Again translated, this means that in tissues where oxygen pressure is low, oxygen is easily released to the hungry cells. Most mammals have hemoglobin dissociation curves of similar shape though some (the deer mouse and llama for example) have somewhat different curves to meet the needs of their habitats.

The shape of the oxygen dissociation curve is affected by other things besides the oxygen partial pressure, as Christian Bohr proved. Increasing the temperature shifts the curve toward the right; cooling shifts the curve to the left. At higher partial pressures of carbon dioxide the curve also moves rightward, and when carbon dioxide falls the curve shifts leftward. When acid, blood has a flatter curve than when alkaline. Consequently there are 'families' of curves rather than one, each being specific for the temperature, carbon dioxide, or acidity of the test conditions.

These shifts (the Bohr effect) are of more than theoretical interest because they affect oxygen transport even under familiar circumstances and make a profound difference at high altitude.

For example, since carbon dioxide pressure is high in the tissues, its diffusion into blood expedites release of oxygen. Moments later, when venous blood reaches the lungs, outward diffusion of carbon dioxide facilitates the entry of oxygen, though not by much because the dissociation curve is so flat at high oxygen pressures. When lactic acid and carbon dioxide are increased by exertion, the tissue acidity stimulates release of more oxygen to cells.

The effect of cold may be seen in the very red cold nose, probably due to reluctance of hemoglobin to give up its oxygen in the well-supplied skin capillaries. By contrast, the blue lips and nails of the shivering swimmer are due to a decrease in skin circulation (to save heat for the core organs) and the skin cells extract all the oxygen they can get; the result is very desaturated blood—which is dark purplish red.

Shunting of blood to central vital organs decreases heat loss and when the body is hypoxic as well, ensures that what little oxygen is available will be reserved for the most essential functions (as we shall see later when we discuss diving mammals). But it is a mixed blessing. By decreasing blood to hands and feet the risk of frostbite is increased, especially at altitude where the oxygen needed for metabolism is already low. On the other hand, when body temperature falls, less oxygen is used, and mammals can survive levels of hypoxia that would likely kill or cripple them at normal body temperature. One dramatic demonstration of this occurred when a young man stowed away in the wheel housing of a trans-oceanic jet which flew for four hours at 29,000 feet; the man was unconscious but alive when the plane landed, and recovered undamaged. Without the cold he would have died.

Another interesting substance affects the transport of oxygen—an organic phosphate which acts much like an enzyme and has the jaw-breaking name of 2,3-diphosphoglycerate, mercifully shortened to DPG. This is sharply increased under conditions of oxygen lack—whether due to altitude or to disease at sea level. But the benefits conferred by an increase in DPG at altitude have recently been questioned and at this writing it seems likely that there is more difference between races, between individuals, and in the same persons under different cir-

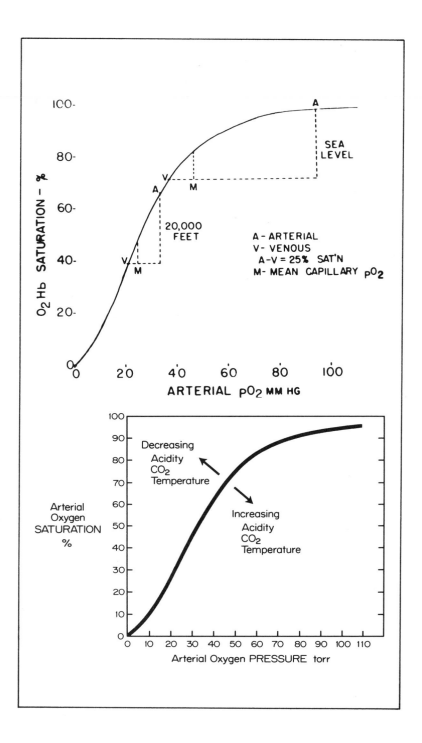

FIGURE 20: OXY-HEMOGLOBIN DISSOCIATION CURVE

Hemoglobin in red blood cells combines with oxygen in proportion to the partial pressure of oxygen in the surrounding air or liquid. When a curve is plotted relating oxygen pressure (abscissa) to percentage of hemoglobin which is saturated (ordinate), we find not a straight linear relationship, but a complex S-shaped curve. The characteristics of this curve are of the utmost importance (upper left): at higher levels of oxygen pressure (as at sea level), virtually all of the hemoglobin is saturated with oxygen and even venous blood, returning to the heart after releasing adequate oxygen to tissues, is well-saturated. By contrast, at high altitude (here shown as 20,000 feet), saturation falls considerably more for a smaller drop in oxygen pressure, indicating that a volume of oxygen nearly equal that at sea level can be released to tissues over a wide range of oxygen pressures. A similar curve constructed for hemoglobin removed from red cells does not have the S-shape and thus is a far less efficient oxygen delivery system. In the lower right-hand drawing note how changes in acidity, carbon dioxide, and temperature change the inflection of the curve, thus altering oxygen acceptance or release.

cumstances than is generally realized. It is interesting that a higher than normal DPG level accounts for at least part of the extra carrying power of fetal hemoglobin.

The red cell is a versatile carrier. It has little need for oxygen for its own life and thus its hemoglobin is mostly used to carry oxygen to other tissues. But hemoglobin has two other roles which are of particular importance at high altitude: the transportation of carbon dioxide and the regulation of acid-base balance, both of which are crucial.

Carbon dioxide diffuses through capillary walls (both in lungs and tissues) more rapidly and completely than does oxygen, and most of it dissolves in the liquid portion of blood — the plasma — forming a weak acid. Only 10% of the carbon dioxide is carried within the red cell, loosely attached to hemoglobin, but even this is important in the pick-up and release of oxygen as noted above. When carbon dioxide is lowered by over-breathing (a normal response to altitude), oxygen transport is impaired — or would be if it were not for other compensatory changes. One of these is the leftward shift caused by the increased alkalinity of blood which has been caused by the fall in carbon dioxide.

Much of the carbon dioxide in blood is carried as bicarbonate, a combination controlled by a special enzyme — carbonic anhydrase — of which there is a high concentration in red cells and in kidneys. The equilibrium between carbon dioxide (in solution as carbonic acid) and bicarbonate is dependent on carbonic anhydrase, and disturbed by an agent which inhibits that enzyme — acetazolamide or Diamox. This medication which has been used clinically for almost thirty years, impedes the release of carbon dioxide by increasing loss of bicarbonate in the kidney. This not only permits a slight increase in breathing without too much loss of carbon dioxide, but also increases the carriage of oxygen. Action of this drug is not completely understood and the small increase in breathing which it causes is not enough to fully explain the increase in arterial oxygen saturation which usually follows use of Diamox. As this medication is being used more and more widely, some of the advice given earlier needs to be modified; we will discuss this important

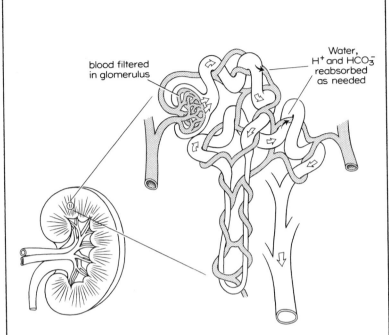

blood filtered
in glomerulus

Water,
H^+ and HCO_3^-
reabsorbed
as needed

FIGURE 21: THE FILTRATION SYSTEM OF THE KIDNEYS

Arterial blood flows through capillaries around the glomeruli (filtration capsules) of each kidney. There are thousands of these and blood flow is large. By active selection the glomerulus allows water and many substances to pass through, entering a network of tubules which are surrounded by veins. Different parts of each tubule have different functions: in some sections water is absorbed, in others sodium, potassium, and other chemical compounds are taken in or allowed to pass under control of many enzymes, of which carbonic anhydrase is one. The selective filtration of the kidney is controlled by both nervous and chemical stimuli and in turn considerably affects the chemistry of blood, thus maintaining the constancy of the internal environment. Losing bicarbonate is one of the measures of acclimatization which improves tolerance for altitude. By inhibiting the formation of carbonic anhydrase Diamox (acetazolamide) allows more bicarbonate to escape, thus (we believe) decreasing altitude illness.

medication more when we consider methods of preventing altitude illness in the next chapter.

The acidity or alkalinity of blood—like any solution—depends on the amount of hydrogen (H^+) or hydroxyl (OH^-) ions in solution; strong acids have an excess of hydrogen ions. The degree of acidity is indicated by the symbol pH, which is the negative logarithm of the concentration of hydrogen ions. The lower the pH the stronger the acid, and the higher the pH the more alkaline the solution. Neutrality is at pH 7.0, at which point the hydrogen and hydroxyl ions are exactly balanced.

Body metabolism produces many substances that threaten the stability of blood pH, normally very close to 7.43: carbon dioxide is formed, lactic acid generated by exertion, proteins break down to amino acids, fats are metabolized into fatty acids, and nucleoproteins give rise to phosphoric and uric acids. Nitrogenous foods and tissue breakdown yield ammonia—the only alkaline substance formed.

With so many strong and weak acids and only one alkaline substance entering and leaving the blood unpredictably, it is remarkable that its pH remains so stable. This is due to the buffers in the blood (which reduce the impact of the ions), to the lungs (which permit rapid loss or retention of weakly acid carbon dioxide through change in ventilation) and to the kidneys (which are able to eliminate either acids or alkalis as needed).

There are six of these buffer pairs in the blood—six combinations of a weak acid with a strong base, and each can resist change in ion concentration by absorbing the strong or releasing the weak acid radical. Hemoglobin has three buffer pairs, and the shift from oxygenated to reduced hemoglobin helps to minimize the change in pH.

Many efforts have been made to manipulate these intricate and intimately interrelated systems. Some are remarkably successful in clinical conditions such as diabetic acidosis or liver failure. To date only Diamox is effective in hypoxia, but it seems likely that as knowledge increases, other effective interventions will be found.

Obviously blood has many other functions such as carrying nourishment to and waste products away from tissues, and carrying the messenger substances or hormones which, even in minute amounts, dictate so many bodily activities. Blood helps to preserve and diffuse body heat and to disperse heat when temperature is too high, depending on how much blood flow is sent to the skin. All are necessary to life, but in our studies of high altitude, oxygen transport is the most important and the only one we can discuss here.

Chapter Seven
ALTITUDE ILLNESS

What does all this add up to? History is interesting to some and valuable to many; basic physiology and chemistry are essential if we want to understand exactly what goes on in our bodies, but what we really want to know is how to prevent, recognize or treat the various problems caused by lack of oxygen. Many ailments can occur on high mountains: heatstroke and frostbite, blood clots and embolism, pneumonia or other infections, all kinds of injuries, and even mental breakdown. I can't deal with these in this book except to the extent that they are caused or aggravated by lack of oxygen.

There is a vast difference between what happened to the passengers in the balloon *Zenith* and the fifteen or twenty persons who have reached the same altitude on Mount Everest breathing only the thin air around them. Response to altitude is determined by speed of ascent, altitude reached, and length of stay — plus individual characteristics, presently unexplained and tantalizingly mysterious. In this section, we will look at the various problems that we call altitude illness and in the next chapter we will see the marvellous adaptive changes which protect the Everest summiter from the death which would rapidly overtake a sea level man abruptly taken to that high place.

For convenience let us consider rate of climb as <u>sudden</u> or abrupt if in minutes or a few hours, <u>fast</u> if over a day or two, and <u>slow</u> or gradual if made over many days or weeks. Let us think of altitudes up to 6–7,000 feet as <u>ordinary</u>, from 7,000 to 12,000 feet as <u>moderate</u>, from 12,000 to 18,000 feet as <u>high</u> and anything over 20,000 feet as <u>very high</u>. Since length of stay is also important, we will call <u>visitors</u> or sojurners those who stay for a few days or weeks, <u>residents</u> those who stay for months, and <u>natives</u> those who are born and reside permanently at altitude.

Sudden ascent is what killed Croce-Spinelli and Sivel on the flight of the *Zenith* as described earlier (page 50–51).

The same thing could happen if an airliner were suddenly to lose cabin pressure; it may also happen in some severe injuries

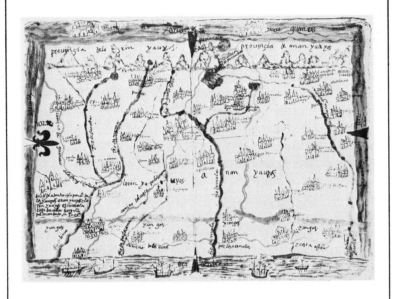

FIGURE 22: WHERE IS PARIACACA?

Father Jose Acosta has been called the Pliny of the New World because of his detailed description of all he saw during his missionary travels in the Andes. His vivid account of altitude illness is the earliest we have, but until recently it was not clear just where or how high the pass he calls Pariacaca actually was. Dan Gilbert has painstakingly investigated this and I am indebted to him for use of this old map — not much perhaps for a journey, but the best available in general terms. Pariacaca, according to Gilbert, was the name given to a whole range of snowy mountains, and to one particular inn along a main road which crossed a 15,750 foot pass which can be identified today — and which was certainly high enough to make travellers sick. The pass is marked just below the dark circle at top center.

or illnesses. The unfortunate who stumbles into a "sink" of carbon dioxide in a desert depression, or enters a deep and stagnant dry well or a vessel filled with nitrogen will die in a minute or so. It is not a problem for those who go onto mountains and not really a form of "altitude" sickness and I mention it only in contrast to the reactions to slow ascent.

Speaking of aircraft, it is worth mentioning that cabin pressure during flight in today's jets is maintained no less than 8.6 lbs. per square inch (436 torr) above the outside atmosphere. Translated, this means that the traveller may be taken from sea level to an altitude equivalent to 6,000–7,500 feet in less than an hour, depending on how high the aircraft flies. Few people are aware of the decreased oxygen which results, but only the very susceptible have symptoms.

The largest number of people who suffer from altitude illness are not Himalayan climbers or trekkers, but the hordes who go from near sea level to a mountain resort in a day or less. Few notice anything at 5,000 feet, but a quarter will have unpleasant symptoms going to 8,000 or 9,000 feet. Those who rapidly go higher, for example by taking the world's longest and highest aerial tramway in Venezuela will have more trouble, and those who are taken in decompression chambers even higher may be dangerously affected.

"The "telefero" is a five minute taxi ride from the airport (6,500 feet) and is in four sections. It takes about one hour to the top (15,600 feet) . . . Two of us went from sea level . . . and were at the top in about three hours . . . I helped carry equipment . . . once and was feeling quite well till afternoon. Then I felt worse and worse—bad headache, lack of energy and very tired. I seemed to feel better if I consciously tried to breathe deeply . . . I had a couple of bowls of soup and a candy bar for supper . . . slept for about 30 minutes . . . and woke and immediately lost the soup. Back to sleep and repeat the performance in a half hour. Morning came finally and I just didn't have any energy . . . Still had my bad headache but as we descended in the tramway I felt better and better and by the time we reached the bottom . . . I took my suitcase and walked to the airport (a couple of miles) . . . and had no difficulty walking up a couple of steep hills at 7,000 feet that afternoon. . ."

Even though this man lives at 8,000 feet in Colorado and often climbs to 11,000 feet feeling fine, he was hard hit by the rapid ascent in Venezuela, because apparently his tolerance for altitude did not carry over long enough to protect him.

In 1920 J. S. Haldane, one of the most respected physiologists of his time, and A. M. Kellas, a physician with Himalayan experience, made an 'ascent' in a decompression chamber and afterwards Haldane described what happened:

". . . *it was our intention to remain for an hour at about the lowest pressure possible without very serious impairment of our faculties for observation. This limit was, however, involuntarily overstepped, in the case, at least, of three of us, and the notes were consequently imperfect . . . AMK and JSH went first into the chamber, and the pressure was rapidly reduced to 445 mm (about 15,000 feet) and kept there for a short time for observation. . ."*

Haldane described their increased breathing and pulse rate and the bluish color of lips and fingernails. After short halts at increasing altitudes, their symptoms appeared to decrease until:

"The pressure was then reduced to 320 mm (22,000 feet). This increased temporarily the hyperpnoea in J.S.H., whose lips were now of a rather dull colour, with pulse 112 and respirations 27. He also had great difficulty in making observations or even counting his pulse, and especially in calculating the pulse from a 20 seconds observation, or remembering at what point on the second hand the observation had begun. Writing was also very shaky . . . He then handed the note-book to A.M.K. who was extremely blue, but felt all right and could still write quite normally, with a pulse of 102. J.S.H. remained sitting in one position . . . but continued to answer all questions so that A.M.K. considered him quite sensible, and mentally alert. Ten minutes later the pressure fell to 300 mm (23,500 ft) . . . J.S.H. asked A.M.K. to keep the pressure steady at 320 mm Meanwhile A.M.K. continued to feel fit, and at various times he noted his pulse was 90 to 93. He could quite easily stand up to regulate the inlet tap or read the barometer. To all his questions about changing the pressure J.S.H. replied with apparent deliberation 'keep it at 320.' Persons outside were somewhat impatient and anxious, and put up messages on the window, but A.M.K. only

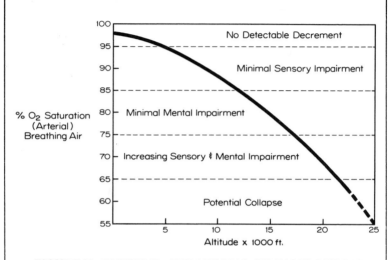

FIGURE 23: PHYSICAL AND MENTAL CHANGES DURING RAPID ASCENT

If an unacclimatized person is taken up in a decompression chamber or aircraft at a climb rate of, say 800-1,000 feet per hour, changes in some functions can be demonstrated as low as 5,000 feet—where dim-light vision is impaired. During the next 5-6,000 feet of climb, higher intellectual functions begin to falter: it becomes harder and harder to do simple arithmetic or puzzles or complicated tasks. By the time one arrives at 15,000 feet handwriting is sloppy and thought processes become disordered and response to instructions slow or faulty. At 18,000 feet five out of a hundred healthy persons will collapse and above 20,000 feet virtually every one is appreciably and often comically altered and more collapse. At 25,000 feet only a few moments of consciousness remain—if one has gotten so high! By contrast consider the scores of Himalayan climbers who have lived and worked hard above this level, thanks to acclimatization (Chapter Eight). The percentage oxygen saturation shown on the ordinate is only an average; it varies with over- or under-breathing and other influences.

smiled and referred to J.S.H., who invariably gave the old answer. After 1½ hours . . . J.S.H. was 'still determined.' Shortly afterwards, however, J.S.H. consented to an increase of pressure to 340 mm. He then began to regain his faculties, and took up a mirror to look at his lips, though some little time elapsed before he realized that he was looking at the back, and not the front, of the mirror . . . and consented to coming down . . . (Later) he had no recollection of the long stay at 320 mm or of anything else after he handed the note-book to A.M.K., but seems to have been conscious and under the influence of a fixed idea that it was necessary to stay at a pressure of 320 mm. On coming out of the chamber he was somewhat unsteady in gait for a short time and inclined to be unreasonable. A.M.K. was much less affected. He could remember everything, and his handwriting had remained quite steady, although his face was extremely blue and presented an alarming appearance to persons who saw him through the window."

This vivid account is particularly important because two men, despite their vast experience, were so affected by lack of oxygen that they might well have died had it not been for the watchfulness of those outside the chamber. Lack of oxygen, much like alcohol, sneaks up on even the knowledgeable and may cripple before one is aware that anything is wrong.

In 1919 Joseph Barcroft did an experiment more closely approximating the experience of the mountain sojurner or visitor when he spent ten days in a "Glass House" in Cambridge, England. The room was specially built so that the <u>percentage</u> of oxygen inside could be adjusted to simulate any altitude, while the <u>pressure</u> remained that of sea level. After slowly 'ascending' to 18,000 feet (in terms of oxygen) he remained there and later wrote:

". . . on the morning of the sixth day I awoke with . . . typical symptoms of mountain sickness: vomiting, intense headache and difficulty of vision. I have recollections of very acute headache accompanied by vomiting as a child, but never in adult life or even in my boyhood can I think of any such attack as occurred in the chamber . . . In the chamber I lived an easy though normal life, reading, writing, making observations,

doing the gas analyses, seeing to the air scrubbers, taking exercise on the bicycle ergometer and so forth . . . There was no cause other than oxygen want to which my sickness could be attributed . . . the partial pressure of oxygen corresponded to about 18,000 feet . . . much higher than the Peak of Teneriffe but, on the other hand, I had not precipitated matters by performance of any such exacting feat as the ascent of a sandhill 1,500 feet in height . . ."

One purpose of this experiment was to test the validity of a theory advocated by Haldane, that the lungs could actively secrete oxygen from alveolar air into the lung capillaries, and that this explained the wellness of some persons who took time to go up or remained for a long period at altitude. Haldane argued that this ability to secrete oxygen was an important part of acclimatization.

Barcroft wished to test this theory by making simultaneous measurements of arterial and alveolar oxygen. Eight years earlier a German scientist named Hurter had drawn blood from the radial (wrist) artery from four patients without mishap, but the importance of this new technique was not appreciated until 1918 when Stadie reported ninety arterial punctures in patients with pneumonia and found the procedure quite innocuous. Barcroft used Stadie's technique which required that the radial artery be exposed and a large steel needle be tied into it while bloods were drawn. What a contrast to the simple procedure now so commonplace! As near as possible to the time of drawing blood Barcroft obtained air from his alveoli at the end of the deepest possible exhalation, and the two measurements gave him the Alveolar-arterial oxygen gradient (discussed in Chapter Four). These analyses consistently showed that air in the lungs had a higher oxygen pressure than did arterial blood, leading Barcroft to conclude that secretion did not take place, at least under these conditions.

But what about more natural circumstances, where mountain people led active lives free of symptoms above 15,000 feet? Did secretion contribute to their high degree of acclimatization? Barcroft and others determined to test this in the Andes, and in December 1921 the International High Altitude Expedition set off 'up the hill', to Cerro de Pasco (14,000 feet) in Peru where they worked for two months and brought back a wealth of information which we will discuss in the next chapter. Alveolar oxygen was always higher than that in the arteries and Haldane's secretion theory was demolished.

Most persons who go rapidly to 10,000 feet will notice headache, rapid pounding pulse, and breathlessness and may feel mentally confused and often nauseated. Of those who continue rapidly to 18,000 feet five out of a hundred will faint and a few may have convulsions; most are pale with ghastly blue lips (cyanosis). Symptoms come on more quickly the higher the altitude but are promptly relieved by oxygen.

A dramatic demonstration was used during flight training in World War II. A group of fliers would be taken up in a decompression chamber, putting on oxygen masks, as required at 10,000 feet. At 25,000 feet one volunteer would be asked to remove his mask but told to put it back on the instant he noticed any trouble. He would then 'fly' a model airplane on a universal joint with stick and rudder while he was told what maneuvers to make. For a few moments he could comply but gradually reflexes slowed and in less than a minute he was unable to control the aircraft. Unaware of his dilemma he soon passed out, smiling foolishly at the oxygen mask held in his hand. Within a few seconds oxygen brought him around, usually with no recollection of what had happened. In both wars many fliers died in this way because they failed to appreciate how swift and subtle lack of oxygen can be.

However we are more interested in what happens to skiers or hikers who go to moderate altitudes, not as rapidly as did Haldane or the *Zenith* crew, nor as fast as aviators, but fast enough to cause distress. These are the people most likely to have altitude illness which may range from trivial to fatal. Today we consider altitude illness not a collection of separate, discrete diseases, but a spectrum or continuum, in which now one, now another may predominate, as shown in this simple diagram:

We can summarize the various parts of this spectrum of illness as follows:

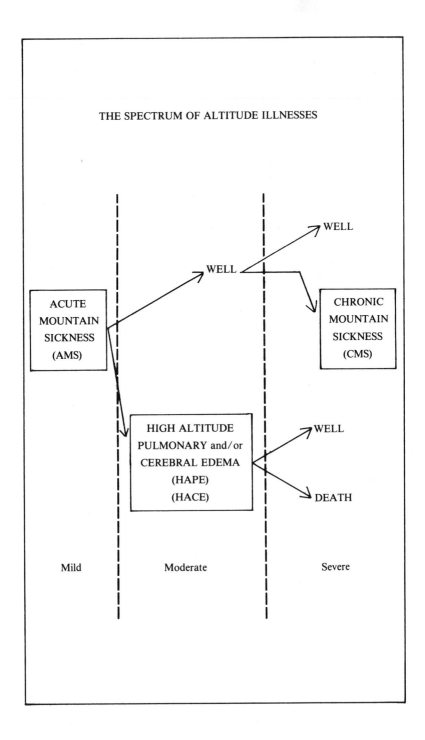

1. Acute Mountain Sickness (AMS) (called 'puna' or 'soroche' in South America): usually occurs above 7-8,000 feet after rapid ascent; characterized by headache, nausea sometimes with vomiting, shortness of breath, disturbed sleep, difficulty with thinking. Self-limited and rarely requires descent or treatment.

2. High Altitude Pulmonary Edema (HAPE): occurs above 9-10,000 feet (rarely lower) and takes thirty-six to seventy-two hours to become obvious, though it probably begins earlier; characterized by shortness of breath, fatigue, cough which sometimes produces bloody sputum, often a slight fever; may rapidly go on to unconsciousness and death. Often mistakenly diagnosed as pneumonia.

3. High Altitude Cerebral Edema (HACE): rare below 12,000 feet, though perhaps the severe headache seen lower is an early form; takes several days to develop but rarely may come on swiftly; characterized by increasing headache, poor judgment, auditory or visual hallucinations, incoordination, stumbling walk (ataxia), drowsiness, coma and death.

In addition to these conditions, two others should be recorded for completeness, though they are unusual:

4. Subacute Mountain Sickness: occurs in a few individuals who never fully lose symptoms of AMS after going to altitude, but remain moderately ill for weeks or months with headache, insomnia, nausea, fatigue, etc.; seldom dangerous, relieved by descent. Some doubt the existence of this category.

5. Chronic Mountain Sickness (CMS): Monge's disease affects a very few persons who either fail to develop any tolerance for altitude, or—more commonly—lose tolerance after long residence at altitude; characterized by fatigue, greatly increased blood count giving a plethoric (ruddy) appearance. Though relieved by descent to low altitude, death may occur from heart failure or stroke if stay at high altitude is prolonged.

Another condition, rare below 17,000 feet, should be mentioned, although it is not a separate entity:

6. High Altitude Retinal Hemorrhage (HARH): usually appears in the form of small bleeding areas in the back of the eye (the retina) which seldom cause any symptoms; occurs in 50% of persons going above 17,500 feet but incidence at lower altitude is unknown; most leave no after-effects. Similar small hemorrhages occur under fingernails and perhaps elsewhere in the body but this is unknown; may explain nosebleeds sometimes seen at altitude.

Different definitions of altitude illness are preferred by some, but this set has the weight of precedent, and it seems to me less cumbersome to label the whole spectrum "altitude illness" and to describe the sub-sets by their principal features.

It is important to remember that one person may have a few, another may have many, signs or symptoms. Hallucinations or a staggering walk may be the first and only prelude to unconsciousness and death from brain edema. Most who are affected at altitude lose some of their judgment, and climbers have made awful decisions, compounding their problems and confounding their companions or rescuers because they were unaware of how profoundly altitude can affect the mind.

ACUTE MOUNTAIN SICKNESS (AMS)

Since Acosta there have been many vivid descriptions of the common form of mountain sickness. Consider Edward Whymper, conqueror of the Matterhorn and most famous climber of the nineteenth century, as he recalled his feelings at 16,000 feet in the Peruvian Andes:

"I found myself lying flat on my back . . . incapable of making the least exertion. We knew the enemy was upon us and that we were experiencing our first attack of mountain sickness. We were feverish, had intense headaches and were unable to satisfy our desire for air except by breathing with open mouths. Headache for all three of us was intense and rendered us almost frantic or crazy."

Edward Fitzgerald, a few thousand feet higher in the Andes, wrote of his ascent of Aconcagua (22,835 ft) in 1897:

"I got up, and tried once more to go on, but I was only able

to advance one or two steps at a time, and then I had to stop, panting for breath, my struggles alternating with violent fits of nausea. At times I would fall down, and each time had greater difficulty rising; black specks swam across my sight; I was like one walking in a dream so dizzy and sick that the whole mountain seemed whirling around with me . . . I shall never forget the descent that followed . . . As I got lower my strength revived, and the nausea that I had been suffering from so acutely disappeared leaving me with a splitting headache."

Fitzgerald spent a month in his efforts to climb Aconcagua, being turned back near the summit because of his severe symptoms. The party retreated to their 9,000 foot base camp where they rested for two weeks while Zurbriggen, the great Swiss guide, recovered from near-drowning while crossing a river. Then in a final assault, the party climbed from 9,000 to 22,000 feet in five days; Fitzgerald could go no further but Zurbriggen reached the summit though completely exhausted.

One more account deserves repeating, written by J. S. Haldane, whose traces are found everywhere in the history of respiratory research. Describing his observations during a five week stay on the summit of Pike's Peak (14,100 ft) in the Colorado Rockies, Haldane wrote:

"Among numerous visitors who came up by train and stayed only about three-quarters of an hour, the most marked and almost universal symptom was blueness of the lips and cheeks, accompanied by great hyperpnea on exertion. As a rule there was no marked discomfort but some persons became very miserable and faint, and actual fainting was observed occasionally as well as vomiting. Among those who walked up or came up on donkeys the symptoms were much more general and severe. The blueness was more marked, and nausea, vomiting, headache and fainting were extremely common. Many persons walked or rode up during the night to see the sunrise especially on Sunday morning and the scene in the restaurant and on the platform outside can only be likened to that on the deck or in the cabin of a cross-channel steamer during rough weather. The walkers straggled in one by one looking blue, cold, exhausted and miserable, often hurrying out again to vomit. Some lay on the floor blue and faint. Others were able to swallow some cof-

fee, but very few had the heart to look at the magnificent sunrise. We saw several alarming cases of persistent fainting, but all recovered after a time."

Notice how Haldane distinguishes between those who reached the summit easily and rather fast by train, and those who walked; he believed that those who rode up Pike's Peak consumed less oxygen and thus might be expected to be less affected than those who took many hours to labor up on foot, and he was probably correct. Haldane was also impressed with the degree of cyanosis (blueness) of the nails and lips of some — but not all — of those who were most sick; what does this mean?

Cyanosis is due to the presence in circulating blood of a certain amount of non-oxygenated (reduced) hemoglobin. Unless four grams per 100 ml of blood is present, reduced hemoglobin is hard to detect. Thus a person who is anemic, for example with nine grams of hemoglobin instead of the usual fifteen, could be very hypoxic and yet not have the four grams of reduced hemoglobin necessary for cyanosis to be evident. By contrast, a full-blooded person with, say twenty grams of hemoglobin (quite common in altitude residents), will show cyanosis even though there is little or no hypoxia.

It seems unlikely that many of the visitors to Pike's Peak were severely anemic, and Haldane took the variations in cyanosis to indicate differences in arterial oxygenation due to differences in the passage of oxygen from lungs into blood, and from this derived the theory that some persons' lungs actively secreted oxygen, uphill as it were, into the lung capillaries. It was this concept, based mainly on the observations on Pike's Peak, which Barcroft doubted and later disproved.

Acute Mountain Sickness can be a miserable affliction. Though few die from it, some wish they would, and it has spoiled many mountain trips, and not only for the victim. The headache, nausea and vomiting resemble sea sickness or, say some, a bad hangover, while many feel only lethargy and depression. Everything tends to be worse in the morning and getting up becomes more of a task than usual. But wallowing in self-pity in bed is little help: symptoms are somewhat improved by moving about, although any real exertion is unthinkable and may make matters worse. Disturbed sleep is common, and periodic or irregular breathing (often called Cheyne-Stokes respiration) is noticeable and annoying.

Periodic breathing consists of a series of gradually deepening breaths, followed by a long pause before the cycle repeats. Mosso first recorded this phenomenon on Monte Rosa almost a century ago, and tried to fit it into his theory that disturbance of carbon dioxide was the cause of mountain sickness. We have recently learned that breathing a small flow of oxygen during sleep prevents this Cheyne-Stokes breathing and improves the morning headache. So too does a medication called Diamox (acetazolamide) which abolishes periodic breathing and smooths out arterial oxygen saturation thus preventing many of the symptoms almost as well as oxygen, and for longer.

Although AMS is usually unpleasant but brief, sometimes it will progress to more serious stages:

"I was called to see a young Turk, aged 23. He was a well-made man with no history of illness, and had lived in the district (at 13,000 feet) for some months . . . He had been below in the port for some weeks, and arrived in the district on July 14th, late in the day. On the 15th he was getting about, though he had slight headache, on the 16th his headache had increased considerably . . . he gradually got worse until the 19th, when I was called to see him. On examination he was profoundly dyspneic, respirations being 60, pulse 144 and hardly perceptible. Air hunger was extreme, he had frequent shivering fits, and the extremities were icy cold . . . During the night he became unconscious while making several attempts to get out of bed . . . Death occurred about 2 PM . . . this case was interesting in that he was evidently suffering from the normal type of puna at first which afterwards developed into a cardiac attack." (pulmonary edema)

So wrote Ravenhill in 1913, dividing the thirty-eight cases he described into 'normal', 'cardiac', and 'nervous puna'. Today we use the terms Acute Mountain Sickness (AMS), High Altitude Pulmonary Edema (HAPE) and High Altitude Cerebral Edema (HACE) in place of Ravenhill's terminology, which appears to have been the first systematic classification attempted.

This can also happen at a lower altitude, as for example this case at 9,500 feet in a well-known ski resort:

B.S. a 40-year-old man drove to 9,500 feet from Nebraska

and soon after arrival noticed shortness of breath, tightness in the chest, and a cough. In the middle of the second night after arrival he began to cough up a great deal of pink watery mucus and breathing became more difficult. Early next morning a doctor thought he was very cyanotic (blue) and heard signs of moisture in both lungs; X-ray of the chest showed pulmonary edema and he was transferred to a hospital at a lower altitude, improving on the way.

What do we know about how hypoxia alters our normal physiology and causes the headache, weakness, nausea and other characteristics of AMS? Granted that lack of oxygen sets in train a number of changes, what are the particular biochemical disturbances which cause the symptoms? In the last few years a good deal of evidence has accumulated suggesting that inability to handle water and salt normally is the main difficulty. This can be traced to the individual cells, where weakening or even failure of the 'sodium pump' (discussed in Chapter Ten) causes "waterlogging" of some or many cells. This in turn leads to puffiness (edema) of feet, face or hands, and probably contributes to the accumulation of water in lungs and brain.

Hormones are also involved. One in particular called ADH (for anti-diuretic hormone) is higher than normal in persons who have AMS; it suppresses urine formation and thus interferes with excretion of wastes and bicarbonate. The water retained may appear as simple weight gain or be obvious as puffiness (edema). Other hormones also play a part as discussed in Chapter Eight. Still, the central problem seems to be failure to handle salt and water appropriately.

But why the headache, the disturbed sleep, the fatigue and often nausea and vomiting? One plausible theory holds that fluid accumulating in the brain, leads to headache and alters the normal activity of the centers which control these functions. This suggests that the primary problem is excess water in the brain tissue. This is not fully accepted at present, although doctors in a ski resort at 9,000 feet in northern Japan have shown by brain scans that there is edema of the brain in their series of several cases. A tragic case occurred in an Andean city:

Soon after arriving at 12,500 feet a healthy 24-year-old woman consulted a doctor because of fatigue, shortness of breath, nausea and vomiting. After a cursory examination the doctor told her she had "flu". Several hours later she was found comatose in bed; she died minutes after transfer to the hospital, and autopsy showed nothing more than cerebral or brain edema.

Another theory, based on the observation that AMS does not appear until several hours after reaching altitude, is that not oxygen lack per se is responsible, but the biochemical changes by which the body tries to minimize the deficiency. We know that overbreathing raises arterial oxygen but lowers carbon dioxide, causing alkalosis and this might cause the symptoms. Mosso may have had this in mind when he wrote:

"Mountain-sickness has been thought a simple asphyxia due to lack of oyygen, whereas, in reality, it is a very complex phenomenon, as the arterial blood loses a considerable part ot its carbonic acid (carbon dioxide) when the barometric pressure diminishes, and even before the effects due to the lack of oxygen in the air appear, the phenomena produced by the diminution of carbonic acid in the blood have already manifested themselves. . . . I became convinced that in air rarefied to less than half an atmosphere, the preponderating cause of mountain-sickness could not be lack of oxygen."

Though most would agree that lack of oxygen is important at much lower altitude than "half an atmosphere" which is about 18,000 feet, it is hard to blame everything on lack of oxygen when we find, for example, that oxygen consumption is not decreased at altitude. That is, we consume the same or nearly the same amount of oxygen as at sea level. On the other hand, breathing oxygen does bring prompt relief from the miseries of AMS, even though the relief may not be lasting and not as great as descending a few thousand feet.

Another puzzle is the alleged benefit of drinking extra water. Is this all mythology, based on anecdotes, or is there some good explanation that makes the observation sound? It has been shown that people tend to get dehydrated at altitude, due to the increased water loss through the skin and from increased breathing in the thin dry mountain air. Blood therefore tends to get thicker, and urine more concentrated, and as William Bean pointed out years ago, the signs and symptoms of AMS are very similar to those due to heat and dehydration. Maintaining normal body water and urine output seems reasonable, and there is good reason for the belief that drinking extra water is helpful. But a word of warning: since alcohol causes many of the same symptoms as hypoxia, it is unwise to rely on the cup that cheers at altitude where in fact one drink does the work of two.

Besides drinking more water and avoiding work that will increase the need for oxygen, how else can one prevent AMS? By taking time to reach 8–9,000 feet or higher, just about all the difficulties can be avoided. How fast is slow enough? This is very much an individual affair. Some can go from sea level to a moderate altitude in less than a day and never turn a hair, while others will be miserable, as Haldane so graphically described on Pike's Peak. Even for one person, the same altitude and rate of climb may cause trouble on one day but not on another. Taking however much time the individual needs, and thus allowing the body to adjust to both lack of oxygen and the loss of carbon dioxide, is the best preventive for all altitude illnesses.

In the most extensive survey yet made, some 5,000 persons were interviewed at six ski resorts, ranging from 8,000 to 9,500 feet high. More than 25% of this randomly selected group reported having had AMS in the past and almost 20% were having typical symptoms at the time. Though the study was done during ski season, there's no reason to believe that summer visitors are any different — both have significant problems which are inversely proportional to the time taken to go from a low to a higher altitude.

It is safe to say that few people will have altitude sickness if they take several days to go from sea level to 9,000 feet, but it is equally safe to bet that few will do so, because most people are always in a hurry. Breaking a journey by over-nighting at 4–5,000 feet is often enough to minimize symptoms if you are planning a skiing vacation at 9–10,000 feet. If you are going with a tour to Cuzco or Machu Picchu in the Andes, perhaps less physically demanding, you may not have this option unless your tour has taken altitude into account. If you are to climb above 10,000 feet, then 1,000 feet a day is usually safe; above 16–17,000 feet each person must find his own best speed.

Athletes who live at low altitude but go to a competition at higher altitude (skiiers as a prime example) present special problems. They need to be in top form, and they should not rely on medication, yet they say they cannot take time for slow ascent which is the only way they can be fully protected.

Unfortunately, as we will see, taking time is not always enough. Thousands of people, of various age, experience, and fitness make the trek to Everest Base Camp each year. Many start from the valley of Kathmandu and walk for 20 days, up and down the steep beautiful ridges, across the grain of the foothills. Then, toughened by the long hike, they usually take five or six days for the final march from Namche Bazaar (11,000 feet) to Base camp (18,000 feet). Even so, about a third will have mild or moderate AMS.

On the other hand, of those who fly to Lukla (10,000 feet) and stagger up the week-long march to Base Camp, most will be uncomfortable, some will be seriously ill, and a few will die. It is rumored that half of the tourists who fly to Lhasa (11,800 feet) have altitude illness. In Cuzco and La Paz, oxygen is routinely available to the newcomer. The Japanese Hotel Everest View has oxygen piped to each room. Several studies show that half of those who climb Rainier (14,410 feet), taking 24–48 hours, will have moderately severe AMS. Go too fast even to moderate altitude, and you are likely to pay a price one way or another.

Yet astronomers who drive from sea level to the 14,000 foot observatory on Mauna Kea (Hawaiian islands) claim to be relatively well during the five or six hours on top, and shift workers, living at 9,000 feet and working for seven hours a day at the summit say they have few problems. In both groups some degree of denial is probably present: like early aviators, they may not wish to acknowledge symptoms, perhaps for the same reason macho types deny any kind of physical weakness.

Many examples confirm the fact that not only the <u>altitude</u> and <u>rate of climb</u>, but the <u>length of stay</u> and the <u>effort expended</u> determine whether an individual will or will not have some kind of altitude illness. Even so there are still other unknowns which make firm understanding of AMS still elusive.

Our society is medication-oriented and it is tempting to believe that some pill or injection will protect us against everything; the search for an 'altitude pill' has been going on for many years, but without striking success. Modern pharmacology does have one promising medication with a rational scientific basis: acetazolamide (Diamox). In addition to being a mild diuretic or kidney stimulant, Diamox inactivates an enzyme which regulates the relationship between carbon dioxide and bicarbonate. It also decreases the reabsorption of bicarbonate in the kidney tubules, thus allowing more bicarbonate to be eliminated in the urine. The loss of bicarbonate allows us to breathe more often or deeply, increasing the ventilatory exchange and bringing more oxygen deep into the lungs without paying the price of excessive carbon dioxide loss. But recent careful studies show that Diamox causes only a small increase in ventilation so that its undeniable benefit must be due to some more subtle, as yet not well understood mechanism. It is known to decrease (though only temporarily) the formation of cerebrospinal fluid — the watery liquid that bathes the brain and spinal cord and transmits chemical signals from blood to brain. Perhaps this may minimize brain swelling due to hypoxia. Diamox also increases the capacity of red blood cells to carry carbon dioxide and may permit retention of more of this in the blood. It also seems to increase 2,3DPG and thus might help hemoglobin to load oxygen.

As Diamox is more and more widely used its unpleasant effects are being described more often. A rare individual may be restless, irritable and unable to sleep, blaming Diamox. The tingling sensation around the mouth or in fingers or toes may not be a bad effect, but rather an indication that the correct dose — for that person at that time — has been taken. But the tingling may not be due to Diamox at all: on an easy walk to 13,000 feet, four of the ten persons had tingling in their fingers, toes, or around the mouth, but only one had taken Diamox — the day before. (It is interesting that the same four also noticed some swelling of fingers and feet, but they were not carryng packs and so the effect of shoulder straps was not the cause.) Some people have commented that tingling may begin within an hour after taking a single dose. For some the increased need to urinate is a deterrent! But for most this diuretic effect is mild.

Even though we have a great deal more to learn about how Dimaox works, double blind studies (where neither the subject nor the investigator knows until later whether a drug or a placebo

A portfolio of pictures of the Mount Logan High Altitude Physiology Study, undertaken by the Arctic Institute between 1967 and 1979.

Mount Logan in the Canadian Yukon is a massive platform for high altitude research and offers many challenges to climbers. Too many severe cases of altitude illness have occurred here in irresponsible or impatient mountaineers.

Kluane Lake was the base of operations for the High Altitude Physiology Study (HAPS) carried out on Mount Logan, ninety miles away and reached by air.

To decrease the incidence of altitude illness, an intermediate staging camp at 9,000 feet was used during several years of HAPS. Scientists and subjects would be flown here and stay for several days before being flown to the 17,500 foot laboratory. It was later abandoned because bad weather often made it inaccessible, and because it was not quite high enough to stimulate acclimatization maximally.

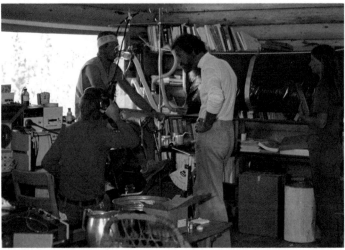

At Kluane Lake (2,250 feet) a sturdy log laboratory provided an ideal setting for the base line studies before the subjects went to the high laboratory where they would stay for six weeks.

During the latter years of HAPS attention was focused on the mechanisms of acclimatization rather than on altitude illness. Since acclimatization develops best during slow ascent, the subjects were flown to 10,000 feet where they remained for a few days before climbing to the high laboratory (17,500 feet) during the next ten days.

Airdrops to the high camps by the Canadian Air Force were very helpful, but sometimes they did not work so well. Here a load has come out of its webbing and will be scattered over several acres of snowfield.

The Wood Laboratory at Kluane Lake was named in honor of Walter Wood who started the research station in 1934 and has been actively involved ever since. It is still headquarters for many different kinds of research under the guidance of the Arctic Institute of North America although HAPS has ended.

Not infrequently Kluane would have bright sunny weather, while the laboratory on Logan was smothered in whiteout due to vicious winds which sweep snow and vapor across the plateau, hiding the camp, making landing or take-off impossible, and often dumping five to fifteen feet of snow on the buildings.

The deep Trench between King Peak and Logan provided an excellent base for the party before starting the ten day climb to the high laboratory. Situated at 10,000 feet it was high enough to stimulate acclimatization but people flown there from Kluane Lake seldom felt more than minor symptoms from the altitude and only for a few days. The route to the high plateau runs up to the low saddle, a long day away.

The Helio-Courier aircraft was ideal transport for HAPS. Taking off from the gravel strip at Kluane, it could land on skiis at Logan, providing snow conditions were right. But when the snow was too deep, the plane had to be turned around by hand (an exhausting job at this altitude), and could not carry a full load.

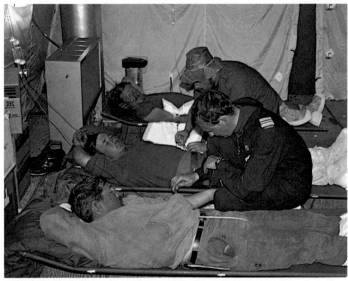

During the first few years of the study Canadian troops volunteered as subjects, and accepted the daily blood drawing with bored tolerance. Scientists came from the Canadian Forces, and from Canadian and American universities. Ten to sixteen subjects and a dozen scientists were involved each year.

One of the major studies examined the ability to work at altitude. Here a subject pedals a cycle ergometer against an increasing load, to determine just how much work can be done before complete exhaustion. This test is called V02Max, and the volume of oxygen consumed is measured before the mouthpiece (white tube, left) carrying exhaled air to a measuring device is removed.

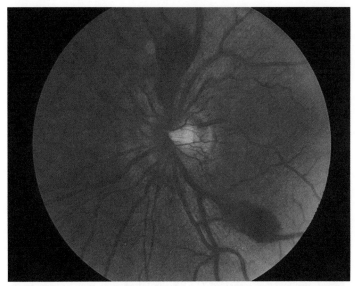

Photographs of the retina were taken on all subjects every few days. From these it was learned that every one showed an increase in blood flow in the retinal blood vessels and more than half showed hemorrhages — the dark pools of blood at 5 and 12 o'clock in this photo.

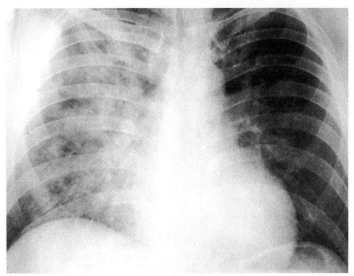

This chest X-ray shows typical high altitude pulmonary edema in the right lung (left side of photo) while the left lung is almost normal. HAPE occurred frequently in other climbers on Mount Logan but rarely in the scientific party because of care given to prevention or early detection and management.

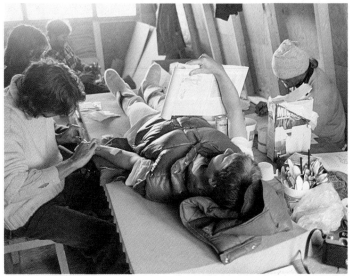

During the last few years of HAPS the laboratory was housed in insulated pre-fabricated wooden buildings which provided excellent accommodations for quite sophisticated studies. Both men and women served as subjects or research workers. Every day was full and tiring.

Severe storms were common at Logan but rarely lasted more than a few days. But during them it was a major ordeal to go outside to change propane cylinders which provided fuel for the electric generators and for cooking. Without snowshoes walking was impossible in the deep snow.

is taken) have conclusively shown that Diamox decreases or completely prevents AMS in most people. The antacid strongly advocated several years ago has been shown by such studies to be ineffective. Some Himalayan climbers have taken Diamox for long periods thinking it may improve acclimatization, but so far there is no good evidence one way or the other.

Ten years ago furosemide (Lasix), which is a strong diuretic, was recommended for preventing all forms of altitude illness, but its value has been disproven by later studies. A female sex hormone, medroxy-progesterone (Provera) stimulates breathing and does decrease AMS, but it also causes feminization which most climbers don't particularly want. It is no longer used at altitude but it can help sea level victims of alveolar hypoventilation. A respiratory stimulant called Coramine has been used but the results are not impressive. Several new drugs are being tried but so far not enough information is available to say one way or another. There is quite a strong psychological effect in altitude illness, and this must always be taken into account.

The leaves of a South American shrub called coca are chewed with lime to ward off fatigue and to prevent altitude illness. Until the Spanish conquest only the aristocracy were alowed this privilege, but today natives use coca and recommend it to visitors. It appears to help, probably because the small amount of cocaine in the leaves makes the user less aware of pain and fatigue. It has no specific effect on altitude illness.

Dietary manipulation is also given much attention by today's health-seeking society. Does diet affect tolerance for altitude? There is theoretical reason to believe that a pure carbohydrate diet (which burns one molecule of oxygen to form one molecule of carbon dioxide, making a respiratory quotient of 1.0) gives an 'altitude advantage' of as much as 2,000 feet compared to a mixed diet which requires more oxygen to produce the same amount of carbon dioxide and has a respiratory quotient of 0.8. Many laboratory studies have confirmed the theory, though not much hard data has come from mountain expeditions so far. It is probable that eating a pure carbohydrate diet during a climb at moderate to high altitude, improves performance and 'takes the climber down' by as much as 1,000-2,000 feet.

However there is a problem. The body must have protein and

fat to replace those 'burned' by hard work (or to a lesser degree in simply living), and these must come from the diet. One might suggest eating protein and fat at night, when exertion ends, but then the arterial oxygen saturation which usually decreases during sleep 'takes the climber up' a few thousand feet so to speak, and the mixed diet would aggravate this! The solution may be to eat a largely carbohydrate diet for all meals on climbing days, but to stock up on fats and proteins during rest days.

Various vitamins or combinations of vitamins and minerals have been advocated for improving altitude tolerance and preventing illness. Elements present only in minute traces in the body (such as chromium, cobalt, zinc, manganese) have been touted. Vitamins C and E and B complex have all had a vogue. As of now, unfortunately, no controlled or reliable studies show that added vitamins or minerals give any benefit at altitude. Only if the diet is grossly deficient (which could happen on long expeditions to high peaks when not only may food be inadequate but appetites fail) are supplements recommended. Even iron — essential for building additional hemoglobin — is normally abundant in food and in body tissues; taking iron pills has no rational justification. Some day evidence may refute these statements — but not today.

HIGH ALTITUDE PULMONARY EDEMA (HAPE)

In 1891 Dr. Jacottet, a robust young physician from Chamonix at the foot of Mont Blanc, took part in a rescue on that mountain, although he had been slightly indisposed a few days earlier. Mosso quotes a description written by one of his companions, Guglielminetti, of what happened in the Vallot Hut at 14,300 feet:

"On the 1st of September, after a day's rest in the hut, during which Jacottet seemed to feel better than he did at first; he climbed to the summit, remained there an hour, and then returned to the hut. During the night he did not sleep and coughed much, and complained at breakfast of headache and lack of appetite. During the morning he wrote a letter to his brother at Vienne, in which he remarked that he had passed so bad a night that he did not wish the like to his worst enemy. His distress in-

creased to such a degree that Imfeld advised him to descend to Chamonix, but he refused. He wrote another letter to one of his friends, telling him that he could not write at greater length because of the sick feeling which was tormenting him, that he was suffering from mountain-sickness like the others, but that he meant to study the influence of atmospheric depression and acclimatise himself. This was, alas! his last letter. He afterwards threw himself on his bed, trembling with cold. On the 2nd September . . . he seemed as paralysed, and began to wander, Oxygen was given to him to breathe, but without result. The respiration was very superficial (60 to 70 breaths per minute), the pulse irregular (between 100 and 120), the temperature 38.3°C. Towards six o'clock in the evening he suddenly ceased to speak, became somnolent, and then the death-agony began. His face grew pale, and towards 2 a.m. he expired in the glacier hut, a victim of his devotion to science, like a soldier on the field of battle.

From Dr. Wizard's post-mortem examination it appeared that Dr. Jacottet had died of capillary bronchitis and lobular pneumonitis. The more immediate cause of death was therefore probably a suffocative catarrh accompanied by acute oedema of the lung."

Dr. Egli-Sinclair of Zurich gave as his opinion that death was due to "mal du montagne" or mountain sickness but did not discuss why the "edema of the lung" had developed. This was probably a case of fatal high altitude pulmonary edema, with elements of brain edema too.

Ravenhill, describing his experiences at a mining camp in Peru at 15,500 feet included several classical cases of pulmonary edema:

"An Englishman, Mr. V . . . arrived in the usual way, by train—forty-two hours' journey from sea-level. Three years before he had lived at the same mine for a period of three months, had not been ill on arrival, and had been in good health the whole time. For some time previous to this latter visit he had been . . . attaining a height of 17,000 feet, and had not been affected. He seemed in good health on arrival, and said that he felt quite well, but nevertheless he kept quiet, ate sparingly, and went to bed early. He woke next morning feeling ill, with symptoms of the normal type of puna. As the day drew on he began

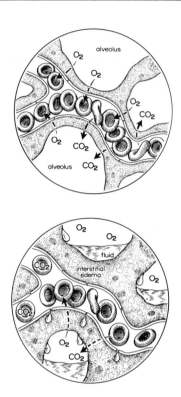

FIGURE 24: NORMAL AND EDEMA-FILLED ALVEOLI

Normally the tiny alveoli, though moist, contain no free fluid and the thin membrane which separates each from its surrounding capillary network is little more than two molecular faces (top). Carbon dioxide and oxygen pass freely through the membrane with little or no drop in pressure. However, when edema begins to form (from heart failure or from oxygen lack), it appears first between the capillary wall and the alveolus thus increasing the pressure drop between alveolar oxygen and that in blood. Carbon dioxide, diffusing more readily, is less affected. As the condition worsens (bottom), fluid seeps through the alveolar membrane into the alveoli where its presence can be detected by gurgles and crackles heard during breathing. The victim tries to cough up this liquid and often raises large amounts of thin frothy fluid which usually becomes pink or even bloody. As the fluid increases, it is more and more difficult for oxygen to enter the blood and the patient begins to drown in his own fluids.

to feel very ill indeed. In the afternoon his pulse rate was 144, respirations 40. Later in the evening he became very cyanosed, had . . . evident air hunger, all the extraordinary muscles of respiration being called into play. The heart sounds were very faint, the pulse irregular and of small tension. He seemed to present a typical picture of a failing heart. This condition persisted during the night; he coughed up with difficulty. He vomited at intervals. He had several inhalations of oxygen; strychnine and digitalis also were given. Towards morning he recovered slightly, and as there was luckily a train . . . he was sent straight down . . . I heard that when he got down to 12,000 feet he was considerably better, and at 7,000 feet he was nearly well. It seemed to me that he would have died had he stayed in the altitude for another day."

This is a classical description of a typical case: gradually developing symptoms within two days after a rapid ascent, growing worse rapidly with signs of moisture in the lungs, and—after seeming near death—improving dramatically after going down only a few thousand feet. Today, however, we would not consider this due to a "failing heart" as Ravenhill hinted. Ravenhill noticed that the longer it took for a person to come up from sea level, the less likely he was to be ill; he felt that prolonged residence at altitude protected most people on return from a brief sojourn at sea level, but he knew that this protection wore off during a long stay at sea level. He puzzled over the curious fact that some persons went down and returned many times without difficulty, but on other occasions of the same duration of stay near sea level, would be badly affected on regaining altitude. Thus he raised the question of frequency of illness among re-entrants compared to the newly arrived—a question we are still debating today.

He reported (but could not explain) the *"well-known fact that in the Andes puna is worse in certain places than in others of the same, or nearly the same, altitude."* He noticed that physical exertion made a person more susceptible and that *"alcohol plays a distinct part in accelerating an attack and increasing the severity of the symptoms."* Ravenhill 'wrote the book' on altitude illness with his perceptive clinical observations.

In 1937, Alberto Hurtado, one of the world's leading experts on high altitude, was inducted into the National Academy of Medicine in Lima, Peru, offering as his thesis a monograph titled *"Physiological Aspects of Pathology of the Life at High Altitude."* He described five cases of altitude illness with detailed laboratory studies. In retrospect four appear to have been cases of sub-acute or chronic mountain sickness, but one may have been high altitude pulmonary edema:

"Man, 58 years old, native of Junin of the Indian race. During the last 29 years he has lived in area of high elevation. He has been in Lima on various occasions and never has had Soroche upon returning. After being in Lima for three days he returns to Oroya by train. At . . . 13,000 feet he feels extremely badly, he begins to cough and he observes that his saliva contains a great deal of 'black' blood. Soon there are added to his symptoms: headache, intense difficulty in respiration and a certain mental incoordination. He . . . remains in his house being in the same condition on the following day when we examine him. At the examination he presents: Orthopnea, very intense cyanosis, expression of anxiety, 120 pulsations and humid and crepitant rales over both lungs. Expectoration is typically abundant, red and foamy (contains blood). An x-ray of the thorax shows an evident diminution of the pulmonary transparency; this alteration is more marked in both bases. Taken down to Lima the patient improves slowly and after two months he ascends again. A detailed examination at this time reveals the signs of circulatory insufficiency (congestion at the base of the lungs, and edema of the extremities). However, this time he does not show acute symptoms of a lack of adaptation."

This is less characteristic of HAPE than are Ravenhill's cases and one wonders whether this patient had underlying heart disease, leading to congestive failure which can so easily be confused with pulmonary edema due to oxygen lack.

In 1958 I was involved in one of those seemingly small episodes which often have large consequences:

On December 28, 1958 two healthy college students on skis crossed a 12,000 foot pass where one of them noted severe shortness of breath, weakness and cough. Within two days the symptoms were so severe that he could not go on, and his com-

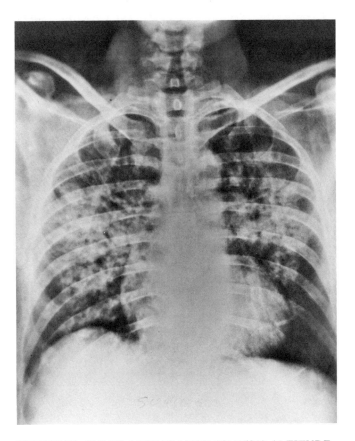

*FIGURE 25: X-RAY APPEARANCE OF HIGH ALTITUDE
PULMONARY EDEMA*

This X-ray photograph is characteristic of HAPE except that the patient was stricken at only 9,500 feet, whereas HAPE usually occurs at a somewhat higher altitude. The neck shadow at the top, and the dense dome of the diaphragm at the bottom are easily identified. In the center of the picture is the flask-shaped shadow of the heart, protruding more toward the right of the photograph (left ventricle). The curved white lines on each side are ribs, and the darker areas represent air-filled lung tissue which easily transmit the X-ray beam. Scattered throughout both lungs, though more in the right one, are fluffy white patches which represent something denser than lung tissue, and in this case are caused by accumulations of fluid.

panion left him in a tent at approximately 9,000 feet to seek help. Early in the evening of New Year's Eve he reached the writer, who spent the next six hours trying to assemble a reasonably sober and competent rescue party; this was done with mixed success, and the party, setting out at dawn on New Year's Day, reached the patient about noon, and brought him to hospital with a tentative diagnosis of pneumonia. More complete study revealed that he had pulmonary edema, and the question became why. He had never been ill, kept in top condition, neither smoked, nor drank, and had nothing to suggest heart disease. Since he lived at 5,000 feet, the added elevation seemed unimportant. It was noted that the year before he and the same friend had tried the same trip, but turned back because the patient became so short of breath at 11,000 feet!

The matter might have rested there: an isolated case is seldom of significance, but some of my mountaineering friends told me of similar episodes which had affected them or their companions on higher climbs. At this point the great cardiologist Paul Dudley White reviewed the case history, agreed that it was not cardiac in origin, and urged that I report it. The short article that appeared in the *New England Journal of Medicine* in 1960 was the first account of HAPE in English since Ravenhill and within a few months I received scores of letters describing similar cases. Half of these could be clearly identified as edema of the lungs occurring at altitude and in the absence of heart disease.

These are examples of what in the last twenty years has become the best known form of altitude illness—the accumulation of fluid in the small air sacs or alveoli—High Altitude Pulmonary Edema or HAPE. The description written by the companion of a young climber who died is graphic and accurate: *"He sounded as though he were drowning in his own juices."*

But case histories, particularly when they are not supported by detailed laboratory and X-ray studies, are only suggestive: to define a new clinical entity requires a great deal of painstaking study. Such work was already in progress. South American doctors were seeing many cases of altitude illness among tourists and workmen traveling between sea level and the high Andes and Hultgren, working with them in 1959, collected clinical details and laboratory and X-ray reports on 18 patients with unquestionable high altitude pulmonary edema. These studies, published in 1962, became the first fully documented description of HAPE. Again there was a flood of correspondence and medical journals contained numerous letters to the editor reporting similar experiences, though some were more likely pneumonia or heart failure than HAPE. This new 'physiological disease' soon became known around the world and recognized for what it was — a temporary, potentially lethal derangement caused by rapid exposure to high altitude and relieved by descent.

In October 1962 fighting that had been simmering for years, broke out between China and India along the high Tibetan border. The Chinese troops had been living in Tibet, usually above 13 or 14,000 feet, since their occupation of that country in 1950, while the Indians, caught unaware, had to rush troops from the flat plains of India high into the Himalayas in a few hours or days. The consequences were predictable: Indian troops suffered more casualties from altitude than from bullets. Singh and his colleagues described many combinations of altitude illness in 1,925 soldiers, reporting an incidence ranging from 0.1% to 8.3% in different companies exposed under similar circumstances — an eighty-fold difference that is hard to explain. These Indian workers have continued to investigate the basic mechanisms of altitude illness and have contributed a great deal to our present knowledge although some of their data and conclusions differ from ours in the western world.

Not only have skiing, trekking and mountaineering become much more popular in the last twenty-five years, but the ease and speed of getting to the mountains has also increased. Where it used to take many days or weeks to walk to the base of a high Himalayan peak, one can now fly in a day or two. Those who might have driven to a ski resort often go by air. We don't want to "waste time by acclimatizing." Too many people think "mountain sickness is for other people, not me." Fortunately people like Phil Synder in Kenya, John Dickinson in Kathmandu, and Peter Hackett, migrating between Alaska and Nepal, have helped the public to realize just what can happen to anyone, and the number of serious cases of altitude illness has not increased as rapidly as the number of persons at risk.

Nevertheless HAPE is still a problem, and a potentially serious one even for the most experienced:

A world class climber spent weeks reaching and climbing to a high camp on one of the great Himalayan peaks. After four days at or above 23,000 feet, and eight days at 25,000 feet, he abruptly began to cough and gurgle; he became very short of breath and weak, recognized that he had HAPE and readily agreed to evacuation. This was difficult, because he staggered so much and was pitifully weak. He improved after getting down 2,000 feet and after two days at 19,000 feet he felt well enough to pack loads to the next higher camp, but since his rales did not disappear for a week, he did not do so.

Certainly one would think his experience and the long period of acclimatization should have protected him, but this and similar cases are further evidence of the remarkable and inexplicable variations between individuals — and in the same person in different circumstances.

But to reiterate the most important fact: altitude illness does not occur on the highest mountains only. In fact more people are affected between 8,000 and 12,000 feet than at higher altitudes. It is the innocent, the ignorant, or the overly bold who get into trouble and sometimes die.

Dr. B. began skiing hard at 8,500 feet two days after leaving sea level, and within a day was short of breath and had a cough producing pink frothy sputum . . . Three days after reaching altitude he was semi-conscious, extremely ill, and unable to walk. By the time he was taken down he was apparently dying. In hospital at 5,000 feet, the diagnosis of pulmonary edema was easily made, treatment started, and he was discharged, well, on the fourth day . . . Three months later taking four days to go from sea level to 8,500 feet, he again developed such severe symptoms that he required a helicopter evacuation; his pulmonary edema was again treated resulting in prompt and rapid recovery.

A 45 year old commercial airline pilot arrived at the 9,300 foot high resort on Saturday, from sea level. He skied without difficulty on Sunday and Monday but that night slept poorly because of headache and cough which produced some blood-tinged sputum. He spent most of Tuesday in bed, but in the afternoon examination and X-ray showed that he had pulmonary edema in both lungs. He was advised to get down to lower altitude and did so within a few hours with marked immediate improvement.

But most people are short of breath at altitude—this is a natural response, so how can the climber or skiier tell when serious altitude illness may be beginning? HAPE is insidious and rarely dramatic in announcing its presence. Though only imprecise advice can be given, the best we can say today is that when the shortness of breath, the tickling cough, the tiredness increase, become more obvious than in one's companions, do not improve with a brief rest—then is the time to suspect something serious. If gurgling can be heard or felt in the chest, if the cough produces frothy blood-tinged sputum, or if the headache becomes very bad or hallucinations, however delicious or mild—begin, then trouble, serious trouble is near, and unless knowledgeable care is given promptly, the person may die. Getting down a few thousand feet is usually dramatically helpful, as it is for AMS. The longer descent is delayed, the slower recovery will be. Oxygen helps, and if given with good medical supervision in a hospital, even at altitude, may be all the victim of mild HAPE needs. But getting down is better. Even an apparently dying patient may rouse, care for himself, and ask to go back up after being taken down a few thousand feet.

There has been a great deal of interest in HAPE during the last few years and new leads toward explanation of the pathophysiology keep turning up. Yet we still do not know the exact mechanism, and research is hampered by the lack of a good animal model. Certain breeds of cattle develop brisket disease when taken to even moderate altitude, but this is a form of heart failure and not analogous to human HAPE, where the heart functions normally. Rats, mice, and guinea pigs do not react to hypoxia as man does. Sheep develop a form of pulmonary edema which has different characteristics, and so do dogs. Bold ingenious studies on human volunteers, especially ardent mountaineers who have had many attacks and are considered to be unusually vulnerable to HAPE, have produced more clues but a

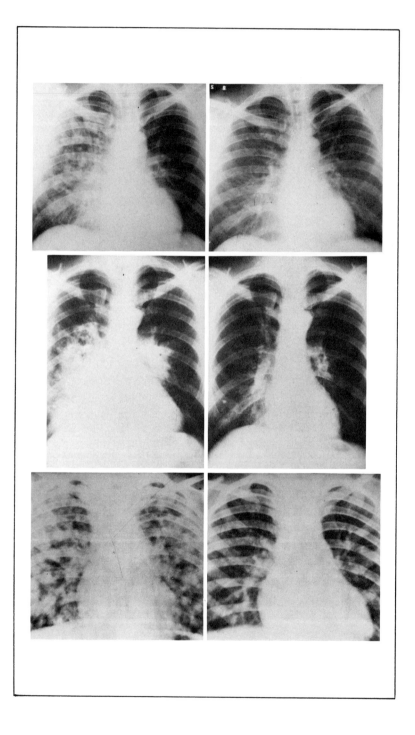

FIGURE 26: VARIOUS X-RAY SHADOWS SEEN IN HIGH ALTITUDE PULMONARY EDEMA

As these three pairs of X-ray photographs show, High Altitude Pulmonary Edema (HAPE) can take several forms.

Top Row: This 35 year old physician was mistakenly diagnosed as having an asthmatic attack when he became very short of breath at a ski resort at 8,000 feet and his doctor heard wheezes and wet crackles in his chest. The X-ray taken when he was admitted to hospital (left) shows fluffy white shadows scattered throughout the right lung, while the left lung seems to be almost completely normal. Three days later (right), both lungs have cleared and transmit the X-ray beam well because the lungs are again filled with air, leaving only the central heart shadow and the ribs to interfere with passage of X-rays.

Middle Row: This young skier (see page 120–2) became very short of breath and weak while crossing a 12,000 foot pass but managed to get down to 9,000 feet where he was later rescued. When he reached the hospital, X-ray (left) showed dense shadows at the 'root' of each lung (close to the heart), which could be due to many things. Two days later (right) all but small normal shadows have disappeared, strongly suggesting (together with the examination and laboratory findings) that the shadows were due to fluid (HAPE). This patient, being tall and thin, has a narrow long chest and a narrow 'vertical' heart.

Third Row: This traveller became very short of breath and obviously extremely ill at 14,000 feet. The first X-ray (left) shows white fluffy shadows scattered everywhere in both lungs almost obscuring the normal rib and heart shadows. Only one day later (right) both lungs are almost completely clear; the shadows of fluid patches have almost disappeared, although here and there (especially in the upper outer part of the left lung) some fluid still can be seen.

These pictures show how variable the X-ray can be and how rapidly the shadows caused by fluid can disappear. From the variety of forms HAPE takes it is not surprising that it is (or used to be) often mistaken for pneumonia or some other serious medical condition.

complete explanation still eludes us. Let us look at some of the less complicated things we know or think we know about HAPE.

Since the pioneering studies of Cournand and Richards more than forty years ago, it has been recognized that the blood pressure in the pulmonary arteries increases considerably during hypoxia. Normally this pressure is fifteen to twenty torr, but at altitude it may reach forty or fifty torr or go even higher during and immediately after strenuous exercise. Hultgren and Grover took to altitude six men who had previously had several attacks of HAPE, and found that they responded to the altitude with considerably more than the average rise in pulmonary artery pressure though they did not develop HAPE on this occasion. They did, however, show a decrease in diffusion of oxygen from alveolus to lung capillary, suggesting that some fluid might have begun to accumulate in the loosely structured space between alveoli and capillaries.

This has since been confirmed by several studies, so that we now believe that many — probably most — people who go rapidly to 8–9,000 feet or higher will develop a small amount of excess fluid in their lungs soon after arrival. In the majority the fluid reabsorbs, but for a few it increases, seeps into the air sacs and HAPE results. It would appear that some persons respond to hypoxia by a greater than normal increase in pulmonary artery pressure which somehow leads to more seepage of fluid out of vessels into alveoli, perhaps between cells in the stretched vessel walls.

But why the excessive increase in pulmonary artery pressure? Why in fact does that pressure increase at all when blood pressure in the rest of the body does not? This we do not know. But we do know that the cells lining and surrounding the blood vessels are capable of producing very powerful substances from an essential fatty acid, arachidonic acid. One group of these substances is the leukotriene family which raises blood pressure in the vessel and causes edema. Another of the substances is thromboxane which also raises pressure and causes blood platelets to clump together. Opposing these is prostacyclin, a member of the ubiquitous prostaglandin family, which relaxes pulmonary vessels, by counteracting thromboxane, thus lowering the pressure in the vessels and also suppressing the tendency for platelets to clump. The balance between these and other substances with equally exotic names determines what the pressure in the small blood vessel will be—and apparently whether or not leakage may occur. These are the frontiers today but too complex and too uncertain to discuss further in this book.

Noting that divers returning from the high pressure under water to normal sea level pressure develop clusters of platelets around the microscopic bubbles that appear in the blood during decompression like bubbles that form in soda when the bottle cap is removed, Gray and Bryan wondered whether these tiny platelet clumps might lodge in the lung capillaries during reduction in atmospheric pressure from sea level to altitude. They reasoned that local injury from such blockage together with the increased pulmonary artery pressure due to altitude might cause capillary leakage. They were able to show that a fall in platelets in circulating blood did occur during ascent and that radioactively labelled platelets did in fact lodge in the lungs of rabbits and of human volunteers decompressed to 14,000 feet. Their studies also suggested that some fluid then began to accumulate in the lungs.

So the possibility that platelet clumps may cause or help cause HAPE needs to be explored. HAPE just might be due, at least in part to imbalance between prostacyclin and thromboxane. To make matters more interesting, aspirin, common every day aspirin, used and abused for so many ailments, can virtually eliminate thromboxane production and thus platelet clumping, but leaves untouched the formation and functions of prostacyclin. Does this imply that aspirin is good treatment or prevention for HAPE? Well, scarcely: we simply do not know enough to say.

Moss did ingenious experiments in which the brain of one dog was provided with ample blood from another dog's lungs. When the donor dog was made hypoxic, thus causing brain hypoxia in the recipient, the lungs of the recipient dog filled with edema even though ventilated with normal oxygen and perfused with fully oxygenated blood. Moss argued that brain hypoxia triggered reflexes which set off pulmonary edema. His work needs confirmation.

An interesting substance in the lining of the respiratory tract, called surfactant decreases surface tension in the alveoli which would otherwise collapse from the large tension (which changes inversely to the square of the radius of a sphere). Surfactant is constantly being made and destroyed; its synthesis is halted by a number of influences, among them hypoxia. Griffith suggests that hypoxia decreases surfactant formation, so that some alveoli collapse here and there, increasing the desaturation of the blood which passes these unventilated areas, and increasing capillary leakage at altitude.

This would fit a hypothesis advanced by Hultgren which reconciles a great deal of information from different sources. He suggests that blood flow may be unevenly distributed in the lung, some areas receiving much more, some much less, during hypoxia, either because of small emboli such as Gray proposed, or because small vessels contract more strongly in some areas than in others under the stimulus of hypoxia, or because of patchy areas of collapse (or atelectasis) suggested by Griffith. As a result some areas are 'flooded' with blood while others experience a 'drought'; capillaries leak in the flooded areas, producing first interstitial and later alveolar edema. This would explain the patchy appearance in X-ray photographs of HAPE, and the other puzzling occurrence of severe edema in one lung, or in some areas while others are completely free.

Support for this theory comes from five cases of severe HAPE, occurring in persons with an extremely rare congenital defect — absence of one major pulmonary artery. The affected lung (which was normally ventilated, but nourished by a net of collateral vessels), did not participate in the oxygenation of venous (less oxygenated) blood, making it probable that the normal lung was 'flooded' as pulmonary artery pressure increased at altitude. HAPE occurred in the normal lung.

M. P. was a previously healthy 21 year old white male who came rapidly from Missouri to 9,500 feet on January 2nd, and skied for a few hours before a slight sprain of the ankle. He 'lay around the lodge' for the rest of that day and developed dyspnea and cough, which grew worse during the night. On January 3rd he was nauseated, vomited and continued to cough, growing worse during the day but did not seek help. Early in the evening his companions decided that he was very sick, and transported him to the local doctor, but he died en route, and vigorous attempts at resuscitation failed. X-rays taken immediately after death on arrival at the doctor's office showed extensive bilateral pulmonary edema. Autopsy done the following day confirmed the presence of pulmonary edema and showed that the right main pulmonary artery was completely absent.

C.C. an 11-year-old boy started on vacation in the Sierras on August 2, 1981, and complained of chest pain when the family reached 7,000 feet. He did not sleep well that night (8,500 feet) because of headache . . . next day though not well, he took a short hike, acted very tired and had a pulse rate of 136. He vomited during the night and began to cough and to bring up increasing amounts of liquid. His mother and physician grandfather thought he had HAPE and started down at 0530, on August 4th, reaching 5,000 feet an hour later where examination and a chest X-ray showed HAPE. He improved rapidly with descent, oxygen and intravenous Lasix and a day later at 3,000 feet seemed well.

What is interesting here is that C.C. was examined five years earlier because of chest pain at low altitude and was found to have no pulmonary artery to his right lung. He is able to play actively with children his age and apparently only gets into trouble if he goes above 5-6,000 feet.

John Bligh and Denise Chauca in sub-arctic Fairbanks, Alaska have found that sheep and cattle are more vulnerable to brisket disease (a form of altitude illness) if they are cold; when taken into a warm shelter, even while at altitude, they improve. This led to suggestions that some receptor in the nose might respond to cold much as it does in diving mammals, raising pulmonary artery pressure higher than it would go from lack of oxygen alone. Barry Burns has found in some preliminary studies that blowing cold air in the nostrils of man does in fact raise pulmonary artery pressure, though cold on the face does not. These studies are at least suggestive, but one must remember that HAPE occurs in warm weather as well as cold.

In the last few years it has become clear that some individuals are very prone to HAPE and will develop it repeatedly, even at moderate altitude, and sometimes even if they take time for ascent. These people are at risk and greatly increase the danger faced by a party on a big mountain. On at least three occasions in recent years not only a climbing party but also rescuers have been endangered because one of the party had his third bout of HAPE. At this time, I would hesitate to recommend for a big mountain expedition any one who has had two episodes of HAPE, unless these could be explained by unusual circumstances.

There are other curious aspects: why, for example, do some unfortunates develop AMS every time they go above a certain altitude, but never develop HAPE? Why should HAPE occasionally appear suddenly in some one quite unaffected a few hours before? Why should one member of a party be smitten while others doing the same work at the same altitude feel fine? We can attribute some of these observations to individual variation, to a mild infection or differences in food or fluid intake—but some puzzles remain.

Then there is the question of whether or not the long-time resident at altitude who goes down to low altitude for a short visit, is at greater risk when returning. Ravenhill observed that some residents were more susceptible on returning, but others were not and that some individuals were sick on one return and not on others. Singh found no difference between returning soldiers and those going high for the first time. Hultgren found that residents at 11,300 feet in Peru ran a considerably higher risk of HAPE when they came back from a stay near the coast than did new arrivals, and Scoggin reported similar observations on residents of Leadville, Colorado (10,500 feet). These studies lack a crucial figure—the number of trips made, or the number of persons going down and returning, without the development of HAPE. To determine the incidence of any abnormality like HAPE, one needs both a numerator (the number affected) and a denominator (the number of persons at risk).

Astronomers commuting from sea level to the observatory at 14,100 feet on Mauna Kea have not gotten HAPE, probably because they stay for only a few hours on the summit. The shift workers live at 9,000 feet and work all day on the summit for six weeks and then spend six weeks at sea level: they report only one case of HAPE in several years, and that was complicated by other factors. Himalayan climbers usually descend to Base Camp for several days of rest in the thick rich air after working for weeks at much higher elevations. They do not develop HAPE when they go back up. I know scores of people who live at 9-10,000 feet and go down to sea level for a few days, and return without any problems.

Nevertheless, despite the deficiency of hard data, persons who live above 10,000 feet may be at slightly greater risk when they return after a visit to lower altitude, and it seems prudent to suggest that they be more alert for signs of HAPE when they go back to altitude.

Men seem to be somewhat more likely to develop HAPE than women under the same conditions, though this may be misleading because of other differences such as numbers at risk and effort expended. Women in the pre-menstrual water-retaining phase do seem especially vulnerable to any kind of altitude illness.

Hultgren has shown clearly that young children are many times more likely to develop HAPE than are adults; persons under twenty are more susceptible than those who are older. Not until other infirmities of age develop are the elderly at greater risk — perhaps because only the fittest of them venture high. Later we will examine who should and who should not go high — and why.

So what should one do when HAPE is suspected? What is the best treatment? Vacationers in a mountain resort, or campers and skiers in areas where good medical care is immediately or soon available may be treated effectively on the spot. In a good facility with medical care, rest, reassurance, oxygen, and perhaps medication, early cases usually clear up quickly although getting to a lower altitude is still the best and most effective management.

High on a mountain the problem may be quite different. If the party can possibly get down, they should do so, soon. They must not wait, hoping "the weather will clear" or the victim will improve, or "perhaps oxygen will work." Far too many tragedies have proven how unwise waiting is. It is much better to go down needlessly than to lose a friend.

In 1960, as HAPE was just beginning to be recognized, a young doctor became seriously ill at 14,000 feet in the Andes after going up too rapidly. He describes hearing moisture when he listened to his own lungs with a stethoscope, and vividly recalls his cough, his shortness of breath and his realization that something dangerous was happening. Finally in the middle of the night, he *"got on a horse and rode as fast as I could down to 12,000 feet. By the time I got there I felt fine."* After a few days he went back up more slowly and was able to reach two 22,000 foot summits. Three years later he went to Everest.

Occasionally descent is impossible and the patient must be cared for on site. Although some new drugs show promise the only treatment we have today is a powerful kidney stimulant (diuretic) — Lasix or furosemide which squeezes water out of the body, particularly from the soggy lungs. But Lasix may decrease the circulating blood volume and cause a form of shock, thus, as Hultgren put it "converting the walking wounded to a litter case." If Lasix is used, and sometimes it is all that one can do, then lots of extra fluids should be taken by mouth to prevent low volume shock — a seemingly contradictory set of recommendations. To date there are no well-controlled studies of the value of Lasix in HAPE, but considerable anecdotal support suggests that Lasix should be part of the high mountain medical kit, for use only when little else can be done. It is not useful as a preventive as was once suggested.

Morphine is another drug with risks and benefits: it is sometimes miraculous in pulmonary edema due to heart failure; it relaxes the anxious and may, by a direct effect on blood vessels, decrease pulmonary artery hypertension and the tendency to edema. But it is also a respiratory depressant and may embarass breathing when the patient is already hypoxic, although the stimulus to breathe is strong at altitude. Morphine has been used infrequently and no definite evaluation is possible except that it may be turned to when nothing else is available. Tourniquets around the legs — sometimes helpful in heart failure, are worthless in HAPE, and despite a few reports to the contrary, digitalis is not thought useful because HAPE is not due to a faltering heart, and that organ probably cannot be whipped to work better.

A reasonable procedure would be to encase the HAPE victim in an airtight box or bag and to pump up the pressure in the bag to simulate the pressure increase achieved by descending several thousand feet. Such apparatus is being tried on an experimental basis and Hackett and colleagues have begun to use it near the Everest Base Camp, for unfortunate or foolish trekkers. This is a promising treatment but there is the problem of decompression to be faced when the victim is taken out of the chamber or bag.

'Pressure assisted breathing' is sometimes used to treat hospital patients with pulmonary edema from other causes. Oxygen is given through a special mask which triggers an increase in pressure at the end of expiration, thus 'driving' oxygen into the lungs during the next inspiration at higher than ambient pressure. Whether this may be beneficial in HAPE has not been adequately tested so far, and it seems unlikely that many expeditions would carry the necessary equipment.

When HAPE is apparent, especially when it seems to be worsening, the best management is to get down, as far and as fast as possible.

HIGH ALTITUDE CEREBRAL EDEMA (HACE)

HACE is a third manifestation of altitude illness, less common but more deadly. Since brain has the greatest need for oxygen of any tissue in the human body, it is not surprising that lack of oxygen affects brain functions early, insidiously, and in a variety of ways. In general terms, the highest or most developed brain functions are the first affected—judgment, difficult decision making, or appreciation of one's condition, among others.

"A 28 year old Korean climber flew to 9,000 feet and during the next week climbed slowly to 14,000 feet, where he felt nauseated and lethargic but insisted on continuing to 16,000 feet, where he became unconscious, nine days after starting his trip. He was carried down to 11,000 feet next day, deeply unconscious, with both lungs filled with moisture and two days later, still deeply unconscious, was flown to hospital at 5,000 feet where he was found to have no pulmonary edema but

severe neurological deficits. Ten days later he had begun to improve and left the hospital after 43 days, still not fully normal."

One of the survivors of a tragedy on Aconcagua wrote:

"For eleven days they had been on the mountain at elevations of between 10,500 and 22,700 feet. They were on the verge of collapse and incapable of any uphill effort to look for their two missing companions. When they arrived at 15,500 feet their condition both physical and mental, was extreme. Even the next day, after a night's rest at the lower elevation, they were still convinced of the reality of hallucinations they had experienced on the mountain . . . that there were trees high up on the mountain, that there was a piece of highway equipment on the summit ridge, that a rescue party had been on the mountain and was stealing their flashlight batteries, that there were dead mules at Camp 3, that there were huts on the route, and that they had heard people talking . . ."

Another example of hallucinations was recorded on a lower mountain:

A 34-year-old physician flew to 10,000 feet and during the next four days carried a heavy pack to 14,500 feet, though he became increasingly weak and short of breath. He noticed some disturbance in vision and had visual and auditory hallucinations (which—though they seemed very real—he recognized as hallucinations). After descending a little way the hallucinations disappeared, his breathing improved, but weakness persisted. Within 24 hours of descent still lower he was greatly improved and fully normal three days later.

Several years later this climber had a similar but less well described episode at the same altitude, and a few years later had a more severe episode at the same altitude, with hallucinations, paranoia (feelings of persecution) and extreme weakness during a slightly higher climb. Although he himself had described the first episode in great detail and though others saw and described the subsequent episodes, he later denied them. This may reflect either a real loss of memory for the acute episodes or an emotional suppression of things he prefers to forget. In any event, for that individual, HACE is a real and possibly recurrent problem at altitude.

These are examples of the lack of insight, the failure to ap-

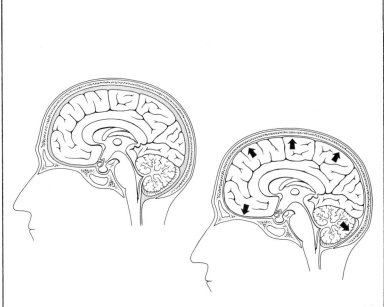

FIGURE 27: THE BRAIN IN ITS BOX — THE SKULL

The soft whitish-gray brain is cushioned within the rigid hard skull by a thin layer of liquid—the cerebro-spinal fluid—which is under pressure little greater than that of the atmosphere. Through the fluid are transmitted many of the chemical stimuli to and from the brain. The 'markings' on the surface of the brain, defining its segments, are usually clear (left). When the brain swells (cerebral edema) because too much fluid is accumulating within the brain tissues, the brain becomes too big for its box (right) and presses against the walls, decreasing the brain markings and increasing spinal fluid pressure. But whether or not pressure is increased within the skull at altitude is still unclear.

preciate one's condition which—on a big mountain—can and has led to many preventable tragedies. Altitude saps the strength and will, but even worse—it weakens our most important mental functions. Tissandier and his companions in the balloon *Zenith* became irrational and unable to do the needful at their highest elevation, and Tissandier's survival was purely by luck. The highly intelligent and perceptive scientist Haldane was so gravely affected in the decompression chamber test that he kept nodding foolishly and ordering "Keep it at 320." The great British climber Frank Smythe for years was reluctant to describe his own hallucination high on Everest, so vivid that he offered his imaginary companion a piece of his candy. Irrational decisions, inability to do even simple tasks well, irritability and lethargy all increase with altitude, and when there is inadequate time to compensate, accidents and tragedies are likely.

Usually headache is the first and worst symptom of HACE. Because headache also occurs with simple mountain sickness (AMS), there is growing suspicion that some edema may develop in the brain at comparatively low altitude—much as we find some fluid accumulating in the lungs, and that this mild, reversible brain edema may be absorbed (again like that in the lung) if the marvellous adaptive processes are given half a chance. But when the headache is very severe, growing worse, and especially if accompanied by other evidence of deranged brain function such as staggering walk, hallucinations, inappropriate talk or emotional reaction, then the threat of progressive HACE is real enough to require emergency management. Once again, descent is the most important treatment.

Coordinated use of hands and fingers may be clumsy or impossible, and double vision may result from weakness of certain eye muscles. The hallucinations may be of any variety: one skier who nearly died of HACE after a climb which took five days to reach only 10,500 feet, continued to see Marilyn Monroe "live and in color" on the wall of his hospital room for a day after most of his problems had cleared (distractingly vivid he reported). The most common hallucination is of a companion nearby, walking, talking, sharing the experience. Most persons with brain edema hear voices, many see bizarre objects. Disorientation in time and space is common. By the time these extreme signs have appeared, the diagnosis is obvious and treatment essential to save life.

Throughout most stories of hypoxic illness is the common theme: loss of higher intellectual functions. The hypoxic person loses judgment and perception and is unable to recognize how serious his problems are. They must be seen by an observer who is unaffected, as by the scientists who observed subjects at altitude through the portholes of the decompression chamber during "Operation Everest." It is much like going late (and without a drink) to a cocktail party which has been going on for an hour or so: the guests (in their own view) are witty, wise, imaginative and sensible, but the new arrival finds them far otherwise.

For the aviator or balloonist such lack of judgment or perception is even more serious — just as alcohol is — because the ability to react swiftly and appropriately, the judgement to recognize early danger, and the wisdom to take the safe course of action spell the difference between life and sometimes a speedy crash. Most air combat during World War II occurred at altitudes which necessitated oxygen equipment (this was before pressurization was practicable) and hundreds of tragic, avoidable deaths were due to unrecognized lack of oxygen caused by equipment failure or delay in using it. Even today this happens, especially under professional pressures:

"On a six hour flight across the Sierras, Rockies and deserts between, in a single engine, pressurized aircraft, we had a cabin altitude of 11,000 feet. Most of us were pilots but no one commented on fatigue and headache from altitude (which we all had), each thinking he was the only one. We exchanged views only after landing and seeing how the others collapsed in the airport lounge! On the return flight we kept a lower cabin altitude but chose to fly above bad weather and planned to make half the trip in darkness. When the engine failed just before dark we made a forced landing in a lucky spot . . . and finally admitted out loud that we had been pushings things foolishly."

Of course altitude is not the only cause of lack of oxygen, and other causes have the same effect on the higher centers of the brain:

Several men were working around a large steel vessel while it was being flushed with nitrogen which was spilling over the brim. Supposedly the ventilation of the temporary shelter was enough to prevent accumulation. One of the men climbed down into the vessel to retrieve a tool despite clear instructions never to enter an enclosed space without a safe entry permit. He collapsed immediately. Ignoring a shouted order not to go into the vessel, a second man climbed in to rescue the first. Both were dead when extricated. The company was sued unsuccessfully on the basis that enough nitrogen might have accumulated in the shelter to affect their judgment.

Carbon monoxide, by combining more readily with hemoglobin than oxygen does, sometimes causes serious hypoxia. A few years ago chronic headaches and irritability of policemen working in traffic control, and of underground garage attendants was traced to poor ventilation which allowed carbon monoxide to build to dangerous levels. Blood tests of drivers on very crowded thruways during rush hour show carbon monoxide levels which are high enough to impair judgment, and even to aggravate pain from existing heart disease which is due in part to inadequate oxygen flow to heart muscle. Of course carbon monoxide can greatly increase the danger from altitude:

A young medical student flew from Florida to Peru and within two days went to 12,000 feet; he felt poorly, but blamed this on diarrhea. Two days later he was taken to 14,000 feet where he was to do volunteer work in a clinic. He felt worse and stayed in his room. Because he was cold he moved to a smaller room which had a gas heater which he turned on high before going to bed. Next morning he was found dead and autopsy showed massive pulmonary edema. A woman in the next room was also affected by the gas which flowed after the burner had gone out but she recovered.

His death was due to the cumulative effect of altitude illness (AMS and HAPE) and carbon monoxide poisoning. The young man's mother sued the sponsoring agency on the grounds that he had been inadequately warned of the dangers of high altitude. Certainly he showed faulty judgment, first in going above 12,000 feet when he felt poorly, and second by going to sleep in a sealed room with a gas heater burning.

Although headache dominates the clinical picture, we have

come to realize that a curious staggering walk (ataxia) appears early and may be the first clue that something is wrong. Seven years ago I took care of a young Japanese climber, evacuated from 17,500 feet because he was unable to walk or even stand, though he denied other symptoms. Even after two days at 2,250 feet he could not sit up, feed himself or stand without help. He made an uneventful recovery, but others are not so lucky.

By its name we imply that High Altitude Cerebral Edema is a swelling of the brain. Is this true? Autopsies on persons dying from altitude illness, usually show swelling, but in addition there often are tiny hemorrhages, large hemorrhages, and clots in veins and arteries. How much of this severe pathology occurs at the time of or immediately after death is sometimes hard to tell, and we fall back on the belief that the brain does swell in altitude illness.

But why does the brain swell? One theory (discussed in Chapter Ten) holds that the bio-electric potentials of cell membranes, which 'pump' sodium out and hold potassium within the cell, are altered by lack of oxygen. The 'sodium pump' falters, sodium is retained, water enters and the cell expands. Wherever this happens edema appears, but in the rigid box-like skull, pressure is not easily dispersed, and ominous signs and symptoms develop rapidly. But whereas loose tissues in the face or hands or feet may swell without causing important symptoms, even a little swelling of the brain, tightly packed in its case, produces serious problems which are self-reinforcing.

Though this book is not the place to discuss in detail other causes of oxygen lack such as carbon monoxide poisoning, head injury, near-drowning, or certain drugs or anesthetics, it is worth noting that these cause signs and symptoms quite similar to those at altitude; all have the common factor of hypoxia. Brain edema at sea level resembles high altitude brain edema more closely than pulmonary edema from other causes resembles that due to altitude.

The brain can withstand more oxygen lack if it is well supplied with blood, but when both blood flow and oxygen supply are compromised, problems develop fast. Perhaps this is why brain edema ebbs and flows (as it were) more rapidly than does pulmonary edema. Neurosurgeons have watched the brain bulge through an incision in the skull when there is not enough oxygen in the anesthetic gas mixture, and shrink back again, in only a few minutes, when adequate oxygen is restored. Breathing oxygen relieves headache more swiftly than would seem possible if cell swelling were the sole underlying cause. Clearly the 'pump failure' theory is not the whole story.

Bo Siesjo, a leading authority on brain patho-physiology, believes that brain function falters and fails during hypoxia because communications between brain cells become disordered — a transmission failure. He reminds us that the flow of blood to the brain is controlled by two major influences (at least): lack of oxygen which dilates these vessels, increasing blood flow, and fall in carbon dioxide which constricts vessels, decreasing blood flow. Consequently when the healthy person at altitude breathes more deeply, thus depleting carbon dioxide, the brain blood vessels receive conflicting orders: hypoxia dictates dilatation, while the fall in carbon dioxide commands constriction. Which dominates is decided by other factors, only some of which are partially understood. Siesjo has pointed out that brain cells are remarkably resistant to permanent damage from hypoxia so long as blood flow is maintained. Several experienced persons have suggested that blood flow is excessively increased during hypoxia, and that this is the cause of headache (from stretching the vessels), and also of leakage (through stretched vessel walls). This would explain why the hypoxic headache is so often 'pounding', and why in early cases there is rarely evidence of increased pressure in the spinal fluid as shown by bulging of the optic nerve (papilledema) in the retina, or as measured by a spinal puncture. This concept would also explain why oxygen so rapidly relieves headache in early cases of AMS or HACE.

Cerebro-spinal fluid (CSF) is the clear, slightly salty fluid which bathes the brain and spinal cord; it is formed in a special part of the brain by filtration through what is called the "blood-brain barrier" and consequently its composition and characteristics — and amount — depend to some extent on those characteristics in the blood and on the filtration process. If these change, CSF is affected. Formation of CSF changes rapidly: acetazolamide given intravenously sharply and swiftly decreases

CSF pressure and alters its composition, but these return to normal over the space of an hour or two. Hypoxia alters CSF formation and pressure, but the magnitude and direction of change depend upon other factors such as the acidity or alkalinity of blood, the flow of blood in the brain and so forth, so how CSF will change is not easily predicted.

What we can say with reasonable confidence is that lack of oxygen affects brain function, increases pressure within the skull, and when both lack of oxygen and decreased blood flow occur, the brain is quickly damaged, often permanently. The mechanisms remain to be worked out in detail. Whatever its cause, HACE is a serious condition which must be treated by immediate and rapid descent.

Descent is mandatory, urgent, and often the only effective treatment. Furosemide (Lasix) has not been used enough to enable any reliable judgment of its value. Intravenous treatments used by neurosurgeons in cases of brain edema due to injury or oxygen lack from other causes might work but have not been adequately tried. Intravenous injection of certain hormones has been used frequently enough to warrant the cautious opinion that steroids such as dexamethasone or betamethasone, given in a dose of 4 to 12 mg every four to six hours do help; their effects are slow which makes it hard to judge whether descent, the steroid, or some other change is responsible. But one of these is the best treatment we have for mountaineers with HACE at this time — best, that is, next to descent. Getting down is still the surest and most important management, and if one starts down before the condition is too far along, improvement is correspondingly fast. Delay not only risks life but may leave long-lasting damage.

"A healthy 25 year old man took 13 days to walk to 11,000 feet and in the next four days to 17,500 feet where he had abdominal pain, fatigue, vomiting, and diarrhea. He became less responsive and had difficulty with balance. Six days after leaving 11,000 feet he could not walk, slept most of the day, becoming unconscious the next day, when he was carried down to 16,000 feet . . . and the next day flown unconscious to hospital at 5,000 feet . . . On the tenth day after admission he was oriented but unable to move his legs . . . The attending physi-

*cian wrote 'I believe he may suffer residual brain damage and I
am not sure he will be able to walk again.' (A complicating
bacterial infection was suspected but not proven.)"*

When either HAPE or HACE is severe and the period of im-
mobilization or unconsciousness is more than a few days, other
complications may occur and kill or threaten the climber. The
most frequent is a blood clot in a leg, which may break off and
lodge in the fine capillary network of the lung, causing
pulmonary embolism. Blood clots are potentially serious even at
sea level, and at altitude—where blood is already thicker and
more sluggish—clots and embolism are major disasters.

*"I knew we were moving up a bit fast for me . . . It was a
surprise to every one when I went unconscious . . . at 21,000
feet . . . I had been going strong to our camp at 20,000 feet
where I even chopped out a tent platform. I didn't even have a
headache . . . It wasn't till after the fifth night that I regained
consciousness at 17,500 feet . . . A blood clot formed in my left
leg and on the sixth day on the carry-out a bit broke off and
went to my lungs. It was agony and I coughed up clots of blood
for two days. I went unconscious on May 7th and reached
hospital on May 20th."*

This young man was lucky to survive what appears to have
been poor management and planning; he lost 40-50 pounds, was
in the hospital for some time but recovered fully. Perhaps his
companions will be wiser on their next expedition.

HIGH ALTITUDE RETINAL HEMORRHAGE (HARH)

Another response to altitude which has received a great deal
of attention in recent years occurs in the retina—a densely
packed layer of light-sensitive cells called rods and cones lining
the back of each eye. The pioneering work of Ross McFarland
before and during World War II showed that these cells (particularly the rods which are sensitive to light and darkness rather
than to color) are extremely sensitive to hypoxia. At 10,000 feet
half of our ability to see in dim light is gone, though restored
rapidly by breathing oxygen. Further loss of dim light vision is
slower with increasing altitude, but this sensitivity is one of the
earliest indicators of lack of oxygen. Just how this may be

related to the increase in blood flow easily seen in the retina at much higher altitudes is not clear.

In 1968 a young climber developed mild cerebral edema at 17,500 feet on Mt. Logan and was evacuated to hospital where, though he had fully recovered, many small hemorrhages were seen in the retina of each eye. No other reason for them was found. Later that year in a physician working at the same altitude I saw similar hemorrhages not explained by other illness. Together these two episodes could not be dismissed, but the only previous observation of anything similar had been made by Singh who saw hemorrhages in the fluid portion of the eyeball in a few of the thousands of soldiers taken ill on the Himalayan frontier. We decided to investigate further and in the next twelve years examined or photographed the retinas of several hundred persons, both acutely exposed and acclimatized, at 17,500 feet. Our observations together with those by Schumacher who examined thirty-nine climbers on Mount McKinley, and other doctors who have looked at the eyes of climbers on many expeditions show that above 12-14,000 feet the blood vessels of the retina dilate, and a larger, more rapid flow of blood courses through them. This occurs in everyone and is not related to symptoms, to speed of ascent or length of stay, or to general condition. Because this increased retinal blood flow appears to be universal at high altitude, we regard it as a normal physiological response to hypoxia. Interestingly enough it is also seen in persons chronically short of oxygen due to certain lung diseases, and also in persons acutely hypoxic from carbon monoxide poisoning.

A second change is more important. Above 17,000 feet more than half of all persons will have hemorrhages of different size and shape, throughout the retina. These appear without warning and most are not noticeable to the person affected. Though most can be seen by a trained individual looking through an ophthalmoscope, retinal photographs are needed to detect them all. Persons with severe HAPE or HACE usually have many retinal hemorrhages but they also appear in persons without any other symptoms, and there is no correlation between HARH and minor altitude illness. They are more likely to occur during or immediately after strenuous exercise, though they do not seem related to the level of arterial oxygen saturation whether awake or asleep. After acclimatization they are slightly less frequent.

Curiously enough though HARH do not seem to happen more often the higher one goes, only a few have been described as low as 12,000 feet (by Japanese doctors at Shinshu University, near a popular mountain resort). Schumacher saw some at 14,000 feet, attributing them to strenuous exertion at that altitude. Neither age nor sex have any influence. Interestingly enough they may disappear during a long stay at altitude, and they heal without a trace a few weeks after descent. So far there is no evidence that a person who has had HARH on one occasion is more vulnerable on another.

Most retinal hemorrhages are not important: they do not cause symptoms or leave scars and—although not something one can ignore—most HARH are not reason either to go down or not to climb again—unless, obviously, accompanied by more serious altitude problems. But there is one important exception.

The macular region of the eye—where we receive central vision on looking straight ahead—is occasionally the site of hemorrhage, and when this occurs, the individual does notice a 'blind' spot or a blur in the center of the visual field. Macular hemorrhages are rare but they do cause symptoms, and they do leave scars. Half of the persons with macular hemorrhages of whom I have personal knowledge still have small but detectable defects in vision. My own, in 1953, left a defect for several years but then was undetectable for 25 years. Recently macular degeneration has begun, but whether there is any relationship whatever to the old insult is unknowable. Prudence seems to dictate that the appearance of a macular hemorrhage or, if no way of examining the eyes is available, the recognition of a central blurred spot, is reason to go down lest the hemorrhage enlarge. But there is no agreement whether or not this is reason not to go high again!

An even rarer retinal insult occurs when patches of the retina swell with edema, compressing blood vessels in the patches and forming what ophthalmologists call 'cotton wool spots' because of their appearance. These cause small blind spots which persist long after descent and are believed to result in scars which leave

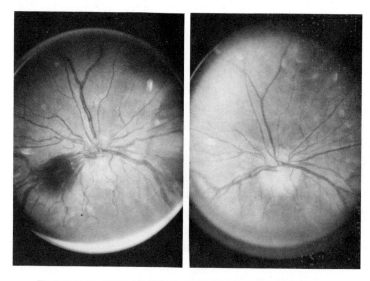

*FIGURE 28: THE RETINA AND ITS BLOOD VESSELS
AT SEA LEVEL AND AT ALTITUDE*

Using a strobe light flashed through the lens of a special camera, photographs can be taken of the retina of the eye, which appears as above right. The round light-colored area to which the small arteries and veins (dark lines) lead is the optic disc, or head of the optic nerve which carries light and color impulses from the sensitive retinal cells to the brain.

Above 15-16,000 feet the veins and arteries almost double in diameter and blood flow in them also doubles (above left). This appears to be a universal and 'normal' response to altitude (and in fact to hypoxia from other causes as well). In addition, over half of all people going above 17,000 feet have small hemorrhages in various layers of the retina (above left), due to leakage, or to actual rupture of small vessels. Some are quite large and blob-shaped; others are small and flame-shaped. Though alarming at sea level, these hemorrhages at altitude rarely cause symptoms and usually disappear within a few weeks leaving no residual damage.

permanent small defects in the visual fields. When they are seen at altitude they are cause for immediate descent because the edematous areas can enlarge, further damaging vision. Similar areas are seen in diabetes and in kidney disease, but whether lack of oxygen is the common cause is unknown. But we know very little about this altitude-related problem today and further advice would be pure speculation.

The first such case which we reported occurred at 17,500 feet, and I have kept in touch with the woman, who still has some small blind spots, though nothing can be seen on examination. She has since been above 20,000 feet on several expeditions without developing any cotton wool spots, although she has had retinal hemorrhages.

It is fascinating to find that about one third of all newborn infants show retinal hemorrhages. A long or difficult delivery increases the incidence, while infants delivered by Caesarean section show fewer hemorrhages. All disappear within a few weeks! The authors of several articles describing large numbers of observations suggest that these may be due to lack of oxygen during the foetal period: while in the womb the foetus receives oxygen in placental blood at the pressure equivalent to that in air on top of Mt. Everest.

Furthermore some patients ill at sea level with diseases which cause severe oxygen lack, show the same kind of retinal abnormalities as healthy persons on high mountains, and these changes also disappear with improved oxygenation.

Of greater concern to the high altitude climber is whether similar hemorrhages may be occurring in other parts of the body where they are less easily seen. Do they form in the brain, or kidneys, or adrenal glands for example? If so, do permanent scars remain? To be blunt — does exposure to high altitude cause bleeding in certain vital organs which causes decreased function perhaps forever? Are we seeing in the eye only a sample of what is occurring elsewhere? Perhaps this is the most important aspect of high altitude retinopathy.

Unfortunately we cannot answer conclusively. Rennie and others have seen tiny hemorrhages under the finger-nails in climbers and in residents at altitude. When urines collected from each of several subjects were meticulously examined for blood, a very small increase in the number of red cells could be found after days at altitude — suggesting that perhaps small hemorrhages had occurred somewhere in the kidneys or urinary tract.

Just what causes retinal hemorrhages is not clear. Some photographed hemorrhages have white centers which might be due to tiny platelet emboli such as Gray postulated as a contributory cause of HAPE. Attempts to show increased fragility or 'leakiness' of retinal vessels, by injecting a dye called fluorescein which readily seeps out of 'leaky' vessels, have not shown abnormal capillary weakness. The blood pressure in retinal vessels does increase during strenuous work or straining — a rather common occurrence in mountain climbing — and there is a definite but weak correlation between strenuous work and the incidence of HARH. On the other hand some climbers have done extremely heavy work without hemorrhage, while others, almost inactive show them. Surprisingly little relationship has been found between mild AMS or HAPE or even HACE and the occurrence of HARH, but usually the more severe is HAPE or HACE, the more likely are hemorrhages.

Dickinson saw many hemorrhages in the brains of persons who died from altitude edema of the brain or of the lungs. Persons dying from carbon monoxide poisoning or asphyxia — and in fact from many different conditions — often show these hemorrages, not only in the brain but in other organs too. These are extreme cases and it would be unwise to extrapolate and conclude that healthy climbers also have these hemorrhages at altitude — a rather sobering thought! We can say with considerable confidence: (1) the more severe or prolonged the lack of oxygen (from any cause), the more likely are widespread hemorrhages, (2) most hemorrhages (except in special spots) are rapidly absorbed by the wonderful healing powers of the body and leave no functional scars, and (3) there is no convincing evidence that being at very high altitude often or for long periods causes permanent damage unless severe altitude illness occurs. Indeed an informal survey of a large number of illustrious Himalayan climbers suggested they were healthier and lived longer than others!

The large number of men and women of all ages who are now scrambling higher and higher without oxygen will be a rich

source of information: I personally am satisfied that no permanent harm is done to the brain or body by climbing as high as
Everest without oxygen, <u>except</u> when serious altitude illness of
any form appears, but there are contrary views!

Hornbein found that some of the scientists who had gone
high on the American Research Expedition to Everest in 1981
had a small persistent inability to tap their fingers rapidly on a
flat surface; this was thought to indicate some remaining nerve
damage although all other tests returned to normal almost immediately after return.

Zdzislaw Ryn in Krakow, Poland has written a comprehensive review of the history of high altitude, and reports his study
of its effect on the brain and nervous system. From 70 "experienced Alpinists" he selected 40 considered healthy and did
many neurological and psychiatric tests before, during and at
intervals after several expeditions.

Thirty-five of the 40 had been on two to five expeditions in
previous years. All spent five to 20 weeks between 17,000 and
20,000 feet and some spent many days even higher. He wrote:
*"All climbers examined experienced acute mountain sickness
with somatic as well as psychic manifestations."* Many described
hallucinations, apathy or complete exhaustion, depression, and
other emotional disturbances. None required evacuation even
though the descriptions given suggest that they were seriously
ill. Tests made at intervals for several years after the expeditions
showed that some of the climbers continued to have emotional
problems, changes in sexuality, or neurological complaints. Ryn
concluded that some permanent brain damage <u>does</u> persist after
long stays or repeated climbs at high altitude.

Unfortunately it is hard to draw firm conclusions from this
major effort, because psychiatric studies at the start of the study
showed that only 11 were considered to be "normal" personality
types, and three had had head injuries (though without apparent remaining damage). During the expeditions all had
altitude illness of one type or another, most suffered hardships
that were more extreme than usual even on big mountains, including starvation, dehydration, and hypothermia, and several
were badly injured in accidents. Ryn's work gives us a lot to
think about but somewhat less to draw firm conclusions from.

Clark made a similar study of 22 persons before and after Himalayan climbs above 17,000 feet and wrote:

"All subjects were at altitude for long periods without supplemental oxygen, but did not suffer any other physical insults such as serious injury or food or water deprivation. Although several climbers experienced acute effects of mountain sickness while at altitude, their post-climb evaluations revealed no evidence of lasting cerebral dysfunction or psychological defect. . . . It was concluded that in healthy people who do not suffer physical insults as well, acute central nervous system effects of low oxygen tensions during high altitude climbs are reversible."

Clark took the additional step of matching the climbers with a control group who had never gone to altitude, and found no important differences between the two groups.

So what do we conclude? The select group of people who have gone very high or stayed very long at great altitude is increasing; those that don't succeed in killing themselves on some incredible climb seem well and healthy for the most part, and as others have pointed out, some of the gretest climbers of the past have lived — mentally intact — to longer than the usual span. There are other hazards in the lives of men . . .

In addition to retinal hemorrhages, and possible bleeding elsewhere, the man at altitude must be aware of the danger of blood clots in legs or arms or elsewhere. Blood tends to clot more rapidly and more easily at high altitude because it is thicker and moves more sluggishly as a result of dehydration and the increased number of red blood cells. Singh and since then several others have shown that hypoxia increases the clotting tendency also. Inactivity or staying in an awkward position which restricts blood flow, is an added insult for the high altitude climber who may have to spend days immobilized in a small tent by bad weather.

After reaching the top of K-2 (28,750 feet) in September 1978, J. W., tired and chilled by the strenuous climb in deep snow, realized he would have to bivouac at 27,800 feet without shelter. His oxygen supply ran out in a few hours and he had to huddle in a cramped position dozing and shivering through the night. He had spilled his water bottle during the ascent and for

Jim Wickwire

30 hours had taken only one small drink of water. In the morning he was still strong enough to descend but began to cough and developed sharp pain in his left chest. During the next week he almost died from pneumonia complicating a blood clot which originated in one leg and was carried to his left lung.

Clots in the legs or arms or, less often, in other veins, ('thrombo-phlebitis') and clots in the brain causing 'strokes' are not rare at high altitude and some have been fatal while others have left permanent damage. When clots in the veins break loose and are carried to the lungs, the resulting embolism can be very serious. Dehydration (discussed below) makes the problem much worse.

"A 38 year old man flew from 5,000 to 9,000 feet and on the same day walked up to 12,500 feet. Two days later he had reached 15,000 feet where he vomited; a day later at 17,000 feet he was weak and had no appetite, and on the sixth day, at 18,000 feet he lost consciousness . . . his condition grew worse and on the 9th day he was carried down to 11,000 feet and next day flown to hospital at 5,000 feet."

There he was unconscious, with severe pulmonary edema, many retinal hemorrhages, changes in the spinal fluid and abnormal electrocardiographic tracings of heart action. He died suddenly on the sixth hospital day, fifteen days after starting his trek. Autopsy showed pulmonary edema and pneumonia, enlargement of the heart, many large and small hemorrhages, both old and new, throughout the brain and many blood clots in the lungs. Clots in some of the large veins in the abdomen were thought to be the origin of clots which broke off and were carried to the lungs. This unfortunate traveller fell victim to a sequence of problems, undoubtedly triggered by altitude illness from which he would probably have recovered had he been appropriately managed much earlier.

CHRONIC (OR SUBACUTE) MOUNTAIN SICKNESS — MONGE'S DISEASE

Finally, there is a rather vague group of problems which can be called sub-acute or chronic mountain sickness, or more simply, mal-adaptation. In 1928 Carlos Monge Sr. described a few long term residents in the Andes who, after a period of good health and apparently full adjustment to altitude, developed fatigue, weakness, sleepiness, depression and other vague symptoms, all too often dismissed as 'emotional'. These persons had unusually flushed faces — almost purplish red in color, and high red blood counts, much above the average for that altitude. (This excess hemoglobin would be expected to result in more cyanosis, as mentioned earlier.) Their hemoglobin was less saturated with oxygen than expected and their ventilation lower than the average at that altitude. The blood was dark, obviously thicker and more viscous than usual. Most of these unfortunates developed heart failure unless they went down to sea level where the majority improved slowly. If this is a real entity of mal-adaptation (which some question), then Monge's disease is probably due to a blunting or weakening of the drive to breathe, which results in under-ventilation of the lungs, less oxygen transport by the blood, and a sharp increase in hemoglobin as a compensatory measure.

A few people never fully recover from AMS, but drag around for weeks, feeling poorly and blaming the altitude for a market basket of complaints! Perhaps this can be called Sub-acute Mountain Sickness, but it is a rather vague problem and may be due to other undiagnosed illness.

Two conditions which in some respects resemble Monge's disease occur at sea level, though they are uncommon. One, which used to be called the Pickwickian syndrome, is now called by the less colorful name of 'alveolar hypo-ventilation', showing that it is due to inadequate breathing. The other is called polycythemia vera or erythremia because of the great increase in circulating red cells and hemoglobin resulting from some unknown stimulus. The symptoms are not unlike those of Monge's disease (CMS) and the victims may develop heart failure too.

The over-production of red cells and hemoglobin in Monge's disease and in alveolar hypo-ventilation at sea level is due to over-reaction to oxygen lack, which is a strong stimulus for blood formation. But instead of improving oxygen transport, too many red cells may worsen it, partly because the thicker blood tends to flow more sluggishly. Also, as mentioned earlier,

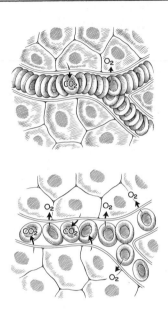

FIGURE 29:
*IS THE INCREASE IN RED BLOOD CELLS HELPFUL OR
HARMFUL?*

Until recently, the increase in hemoglobin and red blood cells which results from long exposure to altitude has been considered a beneficial adaptation on the gounds that more hemoglobin would carry more oxygen to tissues. Although Jourdannet found most high altitude residents to be slightly anemic, Viault later found just the opposite. Most observers today feel that Jourdannet's subjects had other problems which made them anemic, for subsequent studies have found long-term altitude residents and acclimatized visitors usually have more than the normal hemoglobin.

But when the number of red cells increases considerably — as often it does — blood becomes thicker, moves more sluggishly, and tends to clot more easily in the small blood vessels. Thrombo-phlebitis (clots in veins) is a significant problem for persons with far too many red cells. In addition, the disc-shaped cells tend to lie flat against one another, decreasing their diffusing surface and thereby actually decreasing the oxygen available to tissues as shown in the top figure. Whether or not withdrawing or diluting this thick sluggish blood is helpful at great altitude is still debated, but we are coming to believe that too much blood may be an adverse adaptation and perhaps no better than too little.

when there are too many red cells, they tend to stack together which decreases the surface area available for entrance of oxygen, an added handicap at very high altitude.

Not long ago some one who should have known better asked me about the dangers of coming down after being acclimatized to high altitude. Specifically, he asked what would be the bad effects of doing strenuous work at 14–15,000 feet after being acclimatized to 20,000 feet. The answer was easy: none, absolutely none. So far as we know there is no problem in deacclimatizing, which takes less time than acclimatization. Within a few weeks the blood volume and amount of hemoglobin have returned to normal, as have all the chemical changes in the blood. After a major expedition there is a sense of euphoria and joy in simple things — which lasts until the daily round catches up, the climber is mired in routine, dulled by trivia, and the shining mountains are a delectable but distant memory. Then comes a feeling of depression and apathy; these are not the by-products of altitude, but of daily life.

HOW FAST IS SLOW ENOUGH?

We have already looked briefly at safe rates of climb, but the more we learn, as climbers strain against the limits of human performance, the less dogmatic we can be. There are too many individual differences, too much variation in day to day conditions, not only of a mountain but of the climber as well. Too little sleep will weaken body and spirit and perhaps decrease his respiratory response to oxygen lack. By breathing less, the 'physiological altitude' is higher, perhaps enough higher to trigger illness. Dehydration, injudicious indulgence, or a minor respiratory infection all may increase the risk at altitude.

Acknowledging these constraints, can we say what is a prudent rate of climb for most people? On pages 112–3 we looked the average skier or tourist. Here let us look at those who have been on the highest summits. Some of their feats may help us.

Back in 1897, as we saw, Zurbriggen reached the 22,835 foot summit of Aconcagua just five days after leaving base camp at 9,000 feet, though Fitzgerald was too overcome by altitude to do the last few hundred feet. In 1907 Longstaff and his guides climbed from 17,500 feet to the 23,400 foot summit of Trisul in twelve hours. Both of these parties were very fit and strong and had spent weeks climbing about on lower mountains before their great climbs. They were the pioneers, during a period when there was some doubt whether man could survive a night spent above 20,000 feet. For that era these were the highest summits reached. In 1975 Messner and Habeler startled the climbing world by climbing the first 'eight thousander'—Hidden Peak (26,500)—from their advanced base at 16,750 feet in three days, over some very difficult climbing. They had reconnoitered part of the route in advance, but made the final push of almost 10,000 feet in under thirty-six hours. Three years later Messner, alone, climbed from 14,000 feet to the summit of Nanga Parbat (26,500 feet) in just under four days, and in 1979 he and Habeler went from 16,500 feet to the summit of K-2 (28,750 feet) in four days after a longer period spent in preparing the route and high camps.

Kamuro went from 7,500 to 14,000 feet on Mount McKinley in four days and then from 14,000 to 21,000 in seven hours without ill effects; he attributed his success to repeated short 'ascents' in a decompression chamber two weeks before the climb.

Rowell and Gillette left their 10,000 foot base at 9 P.M. and reached the top of Mount McKinley (20,200 feet) in mid-afternoon next day after nineteen hours of climbing during which one of them had moderately severe AMS. During the descent they were exhausted and may have hallucinated; one of them described gurgling in his lungs as they reached 17,300 feet but after a long rest at base they recovered uneventfully. They had been partially acclimatized by a failed attempt on the summit five weeks earlier after many days of skiing at lower levels around the mountain, but had probably lost much of their acclimatization before the 'Alpine style' assault, and seem to have been on the edge of serious altitude illness.

J. W., after ten days of trekking in Nepal, reached a 21,000 foot summit ten hours after leaving 16,000 feet, but during descent rapidly developed such severe shortness of breath and fatigue that she very nearly could not reach camp, where it took three days for her to regain strength. Since others in the party had had a 'flu-like' illness, her probable pulmonary edema may have been partly precipitated by infection, though the speed of ascent was the prime cause.

The ultimate climb, at least to date, is the solo ascent of the north side of Everest by Messner in 1980. In August, with only his girl friend as support, he climbed from an advanced base at 21,300 feet to the summit in three days, alone, without oxygen, and with little to eat or drink. Although his description suggests that he was ataxic and hallucinating at the end, he then went down in twenty hours, unharmed. He had spent six weeks acclimatizing before starting the climb.

These extraordinary feats were accomplished by brilliant climbers, superbly fit, and able to climb rapidly together or alone with minimal wasted effort. More importantly, they had spent weeks or even months on peaks of 14–20,000 feet, and thus were quite well acclimatized. (Just how valuable are the short 'ascents' in a decompression chamber, or running while breathing a low oxygen mixture is difficult to say). Do these world class climbers also have some unique physical trait? We can only speculate. We do know that others have attempted similar climbs and failed; some have succeeded but others have died.

It seems that getting up and down rapidly, before HAPE or HACE is fully developed, may be safe for some people—but only barely so. Rowell and Gillette and J. W. developed their illnesses after the climb, on the way down. Messner was very close to the edge on Nanga Parbat, again on K-2, and twice on Everest. Others have not been so lucky—or been able to judge their abilities so closely. Alpine style climbs are only for the few.

Despite such spectacular achievement—and doubtless even more amazing ones will come—for most visitors to altitude, slow ascent is the only safe way. On a major mountain, pace must be dictated by how the weakest or most susceptible member of the party feels, and when warning symptoms appear the victim should start down or at least stop climbing. The average vacationer to moderate altitude will learn from experience how fast or slow he or she should go, but again—when warning symptoms are obvious, descent is wise.

*   *   *   *

Computers have become such a part of our lives that it would indeed be surprising if a computer model of the oxygen transport and supply system could not be developed, and indeed several have been. Milhorn, Tenney, West and Miller have all made simulations of how the many independent variables interact in the delivery of oxygen to cells. A graduate student, Gary Kessler worked with me for two years on his master's thesis and finally brought together into a comprehensive program several dozen cardiac and pulmonary functions which normally vary in health and illness. Using this program we were able to change one or many variables and determine the impact of these changes, separately or together, on the bottom line — and thus to ask how much oxygen the cells receive under different conditions.

Our program began with the ambitious attempt to sort out the most beneficial from the least helpful or even counterproductive responses to high altitude. Using many formulae generated by others over the last thirty years, Kessler wrote a program in FORTRAN (computer language) based on a concept which Barcroft had proposed in 1938 — that of a "mean capillary oxygen pressure, which, if it prevailed throughout the body, would represent accurately the oxygen consumption of the entire body." Obviously this is a theoretical concept, because as we have seen different tissues have very different oxygen needs and each is differently but profundly affected by hypoxia. In fact acclimatization is the body's re-arrangement of tissue priorities to ensure that "those that needs gets, and those that don't need don't get."

One of the interesting paradoxes in altitude physiology is that the total oxygen consumption of the body is not very different at altitude from what it is at sea level. One explanation often given is that during hypoxia, some organs actually get more blood flow and use more oxygen than they do at sea level, while others need and use less. Even when we take into account the rather small amount of additional oxygen used by the increased work of breathing, it seems that the words "lack of oxygen" are not very accurate. Barcroft's simple concept takes this into account. It has been refined, of course, and there are many different models of capillary blood flow and oxygen extraction, but for our purposes the simple model is good enough.

Using this program we can ask, for example "At 16,000 feet, which improves tissue oxygen supply more — an increase of three grams of hemoglobin, a 10% increase in the output of the heart or a diet which is pure carbohydrate instead of a mixture of fats, proteins and carbohydrates?" We can calculate the benefits — and the liabilities — of a voluntary increase of 50% in breathing. It is even possible to estimate what are the limiting factors at extreme altitude and to suggest which can be overcome most effectively and how.

Now this is all very fine but mountaineers know that the only way to be sure of what you can or can't do at altitude is to try and see. Even if the program could do everything it says it can, and do it accurately, would this matter? Yes, to a limited extent. We might be able to predict whether withdrawing a pint of blood would improve or interfere with performance. We could suggest with assurance what kind of food to eat on a climbing day or on a rest day. We might be able to predict with fair accuracy just how much and how fast a man could work at various altitudes.

But where the program might be most valuable would be in the care of critically ill persons whose oxygen supply was in jeopardy because of heart or lung problems, poisoning, shock, or many other conditions which interfere with the acquisition and transport of oxygen. It might be possible to decide whether a given patient would benefit more from breathing a higher percentage of oxygen, or from a transfusion of blood, or a heart stimulant such as digitalis, or should have treatment to change the acidity of blood. Which of these would take priority? We might even give an educated estimate of the chances for recovery without permanent brain damage. We could do all of these providing certain key data were available — including some measurements which are routinely made on critically ill patients. Although this particular program has not yet been tried at the bedside, it seems to have some promise.

Delicate probes now make it possible to measure the oxygen pressure in capillaries as well as in certain easily accessible cells.

The amount of blood pumped by the heart with each beat can be determined as can the oxygen consumption of the whole body and even of certain organs. But without inserting a long thin catheter into the heart we cannot yet measure the amount of oyxgen returning from all parts of the body to the heart (the mixed venous blood), and this limits how accurately we can measure the adequacy of whole body oxygen supply. These things will come. It is fair to say that computer simulation may have as much value at the bedside in a hospital as in making certain predictions on high mountains — or under other conditions where oxygen is reduced.

Altitude illnesses are fascinating and important not only because they give us insight into some basic processes, not only for the growing number of people who go to the mountains where they may either enjoy a marvellous experience, or be ill and miserable or even die, but also for the hundreds of thousands of those who have some impairment in the oxygen transport system. Chronic lung disease or paralysis of the respiratory muscles, transient asthma or permanent emphysema may impede movement of oxygen from outside air to lungs and thence into blood. Anemia may limit the amount of oxygen that can be carried, or the failing heart may not be able to move blood fast enough. Tissue circulation may be inadequate, or interstitial fluid may slow the delivery of oxygen. Even the cells may lose some of their ability to use oxygen. Though not all of these resemble altitude illness, many do — enough to excite our interest beyond the needs of mountaineers. Next, as we look at wellness at altitude, we will see how the body protects itself against hypoxia, by acclimatizing.

Chapter Eight
ACCLIMATIZATION

So far we have been discussing what happens when a person goes too high too fast, whether on foot, by car, balloon, or aircraft. We have seen that wellness or illness at altitude are determined by several major factors: speed of ascent, altitude reached, length of stay, and by other important individual factors such as diet, emotional or physical stress, general health, and genetic heritage. Unknown today is the influence of temperature, latitude, acquired or inherited biological characteristics, and probably many others.

A marvelously integrated series of changes are initiated by oxygen lack. Some begin almost immediately while others take days, weeks or even years to mature. Collectively the changes are called "acclimatization" though some use "adjustment" or "accommodation" to differentiate the immediate changes from those that take longer. Those who believe that only after generations of residence at altitude is full acclimatization achieved, use the term "adaptation" in the Darwinian sense for the high altitude native.

Acosta vividly and accurately described acute mountain sickness as he saw and felt it while crossing the 15,000 foot Pariacaca Pass, but it is less clear what he thought about acclimatization. According to one translation he did notice a difference between persons who reached the pass by the longer more gradual route from the east, and those who took the steeper western approach. Some Andean scholars believe that the Incas understood the effects of altitude because laws were made which affected the movement of laborers and soldiers, forbidding people to *"change residence from one air temper to another because of the injury it does them."* Our contemporary, Carlos Monge believes that these rules were made to resist what he calls "climatic aggression" and not solely for political or military convenience or to minimize the danger of spreading infections to persons from a different environment.

In the Himalayas the much-travelled Schlagintweit brothers did notice the benefits of prolonged stay or repeated ascents, writing in the middle of the nineteenth century:

"... *so far as the symptoms to be considered in acclimatization, we can speak from our personal experience. When we crossed passes at an elevation of 17,500 to 18,000 feet for the first time we felt serious symptoms. A few days after, when we had traversed the highest points and passed several nights at these altitudes, we were almost completely free from these disagreeable symptoms, even at the elevation of 19,000 feet.*"

Dr. Denis Jourdannet, friend and patron of Paul Bert, spent some twenty years in Mexico studying the country and the people. In a book published in 1861 he recognized the ability of the altitude resident to do harder work than new arrivals, attributing this in part to *"the vast chest (which) makes him comfortable in the midst of this thin air."* He did not involve Bert in his studies, but Bert did speculate about what changes might be most effective in counteracting the effects of altitude. He considered that an increase in the oxygen carrying capacity of blood would be beneficial, although he knew that Jourdannet had found most of the altitude residents in Mexico to be slightly anemic. He knew that Jourdannet and others had found no increase in breathing among Mexicans living at altitude but he predicted that some increase in ventilation would be beneficial. He also hypothesized that cells might adjust their metabolic activities to use less oxygen more efficiently though of course he had no way of confirming this idea. Today almost all of Bert's speculations have proven correct and together they form a good foundation for the intricate relationships between functions which we group together as acclimatization.

Bert and Angelo Mosso were the great pioneers in altitude research, though others contributed important details, and by the beginning of our century the basic mechanisms were understood and technology had advanced far enough to confirm or refute the hypotheses. J. S. Haldane and C. G. Douglas, two giants of physiology at the turn of the century, and an American biochemist Lawrence Henderson spoke at an international congress of physiologists in Vienna during the summer of 1910. A young physician, Yandell Henderson, was there from Yale and as he wrote much later:

"For me the greatest event was to meet Haldane and Douglas

whom previously I had known only from their papers. All one afternoon and evening we discussed respiration, and it was during that talk that Haldane told me of his wish to spend sufficient time on some high mountain to study the development of acclimatization. . . . 'I want a nice comfortable, easily accessible very high mountain with a fairly good hotel on top' said Haldane. And I replied: 'Come to America next summer and we will spend a month or two on the top of Pike's Peak'. "

Sure enough, next summer Haldane and Douglas met young Henderson and Erling Schneider (whose index of physical fitness would soon be used during WWI to estimate whether or not pilots should fly) in Colorado Springs. A few days later they rode the cog railway to the 14,000 foot summit in an hour and a half. Henderson describes their reactions:

"For the first hour or so after arrival we were all very cheerful, unpacking apparatus and fitting up the room that was to be our laboratory. Then, one after another, my three comrades began to exhibit in their mental attitude the blueness which was already a striking feature of their lips and faces. Dinner did not interest them, society was not wished for. The question which seemed principally to concern them was whether they should take themselves to bed, or in the language of the ocean liner should 'go to the rail.' Owing to an unusually sensitive respiratory center, I got off much easier, and suffered nothing more than a slight feeling of tightness across the forehead. Haldane, who was next best, was quite uncomfortable for a day or two. Douglas was speechlessly miserable until the third day. And Schneider for the better part of a week suffered from frontal headache, nausea and sleeplessness . . . although he had lived for several years at Colorado Springs and had made frequent trips into the mountains. Night after night he lay awake with a throbbing headache and listened to me—we shared the same room—snoring in Cheyne-Stokes breathing."

Schneider may have had sub-acute mountain sickness though he like the others did acclimatize eventually. Henderson's graphic description underscores the differences between individuals' ability to tolerate altitude.

Despite this unhappy start the dauntless party stayed on the summit four weeks, measuring alveolar air taken at rest and

164

FIGURE 30: HALDANE AND OTHERS ON PIKE'S PEAK IN 1911

Although De Saussure, Mosso and a few others had made some short-term studies of human reactions on high mountains, the expedition to Pike's Peak inspired by Yandell Henderson was the first to examine changes during many weeks of residence at 14,000 feet. They are shown here collecting, in large rubber Douglas bags, the air exhaled during a period of exertion on top of Pike's Peak. They also collected samples of alveolar air for analysis by catching the last portion of the deepest possible exhalation. The clinical observations of each other and of the hordes of tourists arriving by train, mule or on foot are particularly interesting when compared with what we see today. A remarkable young lady, Miss Mabel Fitzgerald accompanied them to Denver but it was not thought fitting for her to remain on the summit unchaperoned. Instead she travelled through the mining camps of Colorado, and a few years later through the Great Smoky Mountains, carrying her equipment in saddlebags on her horse; she collected and analyzed alveolar air samples from hundreds of long-term residents at altitude, a profile of data that has never been duplicated. Many other mountain expeditions have tried to match the standards set by this early and splendid effort.

during and after exertion, recording breathing patterns (including the Cheyne-Stokes rhythm), and making many clinical observations. Above all they talked for endless hours about pulmonary and circulatory physiology, and the effect of these long conversations upon their future work and through them on generations of students was a major result of the expedition. Henderson wrote much later:

"To those of us who were privileged to participate in the Pike's Peak expedition the memory of that time has remained a life-long inspiration. . . . It was a golden time. Men who are friends under 460 mm of barometric pressure are friends until the end of life" a sentiment shared by those climbers fortunate or generous enough to have appreciated each other's company on high peaks.

Fifteen years later, Joseph Barcroft confirmed Jourdannet's early comment about chest size, taking a remarkable series of X-rays of miners living at 14,000 feet in Peru and expanding Bert's theories. After spending three months at altitude he wrote:

"The acclimatized man is not the man who has attained to bodily and mental powers as great in Cerro de Pasco as he would have in Cambridge (whether that town be situated in Massachusetts or in England). Such a man does not exist. All dwellers at altitude are persons of impaired physical and mental powers."

Carlos Monge the elder indignantly responded:

"For our part, as early as 1928 we proved . . . that Professor Barcroft was himself suffering from a sub-acute case of mountain sickness without realizing it. His substantial error is easy to explain as resulting from an improper generalization on his part of what he himself felt and applying his reactions to Andean man in general. . . . Andean man must be physically distinct from sea level man requiring much further research before one may define, let alone apply the terms inferior and superior."

In 1935 ten distinguished scientists from England and the United States spent six weeks at 17,500 feet in Chile, producing the first comprehensive study of acclimatization. Bruce Dill, another great pioneer in altitude physiology who had been a leading participant in that expedition recently commented on the differences between a longtime resident and one member of the group:

"Keyes, judged by us to be the best acclimatized, had a hematocrit of 51.4% and could climb slowly up the zig-zag trail from 17,500 to 19,000 feet, stopping however for short periods. Campos, mine foreman, had arrived from the lowlands six years before and was said to be one of the most productive workmen. His hematocrit was 74.7%. Though the other native workmen followed the zig-zag trail, Campos walked straight up. My guess is that Keyes' oxygen consumption was about one liter per minute, and that of Campos about 2.5. Their different capacities for work might be calculated from the different ways they altered their oxygen cascades."

There is the core of acclimatization—alterations in the oxygen transport system, from ventilation to cellular utilization. The published papers from the 1935 expedition are the first to clearly identify this integration of many changes, and they are the foundation of what we know about acclimatization today.

During and after World War II there was a resurgence of interest in high altitude, at first for military purposes, but later with a broader vision. One project called "Operation Everest" was designed to see whether or not man could survive and work on the highest point on earth without supplementary oxygen. But it also tested whether or not acclimatization would increase the altitude at which men could work while breathing oxygen—an important aspect of military aviation before the days of pressurized cabins and pressurized breathing equipment.

Operation Everest was possible only through the cooperation of a splendid team of naval and civilian workers at the Naval Air Station in Pensacola, Florida—cooperation which though skeptical at first, soon became enthusiastic. Four healthy volunteers lived in a cramped steel decompression chamber for thirty-five days while the pressure was gradually lowered simulating the slow ascent of a major Himalayan peak. Each day an extensive battery of tests was done, looking at as many parts of the oxygen transport system as possible with the technology then available. After several days at 22,500 to 23,500 feet, the four made a "dash for the summit," and after six hours of slow decompression reched a simulated altitude of 29,100

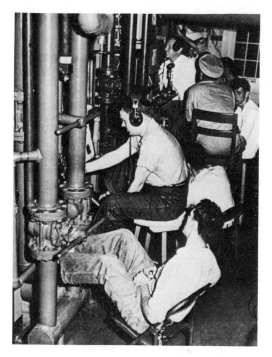

FIGURE 31
"OPERATION EVEREST"—A STUDY OF ACCLIMATIZATION

In 1946 the U.S. Navy supported a study of altitude acclimatization called "Operation Everest." The four volunteers lived in this large steel decompression chamber for thirty-five days, while the pressure was reduced each day by an amount equivalent to that lost in climbing on a high Himalayan peak. A great many studies of blood and breathing and of heart function at rest and during and after work were done each day as the four men 'climbed' over the weeks to 23,500 feet, and, on the final day, made a 'dash for the summit.' Two of the four stayed above 29,000 feet for a half hour; two others had to have oxygen. This was the first study, and in fact is the only kind in which the scientific observers (shown here watching through the windows) were not themselves affected by the altitude they were studying. When they entered the chamber through a lock, they wore oxygen masks to preserve their physical and mental faculties. The study proved (among many other things) that men could survive and even do a little work as high as the summit of Mount Everest.

feet where two of them pedalled a cycle for twenty minutes while many tests were done. Though two had asked for oxygen on the way up, the project showed that man could indeed live at that altitude and perhaps do light work, as I had somewhat optimistically predicted the year before:

"Can men reach 29,000 ft (or higher) without oxygen? Until it is actually done the answer will be doubtful at best. But by the best calculations which we know how to make at the present time, we can say that 29,000 ft is only imperceptibly worse than 28,000 ft. On paper at any rate man can climb to 29,000 ft and perhaps higher. He will need magnificent physical condition and climbing ability. He must have sound judgment and great perseverance and courage. His food, his creature comforts and his climbing stages must be elaborately planned. He will probably be as well off without oxygen as with it.

One day a man will do it."

After the summit climb, the four slept at 20,000 feet and next day, we tried to determine how their acclimatization had affected their ceiling while breathing oxygen.

Two men were removed to the lock, while the other pair donned regular issue military oxygen masks and the ascent began.

"Both men felt well up to 46,000 feet, the highest that men have gone without pressure suits. They climbed upward and at 1601 touched 50,225 feet. There was no cheering; instead every one inside and outside the chamber took the first deep breath of the entire afternoon. Both were mentally alert . . . but complained of weakness and dizziness and after two and a half minutes they descended to 46,000 feet. The next objective was to determine the maximum altitude at which they could work effectively, and during the next half hour the chamber was slowly climbed to 48,500 feet. Each 500 foot step brought an increase in symptoms of oxygen lack. At 46,000 feet both men felt they could do light work indefinitely. When they reached 47,000 feet they believed their time reserve would be several hours, and at 48,500 feet they felt their efficiency would not last for more than thirty minutes . . . the chamber started down at 1648. To them 20,000 feet seemed like home."

We had shown that acclimatization did have a major effect

on the absolute ceiling—but of course with the advent of pressurized cabins this observation has lost significance. Today men live comfortably for weeks or months in the absolute vacuum of space, safely pressurized in their capsules.

We worried a good deal during the last few days of "Operation Everest" that when the subjects abruptly returned to sea level, their respiratory drive—so long stimulated by severe lack of oxygen—would weaken and they might stop breathing. Looking back from what we know today, this was ridiculous and in fact they emerged from the chamber well and happy. Our large collection of data was analyzed and subsequently published, and Dick Riley and I described the process of acclimatization as:

"a series of integrated adaptations which tend to restore the oxygen pressure of the tissues toward normal sea level values despite the lowered pO2 of the atmosphere." An accurate though not particularly original definition.

For me one of the unforgettable impressions was how badly the 'acclimatized' subjects looked and acted. Here for the first time scientists, themselves unaffected by altitude, were able to observe men living and working at altitude, men who considered themselves in good shape and fully competent and who had reached altitude at a rate common to most expeditions. Yet to us looking through the portholes at them, or working in the chamber (but wearing oxygen masks) the subjects were considerably impaired. Truly they looked as Mallory had put it: *"like sick men walking in a dream."*

In 1961 came another extraordinary mountain expedition, which included some of the most distinguished American and British mountaineers and altitude physiologists. A prefabricated insulated building was set up at 19,000 feet not many miles from Everest and continuously occupied for five and a half months during which extensive studies of the changes of acclimatization were carried out. Some of the party stayed at the high laboratory for up to nine weeks without descending, but others had to go down to 15,000 feet for periods of rest, and the party concluded that 19,000 feet was too high for full acclimatization. All of the group lost weight, despite plentiful good food and living conditions luxurious compared to most

*FIGURE 32: LONG RESIDENCE AT HIGH ALTITUDE—
THE SILVER HUT*

In the winter and spring of 1960–61, British and American moun-taineer-scientists occupied this spectacular site at 19,000 feet near a shoulder of Ama Dablam, one of the beautiful peaks south of Everest. During the four months they examined many of the changes of exposure to high altitude on themselves. In the "Silver Hut" they were protected against the cold and wind and could do a number of sophisticated studies on heart and lungs and blood, at rest and during work. They had good food and were able to get ample outdoor exercise skiing and climb-ing nearby, but nevertheless they all lost a great deal of weight, strength and ambition and concluded that 19,000 feet was too high for long-term acclimatization. From this study came a great deal of insight into the physiological changes which occur at great heights. There are no per-manently inhabited villages above 17,000 feet.

climbing expeditions. Some of their more important findings were:

• After some weeks of altitude, the primary drive to breathe was still lack of oxygen, although carbon dioxide seemed to be catching up as shown by an increased carbon dioxide sensitivity.

• Newcomers after four to six weeks of residence were if anything fitter than those who had wintered over.

• Work seemed to be limited by fatigue of the muscles of respiration, but the most work the heart could do was about two-thirds that possible at sea level.

• Contrary to the impression of most climbers, oxygen restored maximum work capacity almost to sea level values. Though not stated in so many words, the implication was that the limited benefits experienced from oxygen were due to poor equipment or misuse.

Only a year later altitude research became critically important when the Sino-Indian conflict erupted along the high Himalayan frontier and thousands of Indian troops, rushed from the low plains to 12–16,000 feet, became actuely ill from various forms of altitude illness. The Chinese forces, having lived for months or years on the high Tibetan plateau were well acclimatized and had few if any altitude related illnesses. Since this experience, Indian research in altitude physiology has been intense and contributes greatly to what we know today. Sujoy Roy has published a summary of the Indian experience with acclimatization.

From 1967 to 1979 the Arctic Institute of North America conducted summer studies in a well-equipped laboratory at 17,500 feet on Mount Logan, in the Canadian Yukon. At first attention was directed at illness — which had become common in persons going rapidly so high, but soon acclimatization became the major focus. Among some forty papers collected in a book published in 1980 and called High Altitude Physiology Study, is the first description of high altitude retinal hemorrhages, the sharp fall in blood oxygen which occurs during the periodic breathing of sleep, the protective value of acetazolamide (Diamox), and confirmation of other observations that the lowlander cannot achieve more than 70% of what he can do at sea level even after eight weeks at this altitude — which, incidentally, is at the frontier above which no one lives permanently.

The most recent and most ambitious Himalayan research was done by AMREE (the American Research Expedition to Mt. Everest) in late 1981. This talented party spent almost three months at and above Base Camp (18,000 feet) and not only brought back a wealth of scientific data but succeeded in placing three men on the summit where they obtained an on-the-spot barometric pressure reading of 253 torr confirming Pugh's prediction in 1961; they also obtained several samples of alveolar air on one climber on the summit as well as a record of ventilation and electrocardiogram tracings during the summit climb.

Maximal work capacity measured at several altitudes was somewhat higher than the trend predicted by Pugh—though within the same ballpark. How the respiratory center responds to low oxygen atmosphere was studied in members of the party and in Sherpas: predictably all increased ventilation but to various degrees. Not expected was the finding that a brisk increase in breathing in response to hypoxia seemed to match the ability of the individual to perform well at higher altitudes. But this was not true of the Sherpas who did not breathe very much more but were able to acclimatize very well. Can this hypoxic ventilatory response in low altitude natives or sojourners at altitude be used to predict success at very high altitude? It is too early to tell.

All of the party—except the Sherpas—lost weight even though some of them ate well, and certain specific studies suggested that absorption of food was interfered with by the altitude. There were some changes from sea level metabolism that were supported by the hormonal studies, but these have not been fully worked out as I write this. Sleep studies showed differences between the Americans and Sherpas: the former almost invariably had periodic breathing, while the latter slept more soundly and usually breathed normally. Red blood counts and hematocrits were almost the same in Sherpas and the western climbers, and a few studies made at Base Camp after hemo-dilution indicated that little benefit came from the blood-letting.

A less scientific but more unusual outcome was that the party remained close friends throughout the expedition and its aftermath—something that is rare in the superheated climbing environment of today. AMREE raised as many questions as it answered but pushed back the limits of our knowledge by a great deal.

Altitude research on high mountains has many attractions: the setting is inspirational, beautiful and challenging even when the party is cold, wet, storm-torn and emotionally far from home. The subjects are free to move about and to do 'normal' activities despite some unpleasant environmental constraints. On the other hand the researchers, however highly motivated and dedicated, are just as impaired as their subjects. Even the miracles of miniaturization do not yet make it possible to do in a mountain laboratory all of the studies one would like.

By contrast, the decompression chamber provides an unreal setting where "pure hypoxia" can be studied without the real world stresses of cold, wind, isolation, and all the rigors of the mountain setting. In the chamber subjects are comfortable—though confined—well fed and coddled through studies which are often painful and tedious, and some of which could not be done on a mountain. Access is easy, it never storms, and food and fluid are plentiful and can be accurately monitored.

Despite these obvious advantages, the chamber is cramped, claustrophobes would be miserable, and even the energetic have difficulty getting their daily exercise. It is a test-tube setting in which to study the basics of altitude illness and wellness, while the mountain is the real world. Both are very valuable for altitude research.

A fascinating aspect of acclimatization is the variety of ways in which different species achieve it. The Andean llama adapts by increasing the extraction of oxygen from capillary blood in his tissues, whereas his Quechua owner is almost as well adapted by decreasing the fall in oxygen pressure at various stages in the oxygen cascade. The Himalayan yak, distant cousin to the llama, has two forms of hemoglobin, one "fast," the other "slow" in the way they pick up and release oxygen, but the alpaca, another cousin, relies on a high level of fetal type hemoglobin to pick up more oxygen in the lung and release it more readily in the tissues. When baboons become very hypoxic they convert adult to fetal hemoglobin with the same result. The Himalayan goose who is more at home far higher than any mammal, shifts his hemoglobin dissociation curve to the left, though not by making fetal hemoglobin, while the deer mouse who lives as comfortably in Death Valley as high on the Rockies, can change from a low altitude form of hemoglobin to high altitude form as he changes homes. Diving mammals, like whales and Weddell seals who can spend over an hour underwater, have developed completely different ways of "living without oxygen," though these capabilities are emergency responses to hypoxia and we cannot call them acclimatization. And the turtle—is he considered 'acclimatized' because he can spend six months—yes six months—under water, with little or no oxygen?

Many studies of different animals and of men with various genetic backgrounds show us that there are different pathways to full acclimatization, some of which appear to be inherited and others responsive to changes in environment. Some of these latter are responses of expediency, necessarily temporary and often carrying price tags. Some changes begin and mature only if the individual is taken to altitude when very young.

One might almost say that whether or not there is a different kind of person who might be called the "Andean" man depends on how old he was when arriving at altitude, which Frisancho argues rather persuasively.

Our knowledge of acclimatization is still limited and in places controversial, but what we know for sure and what we think likely, is summarized below.

Ventilation: Rate and/or depth of breathing increases almost immediately on reaching altitude, peaks within a week of residence, decreases slowly over the next months, but probably remains above the sea level average however long the stay. This produces better mixing of outside and alveolar air, raising the oxygen and lowering the carbon dioxide pressures in the lung. The sensitivity of the respiratory center to lack of oxygen determines the extent and duration of over-breathing at altitude. It is different among individuals and is also affected by extreme fatigue and lack of sleep. Current concepts suggest that persons with high hypoxic ventilatory drives (as this stimulus to breathing is called) do better at very great altitude than those with low or blunted drives. Astonishingly, some high altitude natives have low hypoxic ventilatory drives, but outperform their sea level companions. Another fascinating observation which needs much more study is that some races with higher ventilatory exchange appear to be born with more alveoli giving them a larger area for absorbing oxygen in the lung.

Gradient: There is always a drop in oxygen pressure between alveolus and pulmonary capillary (the A-a gradient), normally only a few torr but — and this is important in disease — sometimes very large. By a combination of better perfusion and an increase in the differential between alveolar oxygen pressure and that in the arriving desaturated blood, the A-a gradient usually decreases with the stay at altitude and, after full acclimatization, is small. (The A-a gradient is the sum of gradients due to shunted blood and membrane resistance; both are usually diminished).

Transport: Soon after arrival at altitude, the amount of circulating hemoglobin increases (the mechanism is somewhat uncertain), increasing blood's oxygen carrying capacity. This 'emergency' adjustment is slowly replaced in weeks and months by formation of new hemoglobin, so that the well acclimatized person may have 30-50% more hemoglobin than at sea level and is thus able to transport that much more oxygen.

A substance called DPG (2,3-diphosphoglycerate), normally present in red blood cells, increases promptly at altitude and shifts the oxy-hemoglobin curve toward the right. For years arguments have gone back and forth over whether a rightward or leftward shift would be a more beneficial adjustment to altitude. A leftward shift would seem to be more helpful at very great altitude, because the curve would be steeper (see Figure 20) thereby releasing a larger volume of oxygen for a small drop in oxygen pressure. The arguments are a bit exotic for this book, but we can say that DPG does not seem very important in acclimatization.

Another mechanism for cushioning the impact of oxygen lack — whether due to the demands of sudden exertion or of altitude, is provided by a relative of hemoglobin called myoglobin because it is present only in muscles (myo-). (In fowl it differentiates dark from light meat). This combines with oxygen much as hemoglobin does, but the shape of its dissociation curve is steeper. It is in fact a sharply left-shifted curve and myoglobin is avid for oxygen, picking it up more readily than does hemoglobin and releasing a larger volume of oxygen for a small drop in pressure. Myoglobin is a kind of storage reservoir or middleman which provides oxygen more rapidly than it can be provided by the arrival of blood from the lungs. It is not surprising to find that myoglobin increases more rapidly than hemoglobin does during acclimatization.

Tissues: To reach the tissues, oxygen-laden blood must traverse thin-walled capillaries in such a way that diffusion is maximized. An immediate response to altitude is the shunting of blood flow from the non-essential to the most important consumers, so the skin loses some and so do the bowels, while the brain and heart receive a greater flow. These transient adjustments are replaced by more equitable rationing with time: 'reserve' capillaries are recruited (as they are during strenuous exertion) and open up to provide greater volume blood flow per unit of tissue. In the longer run, new capillaries actually form. As a result the distance any cell is from a functioning capillary is reduced and the diffusion of oxygen thus improved.

Cells: These of course are the ultimate consumers: for their life support and function the whole system has evolved. We know a little about what goes on inside the cell during hypoxia. For example we know that different metabolic pathways are followed, that the bio-electric potential of cell membranes is altered, and that water and electrolyte distribution is disturbed. We know these changes are transient and revert to or at least toward normal within days or weeks of arrival at altitude. The oxygen pressure within cells is never much more than a few torr at best, so the impact of oxygen lack, though small in absolute terms, may be huge in percentage. One change observed is an increase in the number of mitochondria in cells whose owners have become well acclimatized. The mitochondria (which make up the powerhouse of the body) while they might function less effectively individually, are collectively able to turn out near-normal energy. (See Chapter Ten.)

These are the major direct responses, but they set off secondary ones which are equally important.

Ventilation and pH: As an inevitable consequence of increased breathing, carbon dioxide is 'washed out' of lungs and blood and the blood becomes more alkaline as the weak acid formed by carbon dioxide and water is decreased. So effective are the buffering systems of the blood that the change is not great, but some bicarbonate is excreted in the urine as a part of acclimatization. But not enough is lost to prevent the blood from remaining slightly more alkaline than normal for weeks or months, or even years. Henderson pointed out that the loss of buffer would allow small increases in lactic acid or carbon dioxide to stimulate the respiratory center more than when alkalinity and buffering systems are normal.

Hormones: These messenger chemicals, secreted in minute amounts, dictate, regulate, and report back virtually every life function, so it is not surprising that they are affected by hypoxia and by the changes which result in acclimatization. It is an immensely complicated communication system, with stimulating, inhibiting, releasing factors affecting the secretion of each implementing hormone. For example: the thyroid gland produces thyroxin which regulates metabolism—the rate at which foods are 'burned'. Release of thyroxin is initiated by TSH (Thyroid Stimulating Hormone) from the pituitary, controlled by TRF (Thyroid Release Factor), also from the pituitary, and monitored by sensors of levels of the free forms of thyroxin and of iodine in blood. But the pituitary hormones are in turn responsive to stimulating and inhibiting hormones originating in other parts of the brain and in other sites throughout the body.

Best known of the hormones are those secreted by the thyroid, pancreas, pituitary, ovaries, testes and adrenal glands. All have different but inter-related missions and each is responsive to changes in others. A major emotional stress, for example, often triggers responses in pituitary, thyroid, and sex hormone secretion, not to mention a surge in adrenaline and a change in insulin release. It is not surprising, in the presence of so many variables, that studies of the effect of hypoxia on hormone secretion have produced confusing and even conflicting data.

What about sex and altitude—a subject nearly everyone is vitally interested in? Anecdotally we find that libido is not affected very high on big mountains unless by cold, cramped quarters, confining clothes and lack of privacy. It is said that a lady became pregnant during a storm at 25,000 feet, a rumor I have been unable to verify, but if so, it would be interesting to know about the child. Remarkable explots have been described, but these may be more boast than reality. Up to the threshold for altitude residence there is certainly no decreased interest. All things considered, sex is sex wherever it may be.

Fertility, however, is affected, both in men and women. Lowland women have difficulty becoming pregnant after migrating to 14-15,000 feet, as shown by the careful work of Baker and Abelson. High altitude natives have a lower fertility rate (statistically significant) than their sea level cohorts, but altitude natives who descend to sea level regain sea level fertility. There is a tendency to prematurity and low birth weight in infants born at altitude to altitude natives, and more miscarriages, premature births, and slightly more birth defects also occur among residents at altitude. Just how far this applies to short-term visitors, or at just what point in pregnancy these tendencies become important, we don't know enough to say today.

What little data there is about menstruation suggests that menses are the same at altitude as at sea level. Women on major climbing expeditions seem to follow their customary sea level patterns though some expeditions have had different experience.

Human Growth Hormone (HGH, or somatotropin), best known for its impact on growth during youth, is believed to be even more important in the intra-cellular metabolism of protein. Growth hormone secretion is affected moment by moment by various stresses, including malnutrition, hypoxia, high or low blood sugar and probably others. It seems to be one of the most important hormones as the full extent of its function is slowly becoming clearer.

The hormones that regulate metabolism are altered inconsistently and unpredictably to our current understanding. Blood sugar tends to be low in acclimatized and adapted altitude residents; liver glycogen may also be low so that these 'emergency' fuels will not sustain long bursts of activity.

An interesting family of substances — the prostaglandins —

which are not exactly hormones or enzymes, is attracting increasing attention, but so far they seem more involved in acute responses and thus in altitude illness, than in acclimatization. Neurological compounds like dopamine, or endorphin (our make-it-yourself form of morphine), and a host of other chemicals made in trace amounts by the body are probably affected by — and affect — our responses to high altitude. But this is an ill-defined frontier where today's discovery is too often tomorrow's disappointment.

How do the changes of acclimatization translate into everyday reality? How completely can they restore sea level capability? Is there such a thing as the 'Andean Man' — one who is fully acclimatized? Can we hasten or perfect the process? first let us look at the limits.

More than twenty climbers have reached the top of Everest breathing only air, but this is very close to man's absolute limit. Those who have done so have been super-climbers whose every effort is made most economically in terms of energy expended for oxygen used. From those who have been tested, and from calculations based on the performance of others, it appears that the Everest summiter can push himself to work at a greater level of ventilation at sea level than can ordinary mortals. Though he may not appear out of the ordinary, he can move more air than others can, even though he is not able to reach that sea level maximum when at great heights.

Rheinhold Messner, who has done more extreme altitude climbing than anyone else, has not been tested, but his VO2max can be calculated: he has climbed 3300 vertical feet in 34 minutes. By making certain reasonable assumptions, his VO2Max is found to lie between 77 and 81 ml per kg per minute which is 25 to 50% more than acclimatized Himalayan climbers. This superior ability to move huge volumes of air — plus his intense emotional and physical drive, clearly place him in the super class.

Dr. Chris Pizzo, who managed to deliver the only alveolar air samples yet obtained on the summit of Everest, had an alveolar oxygen of about 36.7 torr, and a carbon dioxide level of 7.5 torr. His respiratory exchange or R.Q. was 1.49 which indicates that he was over-breathing very greatly and was in what we call an "unsteady state" metabolically. He had removed his oxygen mask (used for the ascent) ten or fifteen minutes before taking the sample, But, while he was resting on the way down, his alveolar oxygen was 35. and carbon dioxide 8 torr, and his R.Q. a normal 0.82. His VO2Max is over 60. He too can move a lot of air.

The pressure drop between alveolar and arterial oxygen levels — the A–a gradient (page 58) in Chris Pizzo could not be measured of course without drawing an arterial blood (a bit impractical there!) but was estimated at 5 to 7 torr. This would mean that his arterial oxygen could have been between 29 and 31 torr, which is not very different from that of some persons who remain active despite severe heart defects at sea level. If these measurements are typical, then it is not so much the low level of oxygen as the extremely low level of carbon dioxide which limits work on top of Everest.

Before going for the top, most Everest summiters have spent many weeks at somewhat lower altitudes, tuning up for the effort. They thus acclimatize to altitudes as high as 18–20,000 feet and thus could adjust better to the ultimate height. On top, however, they were very close to the physiological limits and could not have stayed so high for very long. Of course cold, dehydration, semi-starvation and weight loss, and lack of sleep all added to their exhaustion. If they failed to over-breathe, hypoxia would get them, but if they over-breathed too much then hypocapnia — carbon dioxide loss — would do them in. The top of Everest is a very delicate survival zone.

There is abundant evidence that modern man deteriorates more rapidly than he can acclimatize above 18–20,000 feet. Whether this is because of all the cumulative stresses, or a limit imposed by lack of oxygen (or carbon dioxide!) is not clear today. Mountaineers can live and work after a fashion for days or even weeks above 20,000 feet, but each day grinds them down a little more and soon body and spirit can take no more.

Although the sea level resident going to 5,000 feet rarely notices any difference in ability to work there is some impairment which soon disappears completely. At 10,000 feet he will notice a small but definite decrease in performance even after many weeks, and at 15–16,000 feet he will never be able to do what he could at sea level, not after weeks or months, and perhaps not even after years. By contrast the native, born to generations of altitude residents, can do more than even the best acclimatized lowlander, but even he prefers to live below 17,500 feet and climb to work rather than to stay higher.

One way to assess work capacity is to measure the amount of oxygen consumed per minute, and this is often done during the final minutes when the subject is working at the limits of his ability. There is some debate over the merits of treadmill as compared to cycle ergometer, but whatever test is used, the amount of oxygen consumed in the minute before the individual has to stop because of exhaustion is called maximum oxygen capacity, or VO2max.

When measured at altitude, after the improvement due to training has reached a plateau, VO2max is often considered an index of acclimatization. But lowlanders taken to moderate altitude (i.e. 12–14,000 feet) are unable to reach their sea level capacity, and although there is some improvement over time, the higher the altitude the less close the acclimatized lowlander can come to his sea level capacity.

The story is slightly different when the individual exercises only to, say 75% of what he can do at sea level (his VO2max). Depending on the altitude, most people will improve over days or weeks until they approach a limit for that height defined by a rough rule of thumb which says that VO2max decreases by roughly 3% per thousand feet above 5,000 feet. This suggests that at 18,000 feet, the most a sea level resident can hope to achieve will be 60–70% of his sea level VO2max. We can draw a series of curves describing how close to sea level VO2max the visitor can come after time at altitude, each curve representing a different altitude. From these, though the exact numbers may be argued, it is apparent that the higher the altitude, the less even the best acclimatized lowlander can do, compared to his sea level relatives at sea level.

But mountaineers do not climb at maximal capacity—they would be crazy to do so except in a dire emergency. Good climbers move at a pace they can keep up for hours—or minutes when at extreme altitude. When we look at the ability to do sub-maximal or endurance work, we find the same general pattern as for maximal work. The sea level resident working at moderate altitude, can go for hours at let us say 75% of what he can do at sea level; this may improve slightly over time, but is less the higher the altitude. On the summit of Everest he can do very little indeed.

Frisancho believes that if lowlanders are taken to altitude when quite young, they develop a level of acclimatization more nearly that of the native, but the older they are when translocated, the less perfect their acclimatization. Frisancho considers environment almost as important as heredity insofar as altitude is concerned. In fact, many observers say that any person born at altitude will be as well acclimatized as one born there to generations of altitude natives. Others disagree! Frisancho, conceding some inherited acclimatization, believes that a single wild migrant, whose acclimatization is incomplete or different, could introduce variations which would undo the acclimatization achieved by many generations!

These observations are confused by the fact that different races use different strategies for acclimatization. Sherpas, for example, come from a genetic stock that has probably lived for many thousand years at altitude: most (but not all) of them have normal sea level hemoglobin whereas the Quechuas (apparently more recent altitude residents) at a similar altitude, usually show considerably higher than normal levels. Quechuas and Sherpas tend to be short and stocky; the former have large barrel chests, but the latter do not. High altitude Ethiopians tend to be taller and thinner and are said to have more mitochondria in their cells, suggesting that they have learned to use oxygen more efficiently. Like the llama, alpaca, deer mouse and turtle, different people have different ways of adapting to hypoxia.

Some obvious and provocative questions spring from these observations. How does the altitude native match the sea level resident in competitive sports? Does training at altitude improve performance at sea level? Conversely, what is the best way for the lowlander to prepare for competition at altitude?

Prior to the 1968 Olympic Games in Mexico City there was great discussion and many studies were done to predict what effect the 7,500 foot altitude would have on the world's best athletes. Equal attention was given to where the athletes should train—at home, or near Mexico City, or perhaps even higher. Though the Games did not answer the last question, performance far exceeded most expectations. Twenty-nine percent of all competitors broke existing world records, and overall performance improved over that of previous Olympics by a larger margin than in the intervals between earlier games.

However, records were broken almost exclusively in events lasting less than two minutes: only in some longer swimming events did a few competitors do better than in the past. In the hundred yard dash, for example, runners do not breathe at all, and for them the decreased air resistance and density and slightly lower gravity at Mexico City were beneficial. Since there was less oxygen available, in the longer races competitors reached the limit of oxygen dependent metabolism (their aerobic limits) sooner than at sea level, and thus accumulated an oxygen debt and functioned less efficiently. In these short duration events the human body is close to maximal effort, and shaving even hundredths of a second from time is difficult indeed.

As to the possible advantage of training at altitude for competition at sea level, perhaps the dollar gives a clue. If there were an edge to be gained, is it not likely that professional football teams—where huge amounts of money are at stake—would train at altitude? But they do not, and I find it hard to believe they have not explored the possibility.

There were few adverse symptoms at Mexico City, perhaps because contestants had spent weeks at altitude before the games. However:

"The rowers had real difficulties competing . . . The altitude may have been of some minor advantage (because of the thinner air) to the sprinters, but the water was just as thick and the exertion required of the crews showed up at the end of practically every competition. Of the U.S. eight oarsmen, three had severe dyspnea and severe coughing which diminished somewhat after about four hours, and then slowly over the next three days. These individuals also had coarse rhonchi all over their chest. . . . Unfortunately we had no X-rays on these three athletes. . . . The rowers were the only ones who experienced this. We saw none in the 5,000, 10,000 meter or marathon runners."

This was probably early pulmonary edema, similar to what is sometimes seen in the most prolonged and extreme exertion even at sea-level—as in the Comrades fifty-six mile marathon which is run over steep hills and valleys—but at low altitude—in South Africa.

One might think that physical fitness would improve altitude tolerance and even speed up acclimatization, but this does not seem to be the case. It is true that the lean marathoner has a higher VO2max than the fat slob and thus might appear to have an advantage on the highest mountains. (But he also has a lower hypoxic ventilatory drive than the average person—which may be a real disadvantage). The very fit person, working at say 75% of capacity, can do more than his less efficient peer, but we cannot accurately call him better acclimatized. It is also true that the skillful and experienced climber, moving economically and smoothly, uses less oxygen than the struggling novice clutching desperately for every hold, but this too is an index of efficiency rather than acclimatization. To the disappointment of fitness buffs, the evidence suggests that fitness neither enhances acclimatization nor prevents altitude illness.

But the data are not completely conclusive. Kenyans, accustomed from birth to run considerable distances at 5–6,000 feet where they live, consistently excel in distance runs at sea level. How much of this is due to their inherited high altitude genes or to being born at altitude, and how much is due to life-long training is hard to determine. But consider the Tarahumara Indians who live between 7,000 and 8,000 feet: they are said to run 500 miles in five days but have not done well in shorter races at lower altitude.

Then there are the Sherpas of Nepal, whose ancestors for hundreds of generations lived on the high Tibetan plateau. These stocky cheerful mountain people have for decades done heavier work on great Himalayan peaks than fully acclimatized Europeans can do. Not many of them have the same obsessive compulsion to reach the highest summits which characterizes far too many modern mountaineers, but those who do can outperform the best. Andean miners can do incredibly hard work for many hours a day at 17,000 feet, and then play soccer; Europeans pale at the thought.

Based on what we know today, we may say with some degree of confidence:

1. The maximum work one can do at sea level decreases with increasing altitude by about 3% per thousand feet and does not improve much with time.

2. Sub-maximal or endurance work, though decreased at altitude, does improve with time until it approaches the limit noted in the sentence above.

3. Natives can do more at altitude than visitors however long they stay, but do not reach at altitude what their sea level relatives can do at sea level.

4. Some races of altitude natives surpass their sea level cohorts in competition at sea level but other races do not.

5. Training at altitude gives no benefit to the sea level native in short intense events, but may give considerable benefit for long events.

If these statements appear ambiguous — they are. Despite a great many studies by talented experts, it is difficult to draw firm conclusions. One of the reasons for this uncertainty is the marked difference between different races and between different individuals of the same genetic stock and experience. Viva la difference! It is these factors that make a horse race.

Before the 1981 expedition to Everest, John West, as had Pugh years earlier, predicted that active work near the top of Everest without oxygen was just barely possible. The breathing necessary to maximize oxygen deep in the lungs would reduce carbon dioxide to intolerable levels. In the event this was shown to be true.

In 1962, using data obtained on lower mountains, Pugh calculated that the barometric pressure on top of Everest would be between 250 and 253 torr, rather than 235 torr as indicated on the standard altitude-pressure curve. This is because the earth, being slightly flattened at the poles, has a thicker blanket of air above the equator than over each pole. As a result, the weight of this blanket of air is lower the further one goes from the equator. In practical terms this means that a mountain measuring 20,000 feet above sea level in the extreme north (or south) has a lower barometric pressure on top than one of the same elevation nearer the equator—mountains most distant from the equator are "higher physiologically" than those nearby. (Appendix One) This is why Bruce Dill has urged so persuasively that we must "Report Barometric Pressure," and not simply altitude.

Based on his calculations, Pugh predicted that a man could exert himself on top of Everest, but would be very close to the limit, and that although he could climb, he would be so slow that night would certainly overtake him. Both predictions were borne out twenty years later by the American Research Expedition to Everest, as we have seen. The alveolar air samples on the single subject showed a rather higher oxygen and a much lower carbon dioxide than expected, though these were measured during an "unsteady metabolic state" and must be accepted with some reservations, as Norman Jones has recently mentioned.

There is a curious twist to these numbers: they indicate that the oxygen in lungs is not impossibly low on top of Everest, but to keep it at that level requires so much breathing that carbon dioxide is washed out to an almost impossibly low level. It is this which makes a long stay or much work impossible. But there is another constraint as well.

Fifty years ago Sir Brian Matthews calculated that because of the evaporation of large amounts of water in the nose, mouth and windpipe, breathing such huge amounts of completely dry thin air would lower body temperature very nearly as much as could be offset by the 'burning' of foodstuffs—metabolism. As a result no amount of clothing could protect against hypothermia—and of course the colder the inspired air the more heat would be lost. It appears that lack of carbon dioxide and loss of heat through over-breathing and evaporation of water are as perilous as lack of oyxgen.

Without oxygen the Everest summiter is near death, but even with a full supply he has problems which are inherent in the acclimatization which enabled him to climb to the higher camps. Perhaps one would do better to breathe oxygen equivalent to that at sea level all the way from 5,000 feet to the top using tremendous stamina and climbing brilliance to make the whole climb in a few days—without any acclimatization. It could be done, though one would be in serious difficulty if the supply were to fail or run out. But why do it?

Not all the changes of acclimatization are beneficial: some carry penalties, and some are definitely harmful. Over-breathing draws fresh air deeper into the lungs to mix more completely with the alveolar air, depleted of oxygen but also 'washes out' carbon dioxide and threatens the acidity of the blood. To carry throughout the body what little oxygen is available, the heart beats more rapidly. So blood rushes through the capillaries of the lung more swiftly. Since the oxygen pressure in the alveoli is quite low, its passage through the alveolar membrane is slowed. The combination of these two factors suggests that passage of oxygen from lung to blood is less complete on top of Everest than lower down.

If a large number of new capillaries form, or too many reserve capillaries open up in the tissues, the circulating blood volume may be inadequate to fill them all with an acceptable pressure, particularly if the body is dehydrated, further decreasing oxygen supplies to the cells.

If too many red blood cells have been formed, the thickened blood moves sluggishly, tends to clot more easily, and the red cells, rather than tumbling end over end through the vessels, stack like dishes, decreasing the surface area through which oxygen diffuses. Consequently the exuberant increase in hemoglobin and red cells, once believed the most valuable adjustment to hypoxia, is seen as a possible villain today — leading to impaired circulation and decreased oxygen transport just when the opposite is needed. A hematocrit of 57% appears to be optimal at altitude — that is, when cells make up 57% of the blood, oxygen transport is acceptably increased without too great a change in viscosity and flow.

For this reason a few attempts have been made to 'normalize' blood by removing a pint or two, replacing it with an equal volume of plasma (the liquid portion of blood). This is called hemo-dilution and so far the results are inconclusive. Exactly the opposite approach was once advocated: six weeks before a climb, 500–1,000 ml of blood were removed and stored, to be given back to the individual after he had made more blood, just before his high climb. The same method has been tried by competitive athletes, in which it is considered 'doping.' The benefits, if any, in either case are not very large and both hemo-dilution and "auto-transfusion" (as returning the climber's own blood is called) are difficult and dangerous high on a mountain.

Are there any medications or exercises or procedures which will hasten or improve acclimatization? During the desperate days of World War II when a thousand feet of added altitude might mean victory to the fighter pilot, many things were tried. That was before the era of pressurized cabins or pressurized oxygen masks and it was thought (and later proven in Operation Everest) that acclimatization to moderate altitude could increase one's altitude ceiling—so pilots were sometimes sent to live at 5–8,000 feet for weeks between missions. This was certainly enjoyable to the pilots (at least for those who loved mountains) and did improve tolerance but had logistic problems. Instead, pilots were 'taken up' in a decompression chamber for a few hours each day, hoping that this would stimulate acclimatization, but this seemed to increase fatigue without improving altitude tolerance.

Forster studied 41 sea level natives who worked for five days a week at 14,000 feet, going down to 9,000 to sleep each night. On the first few days of each shift their symptoms were worse than later in the week, but each week seemed slightly easier. Blood gas levels improved toward the end of the week, and their exercise tolerance improved as well. But during six weeks of work at sea level, their partial acclimatization disappeared. This carefully done study certainly suggests that eight hours a day of exposure to a higher altitude produces some acclimatization, but a good deal more work is needed before we can accept this and the reports of Soviet and Japanese mountaineers without reservation.

Another approach is for athletes to train while breathing a low oxygen mixture. One occasionally sees runners jogging about like visitors from outer space, with mask on face and cylinders of 14–15% oxygen in nitrogen on their backs. They are breathing the same partial pressure of oxygen available while breathing air at 9–10,000 feet in the hope that this will stimulate better performance at sea level, or more rapid and complete acclimatization on a mountain. It is an interesting approach which needs careful evaluation before acceptance. It sounds rather boring.

Anabolic steroids—hormones which stimulate muscle building—have been used by athletes and some believe they were responsible for the improved performance in the Mexico City Olympics. They have since been considered doping and banned. Only one group have examined the use of anabolic hormones at altitude but the benefits they claimed have not been confirmed by others.

Does acetazolamide (Diamox) improve acclimatization? This interesting question cannot be answered yet. Some persons who took it regularly on a few Himalayan expeditions thought it did help them; others disagreed. Diamox causes acidosis in muscles which might interfere with unloading of oxygen, but would this be more than offset by the increased stimulus to breathe? Or is breathing already maximal? Twenty years ago Diamox was used for long periods—apparently with benefit—by patients with chronic lung disease causing hypoxia; other treatments have mostly replaced it today. Diamox is widely used by mountain visitors and trekkers and occasional undesirable side effects, though rare, are being reported. It is undoubtedly beneficial in minimizing acute mountain sickness but a good deal of controlled study is needed before we can judge whether or not it improves long-term acclimatization.

Different diets, cocktails of trace elements and vitamins, and many drugs have been tried, acclaimed, and disappeared into oblivion. Yet we are so fascinated with modern polypharmacology that we believe there must be a magic medicine which will minimize oxygen lack, and restore full capacity—for climbers and hypoxic patients alike. What would we ask of this magic medicine?

It should stimulate breathing, a little but not too much and at the same time diminish the loss of carbon dioxide, thus permitting better ventilation of the alveoli without the alkalosis due to lack of carbon dioxide. It should increase the capacity and attraction of hemoglobin for oxygen at the higher pressures but loosen the bond at lower pressures to expedite unloading in the tissue capillaries. It should open new capillaries, prevent red cells and platelets from clumping, and stimulate formation of new blood—but not too far. It should normalize the cell membrane electric potential, so that sodium and potassium are maintained at their proper levels and water does not over-fill the cell.

Perhaps it could even stimulate mitochondrial efficiency, increase their number, and sustain normal metabolic pathways in the cells. Could it also enable man to mix aerobic and anaerobic metabolism better, perhaps as some diving mammals do? We have medications today that will do one or two of these things, but always demanding that a price be paid, often an intolerable one. No single medicine or combination will accomplish all we ask.

There is one widely known product — diphenylhydantoin — Dilantin which normalizes cell membranes very effectively. A wide variety of studies in animals and some in man, indicate that Dilantin restores the cell to normal function without overshooting, when the bio-electric potential is disturbed, as we believe it is in hypoxia. Because it is such a remarkable treatment for one illness — epilepsy (where membrane disturbance is present), it has become associated with only that affliction, and efforts to apply it to other problems — notably altitude wellness and illness have been limited. Much more should be done with Dilantin. It might turn out that in combination with medications that do some of the other tasks we request, Dilantin would be our magic drug.

What happens when the well-acclimatized climber comes down to sea level after weeks or months high on some great mountain? Few studies have been done but the shift back to normal physiological function is rather unremarkable. Deacclimatization is more rapid than acclimatization. The overventilation from altitude persists for a few days or weeks, and there is slight breathlessness on exertion for a few days until the buffering system returns to normal. The heart beats more slowly, and the increased blood count gradually falls to normal.

There is a feeling of elation, of euphoria and well-being, and joy in simple things like grass and flowers, warmth and space to move about. Life seems a very precious, many-splendored thing. But in weeks or months the trivial irritants erode this joy, and the daily round seems dull and unimportant compared to the continuing drama of high mountains. Depression is quite common; broken marriages have occured, blamed by some on brain damage from hypoxia, but by others on the end of a great adventure. High mountains are exhilarating, but return to sea level rather dull.

The altitude native or long-time resident also adjusts to the richer air, and in the same way. A few anecdotes describe palpitations, unusual breathlessness, vague pains and weakness in persons well-adjusted to altitude who go to sea level, but there is no firm data. Monge's disease (chronic mountain sickness) affects the long-time residents while at altitude, and it is improved or cured by going down. The Great Inca's order forbidding downward migration was most likely inspired by the dangers of tropical illness rather than de-acclimatization. But altitude natives—like the addicted mountaineer—long for the mountains and all the rewards they give to those who honor them.

CHAPTER NINE—
WOMEN AT ALTITUDE

More than a hundred persons have reached the top of Everest, and four of them have been women: the first, a Japanese housewife named Mrs. Tabei got there in 1975 and within a few days was followed by Mrs. Phantong, a Tibetan mother of three. Considering that the vast majority of those attempting Everest have been men, the success of these four would seem to establish the capability of women at altitude, as is further attested by the literature which shows that at least twenty women have been over 26,000 feet.

But should this be surprising? Women have shown that they can do many—perhaps most—things as well as men, and there is nothing about high altitude that should make it a strictly male reservation. Great climbers at any altitude learn to move gracefully and in rhythm, and seldom rely on brute strength; this is even more essential at great altitude, and should suit women well. To drive toward a summit when one is blunted by hypoxia and many other privations requires immense determination—but are women lacking in such single-mindedness? Don't women tolerate pain and discomfort as well as men? Among the ill-fated Donner party some were even stronger.

Mountain climbing began as a man's game and was dominated by men all through the golden age of Alpine climbing, when virtually every summit in Europe was reached in the last half of the nineteenth century. The culture and mores of those years dictated women's role until our lifetimes, and only a few had the courage—or temerity—to step out of their 'proper place'. Among the earliest female climbers were the three Parminter sisters, whose photograph made after climbing one of the Alps just before 1800 is all that we know of them today.

A few years later Maria Paradis who owned a small dairy (cremerie) along the path that led up to some of the lower peaks near Chamonix in the French Alps, determined to make herself a reputation which would be good for business and so chose to climb Mont Blanc, at 15,780 feet the highest peak in Europe, in 1808. She was the first woman to do so and on the summit her guides lifted her above their shoulders. Thereafter she loved to tell the story to her customers (were there more as a result of her efforts?), but no mention of her reaction to altitude has survived. Two books listing successful ascents of Mont Blanc before 1834 do not mention her at all. Auldjo (whose History of Mont Blanc, written in 1828 is a classic) lists all the ascents and adds in a final paragraph. *"Some years ago a party of guides made the ascent for pleasure. With them was Maria de Mont Blanc, a high spirited girl."* This was the name she chose to be known by, but her fame was fleeting.

A Mrs. Campbell and her daughter crossed the Col du Geant (an 11,000 foot pass between France and Italy) on August 18, 1822, led by guides who had trouble using the rope; the ladies had most inadequate dresses; the bivouac was hard. All in all it was a difficult climb which they handled well, saying they would return the following year to do Mont Blanc, but nothing more was heard from them in the mountaineering world.

A much more notorious lady (or one more notable — depending on whom you choose to believe) was Mlle Henriette d'Angeville who described her mountain sickness while climbing Mont Blanc in September 1838:

"From the base of the Mur de la Cote to the summit I fell into a kind of lethargic sleep which required a halt every ten or twelve steps and an unheard of effort of will to overcome . . . as soon as I sat down a leaden sleep weighed down not only my eyes but all my limbs . . . it was in such a state that I passed the final two hours of the climb, but the thought of abandoning the effort never crossed my mind. . . . Once on the summit my resurrection was immediate: I regained all my mental faculties and was able to enjoy fully the magnificent spectacle . . ." She does not mention headache or nausea (perhaps unmentionable in that era).

Claire Engel describes her as *"a romantic woman longing for glory and excitement; a thwarted maiden lady in her forties, eager to become a society lion, possibly jealous of other well known women, George Sand for one. She was fascinated by Mont Blanc . . . and pined for years before being able to do as she wished and at last succeeded in accomplishing her long cherished desire. She had a strange craving for publicity; she wanted glory as a mountaineer, as a writer . . . thought of going*

FIGURE 33: EARLY WOMEN CLIMBERS

Maria Paradis was the first woman to climb Mont Blanc and being a local restaurant owner, probably was not as finely dressed as the next successful woman, Henriette d'Angeville (shown here, top) who reached the summit in 1838. The tall alpenstock, with a chamois horn on its end, was standard equipment until early in this century. Fortunately, more sensible, though less dramatic, women's clothing came into common use, though not until after WWII.

The Golden Age of Alpine climbing ran from 1854 to 1885 and among the finest climbers of that glorious period were a few women. Mary Isabella Stratton (bottom, first on right) was one of the best: she made the first winter ascent of Mont Blanc and was actively climbing all over the Alps until she was eighty years old. Studio portraits like these were often kept as souvenirs and provide us a nostalgic look at accomplishments, fashions, and relationships in a period which seems much more than a hundred years ago.

to the bottom of the channel in a diving bell and in the air in a balloon . . . she was a sort of femme fatale who loved Mont Blanc because she had no one else to love . . ."

But R.L.G. Irving writes that she was *"a genuine lover of the great mountain. She had no sort of scientific object in view. She climbed the Oldenhorn in her seventieth year in city clothes and boots. . . . A love of adventure without a trace of the adventuress, a quite remarkable emancipation from convention and a magnificent reserve of strength and determination characterize this vivid personality. . ."*

Another Englishwoman soon became almost as well known. Mary Isabella Stratton made four ascents of Mont Blanc, one of them (the first winter ascent) in January 1876 when she had frostbite of her fingers and what sounds like hypothermia. She married a famous guide, Jean Charlet, and together they made many climbs until she was almost eighty. In a lengthy correspondence with a would-be biographer she does not mention altitude sickness.

The best known American woman mountaineer of the last century is Annie Peck who went higher than her predecessors when she climbed Orizaba (then believed to be 18,700 feet high) in Mexico, in 1897. She had loftier ambitions—to reach the highest point in the Americas because

" . . . being always a believer in the equality of the sexes, I felt that any achievement in my line of endeavor would be of advantage to my sex."

Though small she was a spirited professor of Latin at two great colleges, (remarkable enough when a woman's place was thought to be in the home), and widely acclaimed as a scholar at home and abroad. Her love of mountains took her to the Andes again and again, until finally, at the age of 59 on her fifth attempt, she climbed Huascaran (22,650 feet) but was disappointed to find it several hundred feet lower than Aconcagua, highest summit in the Americas which Fitzgerald's party had climbed eleven years earlier. Miss Annie's knickerbockers, frowned on at the time, became famous around the world, and were later adopted by other liberated women climbers. Unlike Fitzgerald, Miss Annie does not mention altitude symptoms.

During the same period, Dr. and Mrs. Bullock-Workman

were exploring the almost unknown Karakoram ranges in north-west India. Dr. Workman had retired from a surgical practice in Hartford, Connecticut, allegedly because of a weak heart, but he and his wife Fannie made eight major expeditions to the Himalayas between 1897 and 1908. Often they crossed 20,000 foot passes, camping even higher, and in 1903 Fannie climbed an unnamed 22,000 foot peak. This remarkable couple spent months above 14,000 feet which may explain why they never experienced mountain sickness, although their locally recruited porters often did. Fannie's accomplishments stirred half serious comment from J. P. Farrar, then editor of the Alpine Journal, premier mountain record in the world:

"I do beg of you, my dear lady, to consider well before you exhort your sex to 'begin to compete with men in the field of exploration.' They may take you too literally. It may be they will eschew the company of any mere male in their journeys . . . I am not sure their cares will be lessened thereby, and do consider our loss!"

His admonition came too late. Women were already showing they loved to climb and could do as well as men. Soon the "all woman party" would be common, but first had to come emancipation—and proper clothing. Miriam O'Brien (who was to become one of the great lady climbers and married a man equally great) wrote of her early climbing days:

"Isobel and I were big girls (this was in 1915) and, though we wore with our middy blouses the big full bloomers of the period, we considered it more seemly to wear a skirt outside. . . . But that was the beginning and the end for me. Trousers for climbing and skiing were just coming into fashion about the time I needed them."

A few years later she was doing some of the more difficult alpine peaks, including the first ascent of two formidable granite needles called the Mademoiselles Anglais (renamed Les Dames Anglais after her climb). By 1930 she was pioneering 'manless climbing', and soon made one of the notoriously difficult routes on a spectacular pinnacle near Chamonix, of which Mummery had written in 1881:

"It has frequently been noticed that all mountains appear doomed to pass through three stages: an inaccessible peak—the

most difficult ascent in the Alps — an easy day for a lady . . . I must confess that the Grepon has not yet reached this final stage."

But after Miriam O'Brien and her friend Alice Damesne had climbed the Grepon, negotiating the Mummery crack without help, one of the great Chamonix guides said sadly:

"The Grepon has disappeared . . . there are still some rocks standing there, but as a climb it no longer exists. Now that it has been done by two women alone, no self-respecting man can undertake it. A pity, too, because it used to be a very good climb."

Today, and for the past twenty years, women have tackled the most difficult routes (including a solo ascent of El Capitan — the 3,000 foot vertical face in Yosemite Valley), and the highest mountains. The best have shown themselves equal to men in their endurance, patience, tolerance for cold and altitude, and even strength. No longer would an Auldjo pass over a remarkable climb by *"a high spirited girl."* Even more significantly perhaps, reports today are less inclined to mention the sex of the climber, and women's parties are dealt with the same as those exclusively male.

But there are differences. Women tend to have lighter frames, to be less muscular and to carry more fat. Their average ventilatory capacity is less than that of men, as is their maximum work capacity (VO2Max), although the very fit woman may have a higher VO2max than the unfit man. Women who are well trained are approaching what men can do in marathons and on long hard climbs at altitude.

Women usually have less strength in the upper body, particularly the arms, compared to men. If they train by running or cycling, their relative weakness is not improved, and Barbara Drinkwater advises women climbers to work harder to strengthen their arms and shoulders as well as their legs — and this they can do. Coupled with their natural grace, this added strength enables women to do as difficult climbs as men, at least up to moderate altitude. There is not enough data to define their capacities on the highest peaks because men still far outnumber women there.

Few studies have sufficient data to permit comparison of the incidence of altitude illness in men and women. Of some 5,000 persons randomly interviewed in a recent study at six ski resorts, about half were women, and acute mountain sickness was equally prevalent in both sexes. On the few all female Himalayan climbs where medical aspects have been described, the women had no more problems with altitude than did the male Sherpas. Among Himalayan tourists, if the data are corrected for the larger number of men, women do seem to have a slightly higher incidence of pulmonary edema and to accumulate more water in hands and feet and face; this may be related to their tendency to retain fluid during the pre-menstrual phase but there is simply not enough information to be sure. On the other hand more men than women seem to develop high altitude pulmonary edema at the moderate altitude of ski areas.

We find conflicting reports—what few there are—about menses. In general, world class female athletes tend to have scanty periods which often stop when training for major contests. On some Himalayan climbs menses are said to have been the same as at sea level—those who tended to be regular remained so, and those who had problems continued with them. But on others the women said their periods became scanty or ceased. Occasionally on long trips, all women tended to fall into the same cycle.

Normally women have somewhat lower hemoglobin levels than men and sometimes are found to have low iron reserves even if they are not anemic. The same prevails at altitude, and women do not increase hemoglobin as briskly as men do as they go higher. This can be a disadvantage, and women intending to try the greatest peaks would be wise to have iron stores checked beforehand, and even to take extra iron—something rarely necessary for men.

Fertility is lower in women born and living at 14–15,000 feet and may be decreased in those who come up from sea level and stay for months or years. Men are alleged to have fewer active sperm after long stays at altitude—but only one is needed and there is little firm evidence about sperm activity at altitude, though some titillating tales describe impregnation—or at least attempts—in high mountain camps.

As we saw earlier, miscarriage and premature delivery are a

bit more common in altitude residents, as are birth defects. But how the length of stay, or the stage of pregnancy, or the additional stresses of the mountain environment affect the fetus is today unclear. Peruvians still celebrate the birth of the first Spanish child to survive after the Spanish conquest, though many had been conceived in the preceding fifty years.

How does altitude affect the fetus? This is difficult to answer from hard statistical data. We know that defects are more common among long time residents and natives, but we don't know when the defects, mostly minor, occurred. We do know that the fetus lives and usually thrives in an environment containing less oxygen than on the summit of Everest, and we have some idea why this is so. This suggests that the fetus is unlikely to be damaged when the mother goes or stays at altitude, unless there are unusually stressful circumstances such as a major illness, abnormal pregnancy, or extreme altitude during the first few weeks.

We also know that at any altitude many environmental influences can harm the fetus: smoking, alcohol, many toxic substances, virus infections and trauma. Do these adverse influences have added effect during hypoxia — as do alcohol and most medications? Trying to determine just what effects are attributable to hypoxia alone is difficult from the data at hand today. Nor can we say for sure which partner is responsible.

We should look at Mrs. Tabei and Mrs. Phantong and scores of western women with admiration not only for their climbs, but even more for the prejudices their predecessors had to overcome. Whether male chauvinism, territorial jealousy, or chivalrous protectiveness was the motive, the result was that women 'did not belong' on high mountains. But today, in photographs of Chinese, Japanese, Americans and Europeans on the highest summits it is not possible to differentiate men from women — and so it should be. Climbing, even Himalayan climbing is no longer an exclusive male sport. Women can excel as well as men — and need pay no greater price. Women's place — and men's is on top.

Chapter Ten
THE CELL

Earlier in this book we looked at the intricate ways in which we acquire oxygen, transport it to the farthest parts of the body, and pick up and carry wastes to disposal sites. We peeked briefly at the complicated control network which maintains the constancy of our "internal environment" despite great fluctuation in the external temperature, pressure, humidity, and oxygen content. In our self-centered complacency we believe that this incredible mechanism has reached its pinnacle in man, even though a considerable part of our sophistication persists in trying to destroy all life.

All this network, all these activities are devoted to one end — the care and sustenance of individual cells. We breathe to acquire oxygen and remove carbon dioxide, and thus to ensure that every living cell has enough of one and not too much of the other. Our hearts pump in order that no cell lack oxygen and nourishment or suffocate in its own garbage. This *"tiny bag of living water that floats in a great dead sea"* (as William Bennett described the cell) is far more than a building block — it is life itself. Albert Claude accepting a Nobel prize in 1974, spoke lyrically about this tiny factory:

"For over two billion years, through the apparent fancy of its endless differentiations and metamorphosis, the cell, in its basic physiological mechanisms, has remained one and the same. It is life itself, and our true and distant ancestor.

It is hardly more than a century since we first learned of the existence of the cell: this autonomous and all-contained unit of living matter that has acquired the knowledge and the power to reproduce; the capacity to store, transform, and utilize energy, and the capacity to accomplish physical works and to manufacture practically unlimited kinds of products. We know that the cell has possessed these attributes and biological devices and has continued to use them for billions of cell generations and years.

In addition, we know also that the cell has a memory of its past, certainly in the case of the egg cell, and foresight of the future, together with precise and detailed patterns for differen-

tiations and growth, a knowledge which is materialized in the process of reproduction and the development of all beings from bacteria to plants, beasts, or men. It is this cell which plans and composes all organisms, and which transmits to them its defects and potentialities. Man, like other organisms, is so perfectly coordinated that he may easily forget, whether awake or asleep, that he is a colony of cells in action, and that it is the cells which achieve, through him, what he has the illusion of accomplishing himself. It is the cells which create and maintain in us, during the span of our lives, our will to live and survive, to search and experiment and to struggle.

*The cell, over the billions of years of its life, has covered the earth many times with its substances, found ways to control itself and its environment, and ensure its survival."**

With the powerful tools we have developed in the last few years we cannot only look at every tiny bit of the cell, but we can dissect out, alter, replace, or replicate the smallest fragments. One might think that no secrets remain hidden, but in fact many still evade us. With breath-taking speed our knowledge has accelerated, though our understanding lags behind. But think how far we have travelled since Robert Hooke first used the word "cell" before the Royal Society on April 13th, 1663, when he used the newly developed microscope to demonstrate the compartments in cork. Though his microscope magnified only 400 times, this was enough to show myriads of neatly arranged boxes, dead skeletons of houses once inhabited. About a century later Henri Dutrochet after looking at thousands of organisms, suggested that all living matter was made up of such individual cells, living cooperatively together, dying and being replaced. But living cells are made mostly of water and thus were difficult to study under the microscopes of those times, so Dutrochet's suggestion took some time to gain acceptance. Then Theodore Schwann picking up some ideas advanced by Schleiden demonstrated that the cell was indeed the basic structure of all living organisms, its life and death and organization contrasting sharply with the static structure of non-living materials. We originate of course from the

---

* Nobel Foundation. For permission to reprint I am grateful.

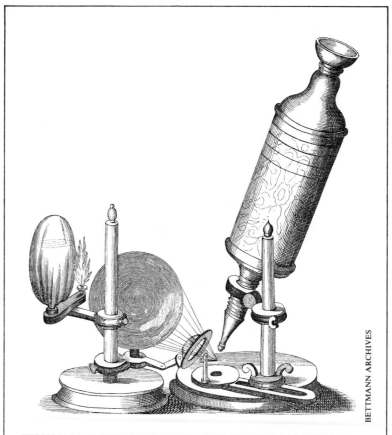

FIGURE 34: ROBERT HOOKE'S MICROSCOPE (ABOUT 1660)

Although Zacharias Janssen and Galileo developed microscopes between 1590 and 1610, the names of Anthony von Leeuwenhoeck and Robert Hooke are more commonly associated with appreciation of the immense value of that instrument. Leeuwenhoeck made several hundred small 'scopes, some of which magnified over 250 times. Hooke's instrument (shown here) was more complicated and gave finer detail and higher power. With it he made thousands of drawings for his great book *Micrographia* which was one of the masterpieces of science in his century. Hooke was charged by the Royal Society (then a fledgling club of the leaders of the day) with preparing several new demonstrations each week, and his microscope helped him to fulfill this impossible task. The microscope shown here magnified 400 times, and led him and others to studies throughout the world of nature—both living and dead.

union of two single cells, each bearing elaborate instructions which direct the result of their union to grow into a human rather than a duck. But just how this is accomplished was explained only a few decades ago by the dramatic uncovering of the genetic code—the "double helix" made up of desoxyribonucleic acid or DNA.

Even the best light microscopes of today depend upon light passing through or reflected from the object being studied and thus are limited in the detail which they can reveal. About 1930 a sophisticated new tool was developed—the electron microscope—which in various ways makes it possible to distinguish individual molecules only a few angstrom in diameter. (The angstrom is 10^{-10} meters long, a very tiny measure indeed.) With this beautiful machine the most intimate structures can be examined, even the living cells of which we are made, and even while they function. Each cell is now recognized to be a complex community of more than forty tiny bits, each with a special function, each requiring nourishment and oxygen. Each cell is a minute factory where busy workers carry on their assigned tasks. Collections of cells form organs, different organs form the animal. Indeed a living body is much like a city where some sections are devoted to casting iron, others to baking bread, others to selling cars or beer, or making clothing. The life of a great metropolis depends upon the interaction of these communities, each of which relies on thousands of individuals to make the food, provide power, or carry off the garbage, and each is a part of the humming whole. Just as a city can adjust to the loss of an industry, so the body can accept loss of, say one kidney, or a part of its blood. Neither city nor man can lose many parts without dying. Neither the city nor the man can survive without a continuing supply of oxygen, and if their air is too depleted of oxygen, both city and human will die.

We have discussed how oxygen is brought to the smallest capillaries where it flows 'downhill' to its destination, the cell. Oxygen must pass through the red blood cell casing, traverse the liquid portion of blood, diffuse through the capillary wall and the fluid which bathes all cells, and finally it must enter the cell and reach the place where it is to be used—the mitochondria. Passage through the various membranes is dictated by physical laws: diffusion depends on the pressure difference or gradient across the membrane, the thickness, characteristics, and surface area of the membrane, and a coefficient characteristic of the gas or liquid and of the particular membrane, liquid, or space to be crossed. Though we can here consider only the passage of oxygen from blood to cell, the same principles apply to movement of any molecule through any medium, though of course the numbers are very different in each case.

But not all diffusion is so simple (if the above is simple!). Some cells are capable of "active transport," that is, they can use energy to move substances 'uphill'. Many substances are transported across membranes in our bodies, but the three we are concerned with (oxygen and carbon dioxide and water) are not. Though Haldane argued strongly that the alveolar membrane could actively secrete oxygen into blood, we have no evidence today that either oxygen or carbon dioxide cross membranes by anything except passive diffusion, subject to the rules defined above.

The integrity of life depends upon separation of *"the bag of living water"* from its surroundings by a membrane, and as Bennett describes this:

"The boundary between a cell and the world is far more than a surface: it is a region that actively creates an interior different from all outdoors. . . . Cell membranes are not . . . featureless, efficient, smooth sheets—a kind of smart cellophane. They are studded with surface features which render the membrane as recognizable as a United States Marine in full dress uniform."

When we examine these surface features with our powerful instruments we find that the cell membrane is a double layer of molecules, some oily, others water soluble, stabilized here and there by cholesterol molecules and cobbled with large proteins, some associated with one face, others with the second face of the membrane while still others penetrate both. These large protein molecules define the unique characteristics and functions of the different kinds of cells and provide "active transport" when that is called for. The membrane is about 100 angstrom thick, and its phospholipids or fat-like molecules are shaped something like tadpoles whose 'heads' facing inwards or outwards present a compact surface, while their 'tails' wiggle freely

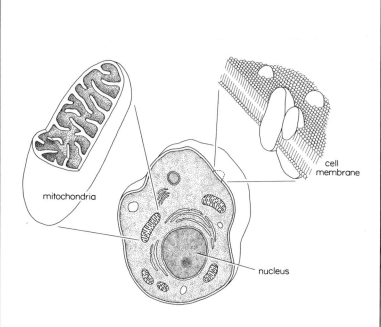

mitochondria

cell membrane

nucleus

FIGURE 35:
THE CELL, ITS MEMBRANE AND MITOCHONDRIA

The cell is the industrial park of the body. In it the mitochondria provide energy while other components recycle products, reproduce, or perform functions unique to each type of cell. A thin two-layered membrane encloses the cell, its molecules arranged in an orderly fashion like tadpoles with their tails facing inward and in constant motion, while between the two faces is an almost imperceptible space. Here and there in the membrane, larger molecules (also in motion) shoulder up as a substance moves in or out of the cell or remains a functioning part of its wall. The permeability or leakiness of the wall depends on a minute bio-electric charge which is affected by many things, including lack of oxygen. The cell membrane, and the mitochondria (whose numbers vary from a few dozen to several hundred depending on the type of cell) are most affected by hypoxia.

back and forth keeping the layers in constant minute motion. The large protein molecules are also in motion, now and then shouldering their way up through the phospholipid heads, bulging outward from the cell here and inward there. The composition of these phospholipids is different in cells of different organs with different functions. Both layers of molecules carry minute electrical charges—the bio-electric potential. Currently the most plausible explanation of the impact of hypoxia on all or at least most functions is that lack of oxygen alters the bioelectric charge on some cell membranes, thus interfering with transfer of sodium, potassium and water into or out of cells. The aggregate impact of this disturbance may explain the entities of altitude illness.

Most simple gases, like other small molecules, pass through membranes as they do through space, by simple diffusion. Their molecules, darting here and there with incredible speed, rapidly scatter. No walls are completely impenetrable and the membranes of living tissue are selectively permeable, some allowing passage of only one type of molecule, others freely passing many different molecules.

Besides the pressure gradient and diffusion coefficient, another influence which greatly affects the speed and completeness of diffusion is the distance to be traversed. Cells may be immediately adjacent to capillaries, or separated by fluid or fibrous tissue, and the further away a cell is from a capillary, the slower and less complete will be the movement of oxygen. Not many cells are far from capillaries, and one of the changes which contributes to acclimatization is the opening up of additional reserve capillaries, and even—after prolonged residence at high altitude—the formation of new ones so that very few cells indeed will be significantly distant from their oxygen supply, as we saw in Chapter Eight.

There are thousands of different kinds of cells in the human body, each with unique capabilities and characteristics, each containing several dozen discrete parts. Two parts are of special interest in our search to understand the causes of altitude illness and the course of acclimatization.

One of the most amazing accomplishments in medicine of the last quarter century is our exploration of genes, the tiny building blocks arranged in neat designs to make up chromosomes which determine our unique individual characteristics. Chemically, genes are contained in long double-stranded spirals of desoxyribonucleic acid (DNA), which control the formation of other substances in cells and thus dictate the genetic code. Only three simple substances (proline, serine, and glutamic acid), arranged in triplets, make up the "code words." Their placement or sequence in the double helix determines whether our hair is red or black, whether we tend to have depressions or are capable of genius, whether we may develop cancer or diabetes or live to be a hundred. If there is an inherited trait which acclimatizes generations to high altitude, it is carried by a special code word or words in the spiral.

In the last few years, incredible though it may seem, we have learned to re-arrange the code words (at least in small organisms) and thus to change their characteristics and their functions. What such bio-engineering may mean to the future boggles the mind and has alarmed many. Genetic engineering may be the most important capability man has ever acquired, for it may perhaps be used to alter any living cell—in man, or bug, or grain—and how wisely and well we use this power will profoundly influence the future of life on earth if we do not destroy it first.

For our understanding of altitude illness and acclimatization, however, the most important bits in the cell are the mitochondria. In these intricate structures are made the molecules of adenosine triphosphate—ATP—which is to life what electricity is to a motor: it makes it run. In response to appropriate stimulus, the ATP molecule breaks down very rapidly, releasing a very large amount of energy and forming ADP (adenosine diphosphate). Three molecules of ADP are then slowly reformed by a less energy-intensive process to make two molecules of ATP and the process is ready to be repeated. Some of these changes occur within and others outside the mitochondria; ATP breakdown to release energy is not oxygen-dependent, but the re-building of ATP from ADP does require oxygen and thus is likely to be affected by high altitude. Some cells with many different functions have many mitochondria (liver cells have 400), while others have few, like the single-purposed sperm which has only forty. Certain stimuli are believed to increase (or decrease) the number of mitochondria and one of these is oxygen lack. More mitochondria might permit the cell to produce more energy by recycling more ATP and ADP with less oxygen.

Mitochondria make the ultimate factory where fuel is burned in the complicated cycles which energize every activity including the creation of new cells. ATP is the molecular configuration in which energy is stored or released, used and rebuilt, as ATP cycles to ADP and back. All life is dependent on the ATP-ADP conversions which we call metabolism. Even though certain portions of it may take place in the absence of oxygen, anaerobic reactions cannot be long sustained: oxygen is necessary for completion.

After oxygen was identified and its role in combustion shown, scientists in the eighteenth and nineteenth centuries were greatly puzzled over how living organisms used food to create energy. How could mammals maintain the body at so constant and reasonable a temperature if food was being "burned" like a candle? (Equally intriguing was the question for cold-blooded or microscopic organisms.) Even the penetrating genius of Lavoisier and Priestley could not grasp how oxygen could be consumed and Joseph Black's 'fixed air' or carbon dioxide be produced, without destroying tissue in which combustion occurred. Then Justus Liebig in the middle of the nineteenth century showed how a metabolic process could produce controllable heat and energy without damaging tissues, and that in fact such control did exist not in the lungs, not in blood, but inside each living cell.

Louis Pasteur, responding to the pleas of French wine makers whose grapes were being ravaged by a mysterious malady (imagine the French losing their wines!) began to study fermentation and in 1858 showed that yeast was responsible. He believed that living yeast was essential and not until 1897 when the Buchner brothers were able to ferment sugared water to alcohol with a cell-free extract from yeast, was it clear that an enzyme, not the living cell, was necessary to make the cup that cheers. Thus began the studies which in the next seventy years deciphered the reactions by which foods are converted to

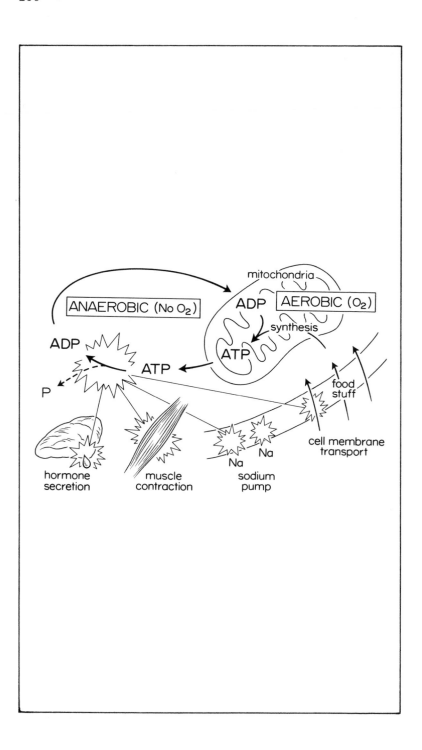

FIGURE 36: METABOLISM AND ENERGY PRODUCTION

After the food we eat has been processed in the stomach and intestines the products of digestion (fatty acids, amino acids, simple sugars, and others) are passed through the intestinal walls into the blood and transported to tissues where they enter cells either by simple diffusion or active energy-consuming transport. The liquid in the cell (cytoplasm) contains enzymes which further break down food substances for diffusion into the mitochondria where energy production is centered.

There, under the influence of many enzymes arranged in an orderly fashion along the ridges of the mitochondria much like chemicals on laboratory shelves, these simpler substances are synthesized to adenotriphosphate, ATP, in a series of steps called the Krebs or tricarboxylic acid cycle. This process is oxygen-consuming or aerobic. ATP is stored in the mitochondria and perhaps elsewhere, and whenever energy is needed can be rapidly mobilized and instantly split, two molecules of ATP forming three of ADP (adenodiphosphate). This is a rapid, almost explosive release of energy which does not require oxygen (anaerobic). The energy released is used (1) to operate the "sodium pump" and to control passage of materials in and out of the cell; (2) to do work such as muscle contraction or secretion of hormones among other tasks; (3) for the synthesis of various substances, especially the slower rebuilding of ATP from ADP, which depends upon oxygen.

These minute biochemical reactions though immensely complex, are surprisingly well known. Lack of oxygen does not affect the quick release of energy in the anaerobic breakdown of ATP, but does markedly affect the rebuilding of ATP from ADP which is oxygen-dependent. Perhaps this partly explains why sudden bursts of heavy work are possible at high altitude while longer sustained effort is not, and why recovery from work takes longer at altitude than at sea level.

energy. The Krebs or citric acid cycle was defined, explaining how substances could be 'burned' by the body without consuming it.

Intermediary metabolism (as the process is called) has since become a major biochemical discipline involving a multitude of enzymes. So ingenious are their inter-relationships that alternative pathways enable metabolism and life to go on without oxygen, though not for long. Such anaerobic ("without air") metabolism makes it possible (with other adjustments mentioned earlier) for whales and other diving mammals to stay under water for an hour, long after their oxygen supplies have been exhausted. Turtles and other more exotic animals can live for six months or longer without air, thanks in part to the anaerobic cycles they possess. Athletes can go beyond their oxygen-dependent limits (though only for a few minutes) thanks to anaerobic pathways. But all must pay back the oxygen debt and recovery from any anaerobic activity takes time with a full oxygen supply. All but a very few organisms (even plants whose main energy pathways depend on carbon dioxide) require oxygen; they may function for a time without it, but sooner or later oxygen they must have or perish.

This book is not the place to dwell on the details of cellular metabolism and enzyme action. What is important here is to realize that mammals depend upon an almost continuous supply of oxygen. After minutes in man, or an hour or so in some other mammals, most functions falter and will soon stop without oxygen. This deterioration of function is altitude illness, and death is not very far away when hypoxia develops.

Three other cell components (water, sodium, and potassium) need special mention because their passage across cell membranes is affected by lack of oxygen. First water. This rather small molecule readily and easily passes through semipermeable membranes to equalize the concentrations of dissolved substances on both sides of the membrane—a process known as osmosis and first described by Dutrochet. One explanation for altitude illness rests on the hypothesis that a derangement of osmotic pressure in cells results from abnormal passage of water and dissolved salts across cell membranes. The concentration of sodium ions within cells is normally only about one tenth that in the interstitial fluid which surrounds the cell, while the concentration of potassium is about twenty times greater inside than outside the cell, although each passes the membrane with equal ease. To explain this discrepant gradient, a 'sodium pump' has been postulated—an energy-consuming transfer of ions across a cell membrane. The 'pump' is constantly pushing sodium 'uphill' as it were, to keep the intra-cellular level down, while at the same time it seems to hold back potassium, retaining it within the cell. About 20% of the energy expended by every living cell is believed to be used by this 'pump' which of course cannot be seen, but whose action is essential to life. As one of the crucial functions of the ATP-ADP cycle it is oxygen-dependent. If the 'pump' malfunctions, sodium accumulates in the cell while potassium leaks out (but at a lesser rate). The resulting derangement affects not only function but also cell size because by osmosis water enters the cell to preserve osmotic pressure and the cell swells. This swelling is believed to be an important contributor to the signs and symptoms of altitude illness.

More than half of the energy generated by the ATP-ADP cycle, called by the jaw-breaking term of oxidative phosphorylization, goes to housekeeping chores like maintaining appropriate levels of electrolytes, water, food and fuel to keep the cell alive and well. But each cell has other important functions too. Each must replicate itself before it dies. Some exist to detoxify the blood as the liver does. Others, in the kidney, excrete, re-absorb, or filter specific substances in response to commands from hormone messengers, themselves made by other highly specialized cells. Some cells make up the web of nerves and brain cells which generate, store, and transmit nervous signals, others make muscles contract or relax or digestive organs to function. Each kind of cell is specialized, each has the requisite number and type of mitochondria, and each is enclosed in a membrane or membranes of special selective permeability. The activities of each kind of cell are dictated by the individual genetic code carried within its nucleus and since each depends on oxygen for life, hypoxia affects them all. There is really no 'typical' cell, but a very large number of quite different ones. Although each may have a similar overall composition, their

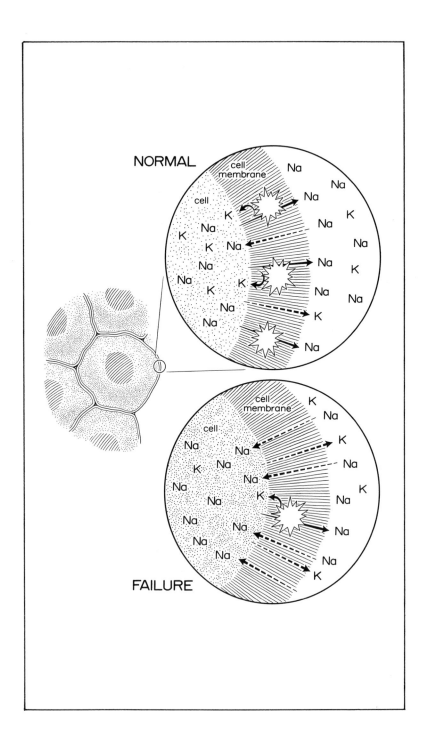

FIGURE 37: THE SODIUM PUMP AND THE CELL

Each of our cells is enclosed within a delicate membrane through which can pass many substances, including sodium (Na), potassium (K) and water. Sodium tends to enter cells in larger amounts than does potassium which tends to leave. To explain how the necessary delicate balance is maintained, an energy-intensive "sodium pump" has been postulated; this is oxygen-dependent and is believed to use up to 20% of the energy each cell generates.

The sodium pump constantly pushes sodium ions out of the cell while hindering the exit of potassium ions and allowing water to pass freely. In this way the concentration of sodium ions is kept lower inside the cells than outside while the reverse is true of potassium. So long as the pump is functioning normally osmotic equilibrium is achieved by passage of water in the appropriate direction. But if the pump falters or fails, as it is believed to do in several conditions, including hypoxia, then sodium is not pushed out as fast as it enters while potassium leaks out. As a result sodium builds up in the cell while potassium falls. To maintain osmotic equilibrium, water enters and the cell swells. Though these changes are extremely small, disturbance of the sodium pump and the resultant swelling of cells, most likely some more than others, is believed to be the basic cause of altitude illness. If true, this might explain why some symptoms are worse in some persons or on some days or in some organ systems. More swelling in the brain may cause the headache, in the face may cause edema of the eyes, while swelling in other specific locations might cause the staggering walk, the hallucinations, or the accumulation of fluid in the lungs.

response to oxygen lack varies widely.

Failure or weakness of the 'sodium pump' is not enough to explain all the problems encountered at altitude however, nor does pump recovery explain fully the process of acclimatization. The complicated cycle through which fuel is converted to energy, requires a large number of enzymes as facilitators. Most are oxygen-dependent, and their functions are deranged unless sufficient oxygen is constantly available. But just how these contribute to illness or wellness is beyond the scope of this book. Barbashova has suggested that one of the adaptive mechanisms at the cell level is an increase in ability to do work with less oxygen (anaerobically), an ability which most tissues normally have to a strictly limited degree, when the immediate demand for oxygen briefly outstrips supply. Barbashova postulated that this increase in capacity for anaerobic work may be held in reserve while other enzyme systems gradually adapt to hypoxia. She calls the immediate reactions to hypoxia (such as increased ventilation and increased cardiac output), the "struggle responses" which sustain the body during the period of slow cellular adaptation. She places great emphasis on the observation that increased resistance of cells to hypoxia is not a response specific to hypoxia, but rather a general response which can be initiated by other agents as well. As Barbashova sees it, tissue adaptation plays a considerable part in acclimatization, and is based on changes in enzyme systems, and an increase in the number of mitochondria which create more effective ways of using what oxygen is available.

F. Z. Meerson in 1975 was referring specifically to the importance of aerobic metabolism in the oxygen transport system, and to acclimatization to hypoxia when he wrote:

"The adaptation of an organism to environmental factors is apparently achieved as a result of coordination at all levels. . . . The main factors of the external environment act indirectly through neuro-endocrine mechanisms with the result that the chain of events, beginning with a deficit of energy and ending in activation of the biogenesis of mitochondria may turn out to be mediated by a cascade of factors . . . the organism has rapidly acting mechanisms for providing the functions with energy; these mechanisms come into play by increasing the transport of

oxygen . . .through such well-known phenomena as hyperventilation, increase in minute volume of the heart . . . this mobilization of the transport system arises before any structural basis of adaptation. . . . With an increase in the capacity of the mitochondrial system, the cells acquire a capacity for absorbing an increased amount of oxygen from a unit of flowing blood. . . . The final . . . process of adaptation . . . is synthesis of nucleic acids and proteins. . . . Thus analysis of the cellular link of the process enables us to come closer to understanding the mechanism of long term adaptation. . . ."*

So there it is . . . short-term immediate "struggle responses" which work to keep the cells supplied with their usual fare, while the cells, within the limits allowed them by their genetic instructions, develop their own ways of using a decreased supply of oxygen more efficiently. The emergency responses taper off or end, and new adjustments in the intracellular materials and processes mature. What a beautifully integrated system it all is . . . and how little of it do we really comprehend!

---

* Physiological Reviews. I am grateful for permission to reprint.

DEFINITIONS AND TERMS
USED IN HIGH ALTITUDE PHYSIOLOGY

Air, Atmosphere, Pressure

Atmospheric, barometric pressure — Usually used inter-changably, referring to the weight of the blanket of air over-lying the earth.

Torr, milimeters of mercury (mm Hg) — One torr (named for Torricelli who made the first merucurial barometer) equals one milimeter of mercury. Used to define barometric pressure.

Ambrient air — The air which surrounds us wherever we are.

Partial pressure — The pressure which one of a mixture of con-fined gases would exert if it were the only gas present.

Percent — Number of molecules of a gas divided by the total number of molecules present gives the percentage of that gas. The percentage of that gas times the total pressure of all gases in a mixture gives the partial pressure of the gas.

Altitude, elevation, height — These refer to the linear distance from sea level to a summit, measured in meters or in feet, deter-mined by survey.

Use of Air by the Body

Ventilation — Usually refers to the movement of air into and out of the lungs, performed by movements of ribs and diaphragm.

Respiration — Commonly refers to the process of breathing; more accurately should include the use of oxygen by the cells as well as ventilation.

Respiratory Center — a collection of highly specialized cells in the lower part of the brain which controls the rate and depth of breathing. There may be several respiratory centers.

Oxygen transport system — Refers to the whole series of pro-cesses by which oxygen in the outside air passes through lungs to blood, is carried by blood to all parts of the body, passes from blood to tissue cells, and is used by the cells.

Trachea, bronchi, bronchioles—The trachea (windpipe) leads from mouth and nose and divides into main bronchi, which in turn divide into even smaller bronchioles that lead directly to air sacs which is where exchange of carbon dioxide and oxygen occurs. Often called the "respiratory or bronchial tree."

Alveolus, Alveolar air sac—The small delicate sac at the end of each bronchiole where gas exchange takes place.

Hypoxia, anoxia, anoxemia. These are used interchangably though they have slightly different meanings: Hypoxia means less oxygen; anoxia means no oxygen, and anoxemia means no oxygen in blood. Asphyxia should be reserved for suffocation.

Hypocapnia, acapnia, hypercapnia. These refer, respectively, to too little, no, and too much carbon dioxide, corresponding to similar words used to refer to oxygen. Eucapnia refers to a normal carbon dioxide level.

Hypoxic ventilatory drive (response). The change in rate and/or depth of breathing dictated by a decrease in inspired oxygen. It is an index of the sensitivity of the respiratory center to oxygen lack.

Carbon dioxide sensitivity. The responsiveness of the respiratory center to an increase or a decrease in carbon dioxide levels in the inspired air.

Maximal Breathing Capacity—The largest volume of air one can breathe in one minute.

Maximal Oxygen Uptake (VO2Max)—The largest amount of oxygen one can acquire while working to utmost capacity. It is used as a measure of work. This test indicates the volume of air one can move as well as the volume of oxygen passing from lungs to blood and is the usual way of measuring cardiorespiratory fitness.

Vital Capacity (VC)—The volume of air that can be exhaled after the fullest inspiration. Forced expiratory flow rate is the volume which can be expired, after full inspiration, in one minute.

Circulation and Blood

Capillaries — The smallest blood vessels which connect the terminal or smallest arteries (arterioles) to the smallest or terminal veins (venules), through which blood passes from the arteries to the veins, delivering oxygen and picking up carbon dioxide in the tissues as it does so. Pulmonary capillaries lie against the alveoli, and enable oxygen and carbon dioxide to move rapidly between blood and air. Tissue capillaries make a network in all other parts of the body.

Perfusion — Flow of blood through tissue such as the lung.

Ventilation-perfusion ratio or V/Q — The relationship — in the lung — between the ventilation of an area and the flow of blood through it. Poorly ventilated but well perfused areas are said to have functional shunts.

Interstitial — Between structures, such as cells or membranes.

Intercellular; intracellular — Between cells; within cells.

Hemoglobin — A complex substance containing four iron molecules which combine loosely with oxygen, picking it up from the alveoli in the lungs where the partial pressure is high, and discharging it to tissue cells where the pressure is low. Usual level is 13 to 15 grams per 100 mili-liters of blood.

Carboxy-hemoglobin — The compound formed when carbon monoxide attaches to hemoglobin, displacing oxygen. Methemoglobin is an irreversible form of hemoglobin formed when the ferrous ion is changed to the ferric form. Mutant Hemoglobins have slightly different molecular configurations and thus carry oxygen differently.

Hematocrit — The percentage of whole blood occupied by cells (mostly red cells). Usually 40 to 45%. Red cell count — the number of red blood cells in one mili-liter of blood. Usually 4 to 4.5 millions.

Oxygen carrying capacity — The amount of oxygen which the blood can carry, usually described in volumes percent — i.e. volumes percent — or volume of oxygen in 100 ml of blood. Combining power is the amount of oxygen which one gram of hemoglobin can pick up. As hemoglobin increases (at altitude for example) the carrying capacity of blood increases, but the combining power does not change.

Buffer—The salt formed from the combination of a weak acid with a strong base, (or v.v.) which is able to absorb hydrogen ions with little change in the pH (acidity or alkalinity) of the solution. Buffering power is used to define the amount of buffer in blood and is an approximation of the blood's ability to resist changes in acidity.

Carbonic anhydrase—an enzyme which facilitates conversion of carbon dioxide to carbonic acid, within the red cells, and probably assists the conversion to bicarbonate in the kidney. It is inhibited by acetazolamide (Diamox).

Clinical Terms

Diuretic—A substance, either natural or synthetic, which increases the formation of urine.

Edema—Fluid which accumulates outside of cells, within the loose tissue between cells, or (in lungs) within the air sacs or alveoli. Most prominent in feet and ankles after standing or sitting, and in face and hands after lying down.

Cyanosis—A bluish color to lips and nailbeds, due to lack of oxygen which leaves some of the hemoglobin in the unoxygenated form.

Ataxia—Staggering walk, an early sign of serious altitude illness. Uncoordinated motions of fingers and hands also occur but are usually not called ataxic.

Hallucinations—Illusions that one is seeing or hearing things that are not there—common in severe altitude illness.

Retinopathy, hemorrhages, cotton wool spots—At altitude blood flow in the back of the eye is greatly increased. Small leakages of blood from the capillaries are common above 17,500 feet. Less common is the accumulation of fluid in the retina, causing white spots that look like cotton.

Signs and Symptoms—Signs are evidences that can be seen or

heard or felt by others; symptoms are appreciable only by the individual who has them.

Miscellaneous Terms

Diffusion — The movement of one substance through another — for example of a gas throughout a confined space, or — more commonly — the passage of a gas through a barrier such as a semi-permeable membrane (which lets some substances through but not others).

Secretion — A process requiring energy which would enable, for example, oxygen to pass through a membrane (the alveolar wall) from a low pressure area to one of higher partial pressure. The lungs were once thought, erroneously, to secrete oxygen into the blood.

Membrane potential, bio-electric stability — Each cell has a very thin membrane encasing its contents. The membrane carries a tiny electric charge which enables it to maintain its integrity and to do its thing. This bio-electric potential requires oxygen to supply its energy. The Sodium pump is a molecular exchange dependent on the membrane potential and thus requiring oxygen, which pushes sodium out while holding potassium within cells. Failure of the sodium pump is thought to be the basic cause of altitude illness.

FURTHER READING

In the bibliography which follows I have tried to list some of the papers which have been most interesting or valuable to me. Obviously it is very incomplete; only one or two papers by some of the most prolific writers are included. A larger shortcoming is the difficulty the non-scientist may have in finding more material on a subject. Different groups and individuals have special talents and interests and publish many of the best papers, so in this section I have tried to indicate who they are, so that persons who have access to a good library, or even better, a medical library, can look up materials I have not shown here.

HIGH ALTITUDE MOUNTAINEERING. The American Alpine Journal (113 East 90th St., New York City 10028), the Alpine Journal (74 South Audley Street, London, W1Y 5FF, England) and Summit (P.O. Box 1899, Big Bear Lake, California, 92315) report most of the major climbs each year, and they (especially the American Alpine Journal) are a rich source. Some of the modern books about a given expedition contain helpful medical appendices. ACCIDENTS IN AMERICAN MOUNTAINEERING, published by the American Alpine Club, covers illnesses as well as accidents.

MOUNTAIN MEDICINE. Though altitude illness is only a part of this big topic, proceedings of various symposia (University of California, Davis) are helpful. Wilkerson's book MEDICINE FOR MOUNTAINEERING is the classic text, and others are in press (Auerbach and Geehr specifically).

HISTORY OF UNDERSTANDING ATMOSPHERE AND GASES. West's collection of classic papers is the best comprehensive source. The special books by Gilbert and Middleton (also referenced here) are very helpful. The Alembic Club facsimile editions are available in most libraries. Singer's SCIENCE, MEDICINE, AND HISTORY is a fascinating collection of essays, and Taton covers the period 1450 to 1800 in THE BEGINNINGS OF MODERN SCIENCE.

PHYSIOLOGY AND COMPARATIVE PHYSIOLOGY. Guyton's TEXTBOOK OF MEDICAL PHYSIOLOGY, and Schmidt-Nielsen's ANIMAL PHYSIOLOGY are excellent reading and about all anyone might want. Hermann Rahn has been giving us intriguing glimpses into little known areas for many years.

HIGH ALTITUDE PHYSIOLOGY. The best modern texts are by Heath and Williams, and by Ward. Van Liere is older but includes materials not found elsewhere. West's collection of old papers is invaluable. All of these are listed in the bibliography.

RESPIRATION. John Severinghaus, Jerry Dempsey, John West and Al Fishman are writing significant papers in this field. John Maher's group at the

224

Army Research Institute in Environmental Medicine (ARIEM) in Natick, Massachusetts, and John Reeves' laboratory in Denver are also very productive. In Seattle, Tom Hornbein and Rob Schoene are opening new areas and refining old concepts.

CIRCULATION AND OXYGEN TRANSPORT. Michael Hlastala, Robert Winslow, John Reeves, Marsh Tenney, Lorna Moore, George Brewer, and Cynthia Beall are major contributors. John Githens is a good source of material on sickle cell disease.

WORK AND INTERMEDIARY METABOLISM. In this flourishing, complicated field, John Sutton, Norman Jones, John West, Barbara Drinkwater, John Faulkner and the group at Natick, Massachusetts have contributed mightily.

ALTITUDE SICKNESS. John Dickinson in Kathmandu, Peter Hackett, Tom Hornbein, John Sutton, Gary Gray, Herbert Hultgren and John Reeves' Denver group are most busy in this field, but new names are constantly appearing.

ACCLIMATIZATION. Alberto Frisancho, Hugo Chiodi, Eugene Robin, Michael Ward, and again, the Natick group are major contributors. Bruce Dill and Ulrich Luft remain the giants of the past and contribute to the present.

SLEEP AND SLEEP DISORDERS. Though this may seem a minor field, it is increasingly important, particularly at altitude, and Kingman Strohl, Sukahamay Lahiri, John Weil, Gary Gray, C. Guilleminault, J. E. Remmers, Neil Cherniak, and A. J. Block have opened doors into promising new areas.

EUROPEAN AND ASIAN WORK. Many individuals working abroad are reporting important data and concepts. Though the majority of medical articles are in English, or have English abstracts, it is difficult to keep up with the world wide literature absent an expensive computer net. Some of the people who are leading the field are named below.

In England: Michael Ward, David Denison, Jim Milledge, Charles Clarke, Joe Bradwell, the indestructible Griffith Pugh, Peter Forster, and of course Donald Heath, and David Williams. In France: One thinks of Jacques Durand, Jean-Paul Richalet, and Pierre Desjours. In Switzerland: Paolo Cerretelli and Oswald Oelz. In Germany: Walter Brendel, Roman Zink, and Johannes Piiper. In Scandinavia: Nils Lassen and Bo Siesjo. In the Soviet Union: Oleg Gazenko, Eugene Gippenreiter and B. Malkin. In India and Nepal: Inder Singh and his colleagues, Balasubramanian, Viswanathan, John Dickinson and Malhotra. Japan, sending more mountaineers to the Himalayas in recent years than all other countries combined, is becoming very active, while China, administering the high Tibetan Plateau is deeply interested in chronic mountain sickness and acclimatization. In South America among the many are Reynarfarjee, pioneer Alberto Hurtado, Penaloza, Marticorena and Carlos Monge, Jr.

*   *   *   *   *

These are the topics and the people I know best. Obviously it is very incomplete and others will have different selections. I have left out many—but by looking at a few papers by those I have listed, sources multiply like branches and twigs on a tree. There is no end to what one can learn, and no end of teachers to learn from.

GUIDE TO REFERENCES

For those who may not be familiar with the names and numbers of the players in altitude physiology, I have listed the names of senior authors of the papers in this bibliography under some major headings. Look up the author and find the article(s) dealing with the subject.

ACCLIMATIZATION
Altitude Natives

Abelson	Houston
Baker	Hurtado
Barbashova	Kellogg
Cudaback	Lenfant
Denison	McFarland
Dill	Maher
Eastman	Matthews
Eckman	Morpurgo
Finch	Murray
Frisancho	Pugh
Haldane	Roy
	Schneider

ALTITUDE ILLNESSES
Acute Mountain Sickness

Cudaback	Rennie
Denison	Schneider
Hackett	Singh
Meehan	Urrie

Chronic Mountain Sickness
Houston
Monge
Ravenhill

High Altitude Cerebral Edema

Austin	Houston
Fishman	Ravenhill
Forster	Rennie
Forwand	Singh
Hackett	

High Altitude Pulmonary Edema

Gray	Lassen
Hanley	Moss
Houston	Ravenhill
Hultgren	Rennie
Hurtado	Singh
Hyers	Staub

High Altitude Retinal Hemorrhage

Cusick	Houston
Dempsey	Schumacher
Frayser	Spalter

Permanent Effects (see also HACE)
- Clark
- Pugh
- Ryn

BLOOD AND HEMOGLOBIN (see also Sickle Cell Disease)
- Jourdannet
- Perutz
- Viault

BREATHING AND LUNG (See also sleep)

CONTROL

Filley	Schoene
Michael	Sheldon
Phillipson	West

PHYSIOLOGY

Barcroft	Green
Cooper	Hefner
Cotton	Lilienthal
Cudkowitz	Schoene
Fitzgerald	West

CELL

Barbashova	Lehninger
Claude	Meerson
Jones	

CIRCULATION AND HEART

Balasubramanian	Vogel
Hultgren	Mortimer

DIET

Eckman	Hansen
Green	Stiles
Hannon	Sutton

EVEREST

Cerretelli	Schoene
Dejours	West
Henderson	

INTRODUCTION TO THE BIBLIOGRAPHY

Since I chose the bibliography for GOING HIGH three years ago, more than 1200 books and articles have been added to the library of approximately 25,000 publications which deal with high altitude and lack of oxygen. Choosing those which would be of interest and value to non-scientists as well as to scientists has been very difficult, and I make no apologies for the many omissions. Those who wish to go further can find rich sources at the end of the papers I chose. I gave preference to those which were most interesting and useful to me.

Some excellent books have appeared in the last few years and these should be the first place to look for more references. The new books tend to be collections of papers by leaders in the field, rather than original works. I made a special point of listing some of the older classics. Often these are distinguished by the elegance and imagination with which they are written — a characteristic woefully lacking in today's precise, dry jargon and complex medi-speak. These older books have stood the test of time and should be models for the writers of today and tomorrow.

BOOKS

AMERICAN ALPINE JOURNAL.
Published in June of each year by the American Alpine Club, 115 East 90th St., New York City 10028.

This journal contains a large section describing mountain expeditions in all parts of the world, as well as occasional medical articles. A yearly summary: ACCIDENTS IN AMERICAN MOUNTAINEERING includes a variety of illnesses and injuries on mountains.

MOUNTAIN MEDICINE.
University of California, Davis, California, 1983.

The most complete collection of papers on all aspects of mountain medicine yet published — the proceedings of the third Mountain Medicine Symposium held near Lake Tahoe in March 1983.

THE NATURAL AND MORALL HISTORIE OF THE EAST AND WEST INDIES
Acosta, Joseph
London, 1604

Early manuscripts such as this are difficult to find, and I am indebted to Ralph Kellogg for copies of the most interesting portions of this first clear description of the effects of altitude. Other translations call the author Jose d'Acosta.

THE RESPIRATORY FUNCTION OF THE BLOOD. PART I. LESSONS FROM HIGH ALTITUDES
Barcroft, Joseph
Cambridge University Press, Cambridge, 1925
This is one of the classics — an elegant discussion of hemoglobin and oxygen transport at sea level and altitude, as well as of altitude illness and acclimatization.

SIVALAYA
Baume, Louis
The Mountaineers, Seattle, 1980
Baume has collected records of all the major Himalayan ascents from the start of Himalayan climbing and in this gives invaluable information about every successful climb and every failure on peaks over 8,000 meters.

EARLY TRAVELLERS IN THE ALPS
de Beer, Gavin
Sidgwick and Jackson, London, 1930 and 1966
This is a fascinating collection of stories of early climbing and travelling in the Alps, with pictures of Scheuchzer's dragons, and stories about Windham, de Saussure and many others.

BAROMETRIC PRESSURE
Bert, Paul (1877)
Translated by M. A. and F. A. Hitchcock, College Book Co., Columbus, 1943
This is the largest collection known of anecdotes, accounts, experiments and speculations about high altitude. Bert spent years collecting records of mountaineers, explorers, balloonists and scientific observations. He describes various types of altitude illness, recounts the tragic and humorous experiences of early balloonists, and gives details of hundreds of experiments he performed in pressure chambers and in the laboratory.

HIGH ALTITUDE PHYSIOLOGY AND MEDICINE. Edited by W. Brendel and R. A. Zink. Springer Verlag, New York, 1982.
Forty-nine short papers presented at an international symposium dealing with high altitude, in Munich in 1980.

LIFE, HEAT, AND ALTITUDE
Dill, D. B.
Harvard University Press, Cambridge, 1938
A classic description of the impacts of temperature and oxygen on man.

A REMARKABLE MEDICINE HAS BEEN OVERLOOKED.
Jack Drefus. Simon and Schuster, New York, 1981.
The author presents a highly readable account of diphenylhydantoin (Dilantin) and why he believes it is not widely used. More than two thousand references are listed, describing the use of Dilantin for many afflictions, including evidence of its effects in hypoxia.

ENVIRONMENTAL STRESS. INDIVIDUAL HUMAN ADAPTATIONS
Folinsbee, Lawrence
Academic Press, New York, 1978.

HARVEY AND THE OXFORD PHYSIOLOGISTS.
Robert G. Frank, Jr. University of California Press. Berkeley. 1980.

A HISTORY OF FLYING
Gibbs-Smith, C. H.
Praeger, New York, 1954
   A complete review of aviation including an important table of dates of importance in aviation from 852 BC to 1953 AD.

OXYGEN AND LIVING PROCESSES.
Edited by Daniel L. Gilbert.
Springer-Verlag, New York, 1981.

DICTIONARY OF SCIENTIFIC BIOGRAPHY
Gillespie, Charles C.
Scribner, New York, 1980
   There are 16 volumes in this fascinating encyclopedia, in which are given biographical and critical sketches of most of the great scientists as far back as we know them. It is difficult not to read like a novel, so well done, and so filled with little-known detail are the sketches. A must for anyone interested in history of science, with a wealth of primary and secondary sources.

THE MONTGOLFIER BROTHERS AND THE INVENTION OF AVIATION, 1783–1784
Gillespie, Charles C.
Princeton University Press, Princeton, New Jersey, 1983
   This is a new, scholarly book about the first hot air balloons and how they evolved sufficiently to lift man from the earth. It is a fine companion piece to Robinson's THE DANGEROUS SKY, and Gibbs–Smith's A HISTORY OF FLYING.

THE EARLY MOUNTAINEERS
Gribble, Francis
T. Fisher Unwin, London, 1899
   Contains stories about Peter III, Domp Julian, Gesner, Leonardo and most other early climbers. Describes Gesner's climbing, and the Pontius Pilate legend in detail. Describes Scheuchzer's travels and has several good dragon pictures. The best source of early Alpina.

RESPIRATION
Haldane, John S.
Yale University Press, New Haven, 1922
Clarendon Press, Oxford, 1935
   One of the great milestones in our understanding of human respiration.

MOUNTAIN SICKNESS
Hackett, Peter
American Alpine Club, New York, 1980

This is a small (75 pp) handbook dealing with practical aspects of altitude illness as observed in the Himalayas; very useful to take on big mountain expeditions.

AN ANNOTATED BIBLIOGRAPHY OF ACUTE MOUNTAIN SICKNESS
Hall, W. H.
U.S. Army Research Institute of Environmental Medicine, Natick, 1964
Twenty-two papers, selected from publications in the last seventy years, are carefully described. Only acute mountain sickness is included. Most of the classical reports are included.

DE MOTU CORDIS
Harvey, William
Thomas, Springfield, 1957
This beautiful translation by Kenneth Franklin contains the Latin text as well and is the complete text of the famous report which Harvey made in the form of a letter to King Charles and to the Royal College of Physicians describing his experiments, logic and conclusions. Harvey does not mention the work of his predecessors; though he was certainly aware of what some had done, he almost certainly did not know that Ibn-Al-Nafis had almost precisely described the circulation four centuries earlier. This is a beautifully detailed and written book.

MAN AT HIGH ALTITUDE
Health, D., and D. R. Williams
Churchill Livingstone, London, 1977
An excellent and very complete book (290 pp) describing the pathology and physiology of adaptation and mal-adaptation in mountaineers and permanent residents. Written primarily for scientists, it is intelligible to anyone and a must for doctors interested in altitude. The second edition (1981) has been considerably expanded and brought up to date, though the bibliography has not been noticeably changed.

BIOMEDICINE PROBLEMS OF HIGH TERRESTRIAL ELEVATIONS
Hegnauer, S. H. (editor)
U.S. Army Research Institute of Environmental Medicine
Natick, 1969
This volume reports a two day symposium of specialists in various aspects of high altitude.

ADVENTURES IN RESPIRATION
Henderson, Yandell
Williams and Wilkins, Baltimore, 1939
Written in a highly readable style, this series of essays describes the early stirrings of research in this century by a friend and colleague of Haldane and Barcroft.

PHILOSOPHICAL EXPERIMENTS AND OBSERVATIONS.
Robert Hooke. W. and J. Innys, London, 1676.

REGULATION OF BREATHING.
Edited by Thomas F. Hornbein. Marcel Dekker, New York, 1981.

HIGH ALTITUDE PHYSIOLOGY STUDY
Houston, Charles S.
Queen City Printers Inc., Burlington, Vermont 1980
   A collection of forty-four papers published between 1968 and 1980 describing the work of the Arctic Institute High Altitude Physiology Study on Mount Logan in Canada.

EXERCISE AND ALTITUDE
Jokl, E., and P. Jokl
S. Karger, Basel, 1968
   An excellent collection of data and theories regarding capability and the constraints on exertion at various altitudes. Of special interest are the chapters on Olympic and Pan-American contests. Excellent reproductions of old photos.

WOMEN AND SPORTS
Kaplan, Janice
Viking Press, New York, 1979.

OXYGEN TRANSPORT TO HUMAN TISSUES.
Edited by Jack A. Loeppky and Marvin L. Riedesel. Elzevier Biomedical. New York. 1982.
   A collection of thirty talks given at a Symposium honoring Dr. Ulrich Luft in Albuquerque, New Mexico in 1982.

THE OUTDOOR WOMAN'S GUIDE TO SPORTS, FITNESS AND NUTRITION.
Maughan, J. J. and Kathryn Collins. Stackpole Books, Harrisburg, PA, 1983.

EFFECTS OF HIGH ALTITUDE ON HUMAN BIRTH.
McClung, Jean.
Harvard University Press, Cambridge, 1969.

THE HISTORY OF THE BAROMETER
Middleton, W.E.K.
Johns Hopkins Press, Baltimore, 1964
   This is a detailed scholarly book filled with anecdotes and examples of the first stirring of knowledge about the weight of the atmosphere, the existence of a vacuum, and the evolution of barometers. Middleton deals with Berti's experiments, with the curious Pascal letter, Torricelli, Baliani, and the pioneering observations by Perier on the Puy-de-Dome. The last sections deal with modern barometers of various types and sensitivities.

ACCLIMATIZATION IN THE ANDES
Monge, Carlos
Johns Hopkins Press, Baltimore, 1948
   Monge senior was one of the pioneers in altitude research in South America and this brief discussion of acquired and inherited acclimatization is interesting, though the viewpoint (and bibliography) are almost entirely South

American. Monge was first to describe the chronic form of altitude illness which bears his name.

HIGH ALTITUDE DISEASES
Monge, Carlos, and Carlos Monge Jr.
Thomas, Springfield, 1966

A brief (96 pages) review of what was known in South America about altitude illness at the time. The bibliography is almost exclusively from South American literature.

LIFE OF MAN ON THE HIGH ALPS
Mosso, Angelo
Fisher Unwin, London, 1898

This book, admirably translated by Kiesow from the second Italian edition, is rich with work done on Monte Rosa and in Milan by one of the major explorers of altitude physiology in the 19th century.

WOMEN AND SPORT: FROM MYTH TO REALITY
Oglesby, Carole
Lea and Ferbiger, Philadelphia, 1978.

THE GASES OF THE ATMOSPHERE
Ramsay, William
MacMillan, New York, 1902

A fascinating collection of anecdotes and experiments done by Boyle, Priestley, Cavendish, Scheele and others written by the man who isolated argon.

L'ADAPTATION A L'ALTITUDE ET LE MAL DES MONTAGNES.
G. Ringebach.
Maloine, Paris, 1983.

A summary (in French) of current knowledge and understanding of high altitude physiology and clinical mountain sickness. Of special value is the bibliography which includes 550 references, many of them not known in this country.

THE DANGEROUS SKY
Robinson, Douglas H.
University of Washington Press, Seattle, 1974

An excellent history of man's attempts to fly, including a great deal of information about lack of oxygen in aviation.

ANIMAL PHYSIOLOGY: ADAPTATION AND ENVIRONMENT.
Schmidt-Nielsen, Knut. Cambridge University Press, London. 1979.

This is a fascinating and delightfully written text which deals with comparative physiology in all sorts of animals. Filled with illustrations, it gives the average reader insight into the myriad ways living organisms learn to live in different environments.

THE PEAK EXPERIENCE: HIKING AND CLIMBING FOR WOMEN
Seghers, Carroll
Bobbs-Merrill, New York, 1979.

HYPOXIA: MAN AT ALTITUDE.
Edited by John Sutton, Norman Jones, and Charles Houston.
Thieme-Stratton. New York, 1982.

Thirty-eight papers and many abstracts presented at the Second International Hypoxia Symposium at Banff in 1981 deal with the effects of hypoxia from many causes, with case reports of several episodes of mountain illnesses. Collected papers from the Third Hypoxia Symposium are in press and will appear in early 1984 from Alan Liss, New York.

GIVE ME THE HILLS
Underhill, Miriam
Methuen, New York, 1956.

One of the most delightful books about women climbers in the early twentieth century, written by an outstanding mountaineer.

ANOXIA, ITS EFFECTS ON THE BODY
Van Liere, E. J., and J. C. Stickney
University of Chicago Press, Chicago, 1962

First published in 1942, this is a complete inventory of the effects of oxygen lack on various organs and systems of the body and probably the richest source of bibliography to that date; the edition of 1962 is a reprint rather than an updated revision of an invaluable work.

MOUNTAIN MEDICINE
Ward, M.
Crosby Lockwood, Staples, London, 1975

This is an encyclopedia of all aspects of mountain medicine, including altitude, cold, sun, illness and injury. Written in a staccato summary style it is most useful as a reference.

RESPIRATORY PHYSIOLOGY
West, J. B.
Williams and Wilkins, Baltimore, 1974

The most compact and readable book on how the lungs work and how oxygen is transferred to and transported by blood. Many diagrams and tables. Deals mainly with normal physiology and thus is an essential basic work in understanding altitude illness. Easily readable by non-physicians.

HIGH ALTITUDE PHYSIOLOGY.
Edited by John B. West
Hutchinson Ross. Stroudsburg, Pennsylvania, 1981.

Most of the important papers in high altitude physiology going back to Acosta are collected in this useful book, one of the Benchmark series of classic papers in physiology.

PHYSIOLOGICAL FACTORS RELATING TO TERRESTRIAL ALTITUDES
Wulff, L. Y., I. A. Braden, F. H. Shillito and J. F. Tomashefski
Ohio State University Press, Columbus, 1968

A collection of some 4,000 references relating to high altitude problems of many types. Though not annotated, it is a valuable resource book, probably the most complete of recent bibliographies.

HOHENKLIMA UND BERGWANDERUNGEN
Zuntz, N., A. Loewy, F. Muller and W. Caspari
Deutsches Verlagshaus, Berlin, 1906.
    A massive collection of studies, in German, by physiologists working in the Alps.

PAPERS AND PEOPLE

Abelson, A., Baker, P. T., et al. Altitude, migration, and fertility in the Andes. Population Biology. 21(1), 12, 1974.
    Using anthropological and sociological techniques Andean populations were examined to determine the impact upon fertility, live births, and infant mortality of altitude hypoxia and of migration from high to low or low to high altitude. Despite the complexity of such studies, evidence suggests that altitude decreases fertility, increases neonatal mortality and increases the probability of birth defects.

Abelson, Andrew. Altitude and Fertility. Human Biology. 48(1):83–92, 1976.

ANAXAGORAS (500-428 BC)
    One of the philosophers during the Golden Age of Pericles in Athens, Anaxagoras built on the principles advanced by Empedocles, holding that matter was infinitely divisible, and that all things were held together in an apparently uniform and motionless form. He wrote only that one important paper and has not had much permanent impact.

ARISTOTLE (384-322 BC)
    Of all the great philosopher/scientists in the Golden Age of Greece, his is one of the most permanently and best known names. His scientific concepts were based on logic: he believed the universe to be finite and centered about the earth. Outside of his universe there could be nothing, inside of it there could be no emptiness, i.e. no vacuum. He believed in the four basic elements of fire, air, water and earth as defined by Empedocles, but rejected the latter's atomic theory. Some consider Aristotle the founder of anatomy, because of his studies of the heart and circulatory system. He believed that the pulsation of the heart was due to "boiling" of the blood, which then flowed to the lungs to be cooled. Because of the way he prepared his animals for study, he did not recognize that there were four rather than three chambers in the heart, nor did he distinguish between arteries and veins or recognize the existence of the heart valves. His influence on all of the sciences endured for a thousand years, being challenged successfully only during the Renaissance.

Austin, F., Carmichael, M., et al. Neurological manifestations of chronic pulmonary insufficiency. New England Journal of Medicine. 257(13): 580-590, 1957.

Avery, M. E. and Frantz, I. D. To breathe or not to breathe? What have we learned about apneic spells and sudden infant death? New England Journal of Medicine:309:107–8. 1983.

Baker, P. T. Human adaptation to high altitude. Science. 163: 1149-56, March 14, 1969.

A summary of knowledge obtained and in progress of being obtained in the high Peruvian Andes, strongly suggesting some aspects of the natives' adaptation to high altitude requires lifelong exposure and may be based on a genetic structure different from that of lowlanders.

Balasubramanian, V., Kaushik, V., et al. Effects of high altitude hypoxia on left ventricular systolic time intervals in man. British Heart Journal. 37: 272-276, 1975.

Balke, B., Daniels, J. T., and Faulkner, J. A. Training for maximum performance at altitude. In EXERCISE AT ALTITUDE. Excerpta Medica Monograph of International Symposium, Milan, September 29–October 2, 1966.

Barbashova, Z. Cellular level of adaptation. Handbook of Physiology, 4:37. Washington, D.C.: American Physiology Society, 1964.

Barcroft, J., Cooke, A., et al. The flow of oxygen through the pulmonary epithelium. Journal of Physiology. 53: 450, 1920.

In this classic paper Barcroft describes the definitive experiments at Cerro de Pasco which proved that oxygen passed from lungs to blood by simple diffusion. This put an end to the secretion theory. Especially interesting from a historical view is the use of arterial sampling for the first time in high altitude research.

BEECKMAN, ISAAC (1588–1637)

Primarily interested in physics, mechanics, and meteorology, he was a progressive thinker, and much concerned with teaching physics and mathematics to the common man. He believed that the universe was infinite, he subscribed to the atomic theory, and he came close to understanding the circulation of the blood. He seems to have understood how pumps worked, and anticipated Torricelli in several theories.

BERNARD, CLAUDE (1813–1878)

Although he is one of the best known physiologists, he was an average student, passing examinations only with difficulty. Fortunately he came under the influence of some of the great physicians of his time, fell in love with physiological experimentation rather than medical practice, and received many honors for his studies of digestive enzymes, liver function, and the autonomic nervous system. He was a great experimenter, and as his studies advanced, his horizons widened and the concept of the constancy of the internal environment became central to most of his experiments and writing. Apparently he was the first to recognize that carbon monoxide killed by replacing oxygen in blood, and he was a pioneer in the study of both toxic and beneficial medications and how they were metabolized. He was the first to recognize the principle of homeostasis—the tendency of living organisms to maintain their own innate stability.

BERT, PAUL (1833-1886)

Truly the father of high altitude physiology, Bert was also a zoologist, physiologist, and a pioneer in transplant surgery. He was also active and prominent in politics, and his textbooks of natural history, zoology, and the physical sciences were widely printed and translated. Claude Bernard had the greatest influence on Paul Bert and was largely responsible for Bert's major work on barometric pressure. Although less well known than his work at high altitude, his studies of caisson disease (bubble formation in the blood of divers brought up from great depth) were equally innovative. He was primarily a teacher, experimenter, politician, and never practiced medicine.

BERTI, GASPARO (1600-1643)

Although he was primarily interested in astronomy and physics, and a professor of mathematics, Berti's major contribution was the apparatus which he built sometime between 1640 and 1643, apparently inspired by Galileo, which led Torricelli toward the modern barometer. None of Berti's own writing has survived, and most of what we know is from secondary sources. Although there is no doubt that he built the first apparatus successfully demonstrating the principle of the barometer, at first he was unconvinced that a vacuum existed above the barometric column, because a sound generated in that space could be heard, but Maignan showed him how this had happened. Torricelli received a letter describing Berti's work in 1644 and immediately realized that using mercury in place of wine, water, or honey would make the apparatus far more manageable. Although Berti made the first "barometer" Torricelli made it practical.

BLACK, JOSEPH (1728-1799)

In addition to carrying on a busy and distinguished medical practice, Black was a brilliant and popular chemistry teacher, lecturing without notes, demonstrating his experiments with unfailing success, and attracting students from all over the world. His experimental methods were very precise, and he was the first to demonstrate the qualities of carbon dioxide, which he called "fixed air" and recognized as a product of animal metabolism. His experiments with heat were even more important. Black recognized that air was necessary for all forms of combustion, was quite ambiguous in his treatment of the phlogiston theory, and after Lavoisier's work was known, gradually abandoned the phlogiston theory.

Block, A., Boysen, P., et al. Sleep apnea, hypopnea and oxygen desaturation in normal subjects. New England Journal of Medicine. 300(10), March 8, 1979.

BOERHAAVE, HERMANN (1668-1738)

Holding three of the five professorships in the medical school at Leiden, Boerhaave was one of the great teachers of his time, attracting students from all over Europe. He not only lectured for four or five hours a day, but he was also a brilliant bedside teacher and established the modern system of history, physical examination, diagnosis, course of illness, and autopsy. He did not have a clear concept of red blood cells, and his somewhat ambivalent interest in alchemy is indicative of the confusion which still existed in science in Europe during that time. With extraordinary patience, he studied the possibility of transmutation of elements, for example, distilling mercury over 500 times, shaking a sample of mercury continuously for 8½ months and then distilling it repeatedly, and even boiling one sample of mercury for 15½ years.

BORRICHIUS (BORCH), OLAUS (1626–1690)
Borch, a Dane, studied medicine first but became better known as a professor of botany and chemistry. He had a large and busy medical practice, and wrote extensively about a wide variety of subjects. In one of his many experiments, he decomposed potassium nitrate to generate oxygen in 1678, but apparently did not pursue the subject.

BOYLE, ROBERT (1627–1691)
Born in Ireland, Boyle achieved major influence through his extraordinary work in philosophy, chemistry, physics, and as a founder and principal influence in the Royal Society. Of his wide interests, his best known work is in the physics of air. He learned of Von Guericke's air pump, adopted Hooke's design, and confirmed the observations of Torricelli and Berti. He demonstrated that sound could not be transmitted in a vacuum (thus showing that Maignan was correct when he told Berti that the bell was heard in Berti's barometer because the sound was transmitted via the metal arm which held the bell). Boyle studied the behavior of gases, the vacuum, and the properties of matter throughout his life. He supported the concept of atomic structure of all matter, although he used the less specific term "corpuscle." He was a great experimenter, and described all of his experiments in immense detail so that others might repeat them.

Boyle, R. Tracts: Containing suspicions about some hidden qualities of the air. London, 1674.

CAVALLO, TIBERIUS (1749–1809)
Though born in Italy Cavallo soon settled in England and took up experimental physics at first with atmospheric electricity, studies inspired by Benjamin Franklin. He then studied the physics of the atmosphere, developed an improved air pump, and wrote a book on the nature and properties of air and "other permanently elastic fluids" as gases were then known. His book "The History and Practice of Aerostation," which dealt primarily with balloons, is a classic.

CAVENDISH, HENRY (1731–1810)
A bachelor who wrote no books and few articles in his long career in natural philosophy, Cavendish was a recluse. Inspired by Newton he extended the studies made by Black on "fixed air" and heat. He was a firm believer in

phlogiston even after Priestley had published his work with oxygen. One of his more extraordinary accomplishments was "the weighing of the world" using a torsion balance, and rounding out Newton's law of gravitation.

Cerretelli, P. Limiting factors to oxygen transport on Mount Everest. Journal of Applied Physiology. 40: 658-667, 1976.

CESALPINO, ANDREA (1519–1603)
Cesalpino was a philosopher and physician, a follower of Aristotle, and a pioneer in the study of circulation. He realized that the heart pumped blood throughout the body, through the arteries and received blood from the veins. He described the valves of the heart and pulmonary vessels although he failed to put together a coherent picture of circulation as Harvey later did.

Clark, Charles F., Heaton, R.K., and Wiens, A. N. Neuopsychological functioning after prolonged high altitude exposure in mountainering. Aviation, Space and Environmental Medicine. 54(3):202–207. March 1983.

Claude, A. The coming of age of the cell. Science. 189: 433-436, August 8, 1975.
This was Claude's acceptance speech for his Nobel prize in Physiology or Medicine in 1974 and is a beautifully written and inspiring summary of what we know about cells today.

Claybaugh, J. R. et al. Antidiuretic hormone responses to eucapnic and hypocapnic hypoxia in humans. Journal of Applied Physiology, 53:815–823, 1982.

Cooper, K. R. and Phillips, B. Effect of short-term sleep loss on breathing. Journal of Applied Physiology. 53:855–858, 1982.

Cotton, E. K. and Grunstein, M. M. Effects of hypoxia on respiratory control in neonates at high altitude. Journal of Applied Physiology. 48:587–595. 1980.

Crawford, R. D. and Severinghaus, J. W. CSF pH and ventilatory acclimatization to altitude. Journal of Applied Physiology. 45:275–283. 1978.

Cudaback, D. D. Effect of altitude on performance and health at 4km telescopes. University of California (in manuscript).
In this comprehensive summary of altitude illness, the author takes an overview of all evidence dealing with the effects of medium altitude (up to 15,000 feet.)

Cudkowicz, L., Spielvogel, H., and Zubieta, G. Respiratory studies in women at high altitude. Respiration. 29:393–426, 1972.

Cusick, P., Benson, O., et al. Effect of anoxia and of high concentrations of oxygen on the retinal vessels: Preliminary report. Staff Meetings of the Mayo Clinic, 15: 500-502, 1940.

Dejours, P. Mount Everest and beyond:breathing air. In A COMPANION TO ANIMAL PHYSIOLOGY edited by Taylor, C. R. et al. Cambridge University Press, 1982.

Dempsey, L., O'Donnell, J., et al. Carbon monoxide retinopathy. American Journal of Ophthalmology. 82(5): 692-693, 1976.

Denison, D. Hypoxia. In Weiner and Edholm, (ed), "Principles and Practice of Human Physiology." Academic Press, London, 1979.

Dill, D. B. Physiological adjustments to altitude changes. Journal American Medical Association, 205: 123, September 9, 1968.

Physiological adaptation to high altitude involves rapid responses in respiration and slower responses in nervous, muscular, and cardiovascular systems. An excellent criterion of adaptation is measurement of the capacity for supplying oxygen to tissues: the oxygen consumption (VO2 maximum). Such measurements reveal four stages of response. At 10,000 feet stage 1 is reached in minutes, VO2 max declines 10%. In one to three days, (stage 2), it declines another 10%; this is the stage of unpleasant subjective responses. In a few weeks, stage 3, performance approaches the level of stage 1. Red blood cell volume increases in stage 4, reaching its maximum after a year or more. Performance improves pari-passu: eventually sea-level performance can be achieved at 13,200 feet. Above 17,500 feet there is deterioration rather than adaptation.

Dill, D. B. and Evans, D. S. Report barometric pressure! Journal of Applied Physiology. 29(6): 914-916, December, 1970.

A brief but authoritative statement concerning the variations in barometric pressure due to weather, different latitudes, and different seasons. A standard atmosphere pressure altitude curve is included.

Drinkwater, Barbara. Response of women mountaineers to maximal exercise during hypoxia. Aviation, Space, and Environmental Medicine. 50(7):657–662. 1979.

Eastman, J. Mount Everest in utero: President's address. American Journal Obstetrics and Gynecology. 64(4): 701, 1954.

Eckman, M., Barach, A., et al. Effect of diet on altitude tolerance. Journal of Aviation Medicine. 16(15): 328-340, October 1945.

Elliott, P. R. and Atterbom, H. A. Comparison of exercise responses of males and females during acute exposure to hypobaria. Aviation, Space, and Environmental Medicine. 49(2):415–418, 1978.

EMPEDOCLES (492–432 BC)

This early Greek philosopher originated the four element theory of matter, believing that earth, water, air and fire were the "roots of all things" and that there were two forces — love and hate — which moved mankind. He believed that animals developed both by chance and by natural selection, and Darwin quoted his work as cited by Aristotle whom he influenced profoundly. Most of what is known about him is overlaid with legend. He is said to have stopped an epidemic by diverting two rivers, to have changed the climate in a valley by building a wall across a gorge, and to have revived a woman who had been without pulse or respiration for thirty days. His alleged leap into the volcanic crater of Etna may be myth, or impelled by belief in his immortality, or a prank!

Faulkner, J. A., Kollias, J., et al. Maximum aerobic capacity and running performance at altitude. Journal of Applied Physiology. 24: 685-691, 1968.

Faulkner, J. A. Maximum exercise at medium altitude. In FRONTIERS OF FITNESS. Edited by R. T. Shephard. Charles C. Thomas. Springfield. 1971.

Faulkner, J. A., Daniels, J. T., and Balke. Effects of training at moderate altitude on physical performance capacity. Journal of Applied Physiology. 26:85–87, 1967.

Filley, G., Swanson, G., et al. Chemical breathing controls: slow, intermediate and fast. Clinics in Chest Medicine 1(1): 13-32, January, 1980.

Finch, C. and Lenfant, C. Oxygen transport in man. New England Journal of Medicine. 286: 407-415, February 24, 1972.

> Oxygen transport is a corporate process involving several organs, each with its own regulatory system. Individual diseases of the heart, lungs or blood may impair the functional capacity of a single component, yet oxygen transport is sustained by adjustments in the remainder of the transport system.

Fishman, R. Brain edema. New England Journal of Medicine. 293: 706, October 2, 1975.

> A brief, tightly written review of the various pathophysiology of brain edema from various causes; management is discussed.

Fitzgerald, M. P. The changes in the breathing and the blood at various altitudes. Philosophical Transactions of the Royal Society. Series B: 203:351–371, 1913.

> This is the full report of this remarkable woman's work on alveolar air samples drawn at various altitudes long before many women were daring such efforts.

Forster, P.J.G. Work at high altitude: a study of the United Kingdom infra red telescope, Mauna Kea, Hawaii. (in manuscript).

> This is an important study of 41 shiftworkers working at 14,000 feet while sleeping at 9,000 feet, and 19 commuters, who lived at sea level but commuted daily to the summit.

Forwand, S., Lansdowne, M., et al. Effect of acetazolamide on acute mountain sickness. New England Journal of Medicine. 279: 839, 1968.

> In a double-blind study, either placebo or acetazolamide was given to forty-three subjects rapidly transported to 12,800 feet for five days. Significant reductions were observed in the most prominent symptoms of acute mountain sickness, but the mechanism of action was not identified.

Frayser, R., Houston, C., et al. Retinal hemorrhage at high altitude. New England Journal of Medicine. 282: 1183, 1970.

> Nine out of twenty-five individuals taken to 17,500 feet were found to have retinal hemorrhages. Of seventeen persons who went up rapidly six had hemorrhages; of eight who climbed slowly to altitude, three showed hemorrhages. Incidence of retinal hemorrhage was unrelated to other symptoms of

altitude sickness, but seemed to be reduced in the nine individuals premedicated with acetazolamide. This is the first report of retinal hemorrhage in healthy individuals exposed to high altitude hypoxia.

Frayser, R., Houston, C., et al. The response of the retinal circulation to altitude. Archives of Internal Medicine. 127: 708, 1971.

Individuals taken rapidly or slowly to 17,500 feet showed increases in retinal blood flow of 89% over control values within two hours, and of 128% over control after four days. Retinal blood flow increased by 105% over control values in acclimatized subjects. Both arterioles and venules show increased diameter and tortuosity beginning a few hours after arrival at altitude.

Freemon, F. "Sleep Research—A Critical Review." Charles C. Thomas, Springfield, 1972.

Frisancho, A. Roberto. Perspectives on functional adaptation of the high altitude native. In press 1983.

GALEN (129-199)

Few physicians have more profoundly influenced medicine than did this Roman who served as physician to the gladiators after completing twelve years of medical studies. He believed in a "four-fold scheme" which included the four humors of the body, the four elements, the four seasons, the ages of man, and other factors in a harmonious whole. His greatest work was titled "Anatomical Procedures" but was based on observation rather than dissection. He accepted the view of Erasistratus that blood entered the right ventricle from the veins, and was prevented from returning by the tricuspid valve. From the right ventricle it went to the lungs by the pulmonary artery and nourished the lungs. He felt that the heart worked as does a bellows, actively dilating and passively contracting. He showed that the heart and vessels always contained blood, while Erasistratus had thought that sometimes they could contain air. Galen is best known for his immense pharmacopeia, which dictated medical treatment for many centuries.

GALILEI, GALILEO (1564–1642)

His is one of the most famous names in mathematics, physics, and astronomy. He was a firm supporter of Copernicus, and for this was examined by the Inquisition, condemned to prison, but the sentence was commuted to house arrest for life. His most famous studies were made possible by the thirty power telescope he developed in 1609, and he is best known for his work in astronomy and in the motions of falling bodies. Galileo treated the existence of a vacuum in a curious way. Having been told that suction pumps and siphons could not lift water beyond a certain height, he explained this with the theory that water had its own inner limited tensile strength just as a rope or wire will break of its own weight if long enough. He failed to understand that the weight of the atmosphere was the cause of the siphon phenomenon and rejected it even after Baliani had clearly explained it to him.

Getts, A. G., and Hill, H. Sudden infant death syndrome: incidence at various altitudes. Developments in Medical Child Neurology. 24:64–68, 1982.

Gilbert, D. L. The first documented report of mountain sickness: the China or Headache Mountain story. Respiration Physiology:52:315–26 (1983).

Gilbert, D. L. The first documented description of mountain sickness: the Andean or Pariacaca story. Respiration Physiology: 52:327–47 (1983).

These two articles, representing years of historical research, define in detail the earliest descriptions of AMS, where it occurred and what was thought about its cause. The China story goes back over 2000 years; the Andean tale is a mere 500 years old. Extensive bibliographies accompany both of these important papers.

Githens, J. H., Phillips, C. R., et al. Effects of altitude in persons with sickle hemoglobinopathies. Rocky Mountain Medical Journal. 72:12: 505-9, December 1975.

Describes several different syndromes manifested at altitude by persons with sickle cell anemia, sickle trait, and thalassemia and concludes that there is appreciably larger risk in patients with sickle/hemoglobin C disease and sickle/thalassemia than with other sickle hemoglobinopathies, but the incidence is not clear.

Gray, G. Studies on altitude illness with special reference to high altitude pulmonary edema. Ph.D. thesis. University of Toronto, Institute of Medical Science, 1976.

An extensive and scholarly review of various theories of high altitude pulmonary edema, with introduction of the concept that platelet emboli may contribute to inequalities of perfusion and result in local patches of edema.

Green, C., Butts, J., et al. The relationship of anoxic susceptibility to diet. Journal of Aviation Medicine. 16(15): 328-340, October 1945.

Green, J. F., M. Sheldon, and G. Gurtner. Alveolar-to-arterial PCO_2 differences. Journal of Applied Physiology. 54(2):349–354. 1983.

GUERICKE, OTTO (1602–1686)

Although he was destined for politics and studied law, he became preoccupied by the concept of space and soon became a convert of Copernicus. He wondered about the possibility of a vacuum, how heavenly bodies might affect each other across the emptiness of space, and whether or not space was indeed bounded or limitless. In 1647 he made the first functioning suction pump and ten years later constructed the famous Magdeburg Sphere, which consisted of two hemispheres made of heavy copper, fitted tightly together with a gasket, and then evacuated. The difficulty of separating the evacuated spheres was convincing evidence of the pressure of the atmosphere.

Hackett, P., Rennie, D., et al. The incidence, importance, and prophylaxis of acute mountain sickness. Lancet. 1149-55, November 27, 1976.

A review of the authors' experience with 273 unacclimatized trekkers to Everest, seen at Pheriche (4,243 m). Several severe cases of HAPE and HACE are reported, and evidence advanced that acetazolamide decreases the severity of illness.

Hackett, P. and Rennie, D. Rales, peripheral edema, retinal hemorrhage and acute mountain sickness. American Journal of Medicine.67: 214-218, August 1979.

This is a clinical summary of studies made on 200 persons trekking in the Mount Everest region in 1977-8. Pulmonary rales were noted in 23%, peripheral edema in 18% and retinal hemorrhages in 4%. The study was conducted at 14,000 feet before and after ascent to 18,000 feet. Half of those who flew to 9,000 feet, and a third of those walking to that altitude over a period of 10-14 days suffered symptoms of acute mountain sickness.

Hackett, P. H., Reeves, J. T., et al. Control of breathing in Sherpas at low and high altitude. Journal of Applied Physiology. 49(3):374–79. 1980.

Hackett, P. H. and Rennie, D. B., Acute Mountain Sickness. In press.

Haldane, J., Kellas, A., et al. Experiments on acclimatization to reduced atmospheric pressure. Journal of Physiology. 53: 185, 1920.

HALES, STEPHEN (1677-1761)

Born to an old and distinguished family, Hales took a general education at Cambridge, where he was strongly influenced by Newton's heritage and by Stukeley, but he himself had no formal medical training. Throughout his life he was a clergyman, but his curiosity and ingenuity led him into pioneering studies of blood pressure and circulation for which he was made a member of the Royal Society. At the time the magnitude of the arterial blood pressure was unknown, some contending that it was very large and might actually power muscle contraction. Hales' simple measurement of the arterial blood pressure in a mare ensured him permanent fame, and led him to further studies of the heart, the veins and capillaries, and the mechanics of blood flow. He was very versatile, and his most original—though less known—work involved the force which could raise the sap in plants and trees often to great heights. He demonstrated transpiration, showing that leaves give off not only moisture but also tiny bubbles of gas. This led him to study the gas laws and the composition of air as defined by Hooke, Mayow, and Boyle. He repeated Mayow's experiments, placing either a candle or a small animal under a bell jar and demonstrating that some element in air was consumed before the candle was extinguished or the animal died. Taking this a bit further in a series of re-breathing experiments on himself, he showed that some element of air was consumed and another gas produced by the body, which would not support life. This convinced him that "fresh air" was essential to health, and led him to invent ventilators for purifying the air in hospitals and on ship-board, a major advance in public health.

Hanley, Daniel F. Health problems at the Olympic games. Journal of the

American Medical Association. 221:987–90. August 28, 1972.

Hannon, J. P. Alterations in serum electrolyte levels in women during high altitude (4300 m) acclimatization. International Journal of Biometrics. 14:201–209, 1970.

Hannon, J. P. Altitude acclimatization and basal ventilatory function of women. Federation Proceedings. 34:410, 1975.

Hannon, J. P. Nutritional aspects of high altitude exposure in women. American Journal of Clinical Nutrition. 29:604–613, 1976.

Hansen, J. P. and Evans, W. A hypothesis regarding the pathophysiology of acute mountain sickness. Archives of Environmental Health. 21: 666-669, November 1970.

Hansen, J. P., Hartley, L., et al. Arterial oxygen increase by high carbohydrate diet at altitude. Journal of Applied Physiology. 33(4): 441-5, October 1972.

HARVEY, WILLIAM (1578–1657)
> After receiving his doctorate in medicine at Cambridge, Harvey studied under some of the great anatomists in Italy, returning to London where he became a distinguished physician and an important influence in the Royal College, doing his historic work on circulation in his free time. He had a broad interest in the arts and a wide circle of friends outside of the sciences and was untiring in his studies of the entire animal world, though he is best known for his "discovery" of the action of the heart and circulation. Most of his papers on other areas of natural history were lost in the Great Fire of London. Though Harvey followed Aristotle rather than Galen, his unique contribution came from his ability to put together many theories and observations of others and his own dissections and calculations, to produce the first complete and accurate explanation of the coursing of blood through arteries, veins and tissues, impelled by the heart as a pump. Many others had accurately described parts of the system—Galen's concept of the greater circulation was one bit, and Colombo's description of the circulation through the lungs another, but Harvey was the first to make a coherent description of the whole, except for Ibn-al-Nafis whose work was unknown for many centuries. The logical steps through which he reached his conclusions are fascinatingly revealed in his great book.

Hedemark, L. L. and Kronenberg, R. S. Ventilatory and heart rate responses to hypoxia and hypercapnia during sleep in adults. Journal of Applied Physiology. 53:307–312, 1982.

Heffner, J. E. et al. Platelet induced pulmonary hypertension and edema. Chest., 83:78S, June 1983 Supplement.

Henderson, Y. The last thousand feet on Everest. Nature. 3631, 921-923, June 3, 1939.
> A brief summary of all of the existing evidence about alveolar and arterial oxygenation at extreme heights with an explanation of why acclimatization imposes a handicap at extreme altitude.

HOOKE, ROBERT (1635–1702)

Although described as sickly all of his life, Hooke was a precocious genius whose talents included mathematics, mechanics, and physiology. Before he was 18 he had mastered geometry, and the organ, and described thirty ways of flying, then entered Oxford where he was befriended by some of the most brilliant men of his time. As assistant to Robert Boyle, he built an improved version of Guericke's air pump, and undoubtedly contributed importantly to formulating Boyle's famous gas laws. By 1660 he had invented a method for using a spring instead of a pendulum to drive a clock, and actually drew up a patent for this in 1660, although Huygens built the first spring watch in 1674. He joined the Royal Society, becoming curator responsible for several new scientific demonstrations for each weekly meeting. He published his most important book *Micrographia* in 1665, containing hundreds of observations made through the newly invented microscope. Less well known are Hooke's studies of air, combustion, and respiration. He showed that the function of breathing was to supply fresh air to the lungs rather than to cool or to pump blood, and along with Mayow, Boyle, and Lower came close to isolating oxygen. He was a tireless inventor producing brilliant and innovative ideas and a variety of scientific instruments. He was described as a "difficult man in an age of difficult men whose life was punctuated by bitter quarrels which refused to be settled."

HOPPE-SEYLER, ERNST FELIX (1825–1895)

Though he was a physician his major work was in physiological chemistry, a discipline which he really established, editing the first bio-chemical journal in Germany. He examined the structures of chlorophyll and blood, and obtained hemoglobin in crystalline form for the first time.

Houston, C. Operation Everest, a study of acclimatization to anoxia. U.S. Naval Medical Bulletin. 46: 12, 1783, 1946.

This report describes a thirty-five day study in which four volunteers were gradually decompressed in a chamber to a pressure altitude of 23,500 feet and then to 29,000 feet while many tests were done to elucidate the factors contributing to acclimatization.

Houston, C. Acute pulmonary edema of high altitude. New England Journal of Medicine. 263: 478, 1960.

A case of acute pulmonary edema occurring in a healthy skier at 12,000 feet is reported with brief review of four similar but less well documented cases among mountaineers. Though the mechanism was unknown, the combined effects of anoxia, cold, and exertion were suspected as causative. This early case report stimulated further studies.

Houston, C. and Dickinson, J. Cerebral form of high altitude illness. Lancet. 785, October 18, 1975.

Twelve cases of severe altitude illness in which neurological signs and symptoms dominated the clinical picture are described. Two patients died and autopsy confirmed the presence of cerebral and pulmonary edema;

other pathology was identified in several of the patients. The importance of early descent is emphasized.

Houston, C., McFadden, M. Long-term effects of altitude on the eye. Lancet. II(8132): 49, 1979.

Houston, C. The quest to understand high altitude: a trip back in time and a look ahead. Postgraduate Medicine: 73(8):307–14, June 1983

Houston, C. Altitude illness: the dangers of the heights and how to avoid them. Postgraduate Medicine: 74(1):231–45, July 1983.
These two papers summarize the history of research in altitude illness, current concepts of cause and management, and what fields for future research appear most productive.

Hultgren H., Spickard, W., et al. High altitude pulmonary edema. Medicine. 40: 289, September 1961.
This early article reports eighteen patients with pulmonary edema at 12,000 feet in the Andes and thirteen suggestive cases occurring in mountaineers. The literature is reviewed and mechanisms examined. Fifteen of the eighteen persons studied in the Andes developed the condition after re-entry to altitude.

Hultgren, H. and Grover, R. Circulatory adaptation to high altitude. Annual Review of Medicine. 10: 119-152, 1968.

Hultgren, H., Grover, R., et al. Abnormal circulatory responses to high altitude in subjects with a previous history of high altitude pulmonary edema. Circulation. XLIV: 759, 1971.
Five men with history of HAPE showed normal pulmonary dynamics and artery pressure at sea level but a much higher than average pulmonary artery pressure and impaired oxygen transfer during a day or two at 3100 m. (10,150 feet). Suggests that interstitial edema may have begun.

Hurtado, A. Physiological and pathological aspects of life at altitude. Lima, Rimac, 1937. (Privately translated from the Spanish by Houston.)
A dissertation delivered to the Faculty of Medicine, Lima describing adaptation to altitude and containing five detailed case reports of maladaptation. Describes myoglobin and its function as well as the first general review of the signs and symptoms and pathophysiology of altitude sickness.

Hurtado, A. Some clinical aspects of life at high altitudes. Annals of Internal Medicine. 53: 247, 1960.

Hyers, T., Scoggin, C., et al. Accentuated hypoxemia at high altitude in subjects susceptible to high-altitude pulmonary edema. Journal of Applied Physiology. 46:1: 41-46, January 1979.
Seven high altitude residents considered to be HAPE-susceptible were compared with nine low altitude, non-susceptible controls in a comprehensive study of several parameters during a twelve hour low pressure chamber stay at 13,500 feet. All HAPE-susceptibles, and none of the controls,

showed exaggerated hypoxemia, relative hypoventilation, and widening of the alveolar-arterial gradient during the altitude stay. A major contribution to understanding HAPE.

Jones, D. P. et al. Intracellular oxygen supply during hypoxia. American Journal of Physiology: 243(5):247-53. November 1982.

Jourdanet, D. De L'anemie Des Altitudes Et De L'anemie En General, Dans Ses Rapports Avec La Pression De L'atmosphere. Paris: J. B. Baillier et Fils, 1863.

Kellogg, R. Altitude acclimatization: a historical introduction emphasizing the regulation of breathing. The Physiologist. 11: 37-57, February 1966.
A delightful and scholarly summary of old and modern understanding of altitude acclimatization.

Kellogg, R. La pression barometrique: Paul Bert's hypoxia theory and its critics. Respiratory Physiology. 34: 1-8, 1978.
This is a charming, and highly readable account of the contributions made by Paul Bert and his associates to our undersanding of oxygen uptake, hypoxia, and altitude illness. Theories and criticisms prevailing in the last part of the nineteenth century are examined.

Kramar, P., and Drinkwater, B. Women on Anapurna. Physician and Sportsmedicine. 8(3):93-99, 1980.

Kramar, Piro, et al. Ocular manifestations and incidence of acute mountain sickness in women at altitude. Aviation, Space, and Environmental Medicine. 54:116-120, 1983.

Koo, K., et al. Arterial blood gases and pH during sleep in chronic obstructive lung disease. American Journal of Medicine. 58: 663-670, 1975.

Lahiri, S., and Milledge, J. S. Muscular exercise in the Himalayan high altitude residents. Proceedings of the Federation of American Societies of Experimental Biology. 25:1392-1396, 1966.

Lassen, N., Ingvar, D., et al: Brain function and blood flow. Scientific American. 239:4: 62-71, October 1978.
This is a comprehensive discussion of relationships between blood flow and brain function under various conditions. It provides important information on which future studies of hypoxia, hypocapnia, and brain function can rest.

LAVOISIER, ANTOINE-LAURENT (1743-1794)

Although best known for his studies of oxygen (and he is usually credited, erroneously, with having been the first to make it) this Parisian was a distinguished chemist, geologist and social reformer as well, and it was indeed his activity as a humanitarian and reformer which led to his execution during the reign of terror in the French Revolution. In his mid-twenties he first became interested in the properties of air, which led in 1775 to his 'discovery' of oxygen, some two years after he had received a letter from Scheele describing how to make that gas. Although Hales, Black, Priestley, and others were also studying the atmosphere, Lavoisier at first knew little of their work, although he immediately appreciated the significance of Priestley's work as soon as he learned of it. In 1782–3, following some leads opened by Cavendish and Priestley, Lavoisier showed that water was not a simple material but a combination of "inflammable air" (hydrogen) and "dephlogistigated air" (oxygen). He immediately understood the importance of the Montgolfier balloon ascents in 1783, and during the next two years made a number of hydrogen balloons which rose even better, but his interest in balloons was soon displaced by work on his monumental chemistry textbook, completed only shortly before his death on the guillotine.

Lenfant, C., and Sullivan, K. Adaptation to high altitude. New England Journal of Medicine. 284: 1298, June 10, 1971.

> A concise and careful review of the process of acclimatization. Major emphasis is placed on changes in the oxygen transport mechanisms in response to altitude hypoxia. Many references.

Lehninger, A. L. How cells transform energy. Scientific American. September 1961.

Lilienthal, J., and Riley, R. An experimental analysis in man of the oxygen pressure gradients from alveolar air to arterial blood during rest and exercise at sea level and at altitude. American Journal of Physiology. 147: 199, 1946.

Long, I. D. Sickle cell trait and aviation. Aviation, Space, and Environmental Medicine. 53(10):1021–1029. October 1982.

> This review notes in part: "Sickle cell trait is a benign genetic abnormality which has been wrongly projected as a health hazard in aviation. Conflicting reports on the relationship between this trait and flying exist in the literature . . . shows both that there is no evidence that the sickle trait is a health hazard, and that most of the literature contrary to this finding is invalid."

LOWER, RICHARD (1631–1691)

> Lower became one of the most distinguished practitioners of medicine in London and was reported to be the finest English physiologist since Harvey. He became interested in the attempts by Christopher Wren to infuse blood and medication directly into veins, and performed the first successful blood transfusion between dogs in 1665, and between humans in 1667. These studies led to extensive work in cardiopulmonary physiology and in 1669 he published definitive experiments showing that the bright red color of arterial blood was due to the oxygenation of dark red venous blood during its passage through the lungs. Thus he rounded out Harvey's work, and laid the basis for much of what would follow.

McFarland, R. Psychophysiological implications of life at altitude including the role of oxygen in the process of aging. Physiological Adaptations Desert and Mountain. Academic Press Inc., New York and London, 1972.

Maher, J. T., Jones, L. G. and Hartley, L. H. Effect of high altitude exposure on submaximal endurance capacity of men. Journal of Applied Physiology. 37:895-898, 1974.

Mahoney, B. S. and Githens, J. Sickling crises and altitude. Clinical Pediatrics. 18:7: 431-8, July 1979.
> Seventy-five black patients with sickle hemoglobinopathies and 172 of their family members were studied. Twenty percent of the 39 persons with sickle cell anemia and 28.6% of the persons with sickle hemoglobin C or sickle thalassemia had developed crises when travelling in the mountains above 6,500 feet. In 103 family members with sickle trait no significant risk was found in travelling in aircraft or at similar altitude.

Matthews, Brian. The Physiology of man at high altitudes. Proceedings of the Royal Society of London. 143:1-4, 1954.

Meehan, R. T. et al. The pathophysiology of high altitude illness. American Journal of Medicine. 73(3):395-403. September 1982.

Meerson, F. Z. Role of synthesis of nucleic acids and protein in adaptation to the external environment. Physiological Reviews. 55:1, 79-125. 1975.
> This is a masterful review of the major changes which make possible adaptation to an alien environment with special stress on cellular metabolism.

Michael C., Khoo, K., et al. Factors inducing periodic breathing in humans: a general model. Journal of Applied Physiology 53(3):644-59, 1982.

Miles, D. S. et al. Absolute and relative work capacity in women at 758, 586, and 523 torr barometric pressure. Aviation, Space and Environmental Medicine. 51(5):439-444, 1980.

Monge, C. High altitude disease. Archives of Internal Medicine. 59: 32-40, 1937.

MONTGOLFIER, ETIENNE JACQUES (1745-1799)

MONTGOLFIER, MICHAEL JOSEPH (1740-1810)
> These two brothers were members of a large and prosperous French family engaged in paper manufacture, and both were self-educated in mathematics and science. How or when they became interested in ballooning is unknown, but in 1782 they (and Lavoisier) used hydrogen to fill small balloons of paper or silk to demonstrate the principles of flight, and then turned (probably because hydrogen was scarce and difficult to produce) to hot air. They then constructed a series of increasingly large balloons using hot air and smoke from moldy hay for lift. Overnight they became world-famous and the term "montgolfier" became synonymous with balloons in general although the brothers themselves made only a few flights. After two years of intense activity both retired to other pursuits, but the science — or sport — they founded endured and spread, bringing notoriety to hundreds of others.

Moore, Lorna G. et al. The incidence of pregnancy-induced hypertension is increased among Colorado residents at high altitude. American Journal of

Obstetrics and Gynecology. 144(4):423–29. October 15, 1982.

Moore, T. The world's great mountains: not the height you think. American Alpine Journal, 1968.
A discussion of barometric pressure variations due to latitude, climate, temperature, including speculations about distance from the center of the earth to the highest summits and about variations in 'physiological altitude' at different latitudes.

Mordes, J. P., et al. High altitude pituitary-thyroid dysfunction on Mount Everest. New England Journal of Medicine. 308:1133–1138. 1983.

Morpurgo, G., et al. Sherpas living permanently at high altitude: A new pattern of adaptation. Proceedings National Academy of Science. 73:3: 747-750, March 1976.

Mortimer, E. A., Monson, R. R. et al. Reduction in mortality from coronary heart disease in men residing at high altitude. New England Journal of Medicine: 296:581-5, 1977.

Moss, G. Shock, cerebral hypoxia, and pulmonary vascular control: The centri-neurogenic etiology of the "respiratory distress syndrome." Bulletin New York Academy of Medicine, 1973.
This is the most complete report of Moss' cross-transfusion experiments and seems to prove clearly that cerebral hypoxia alone (in dogs) can cause pulmonary edema even when the lungs and body are normoxic.

Murray, R.H.S., Shropshire, S. and Thompson, L. Attempted acclimatization by vigorous exercise during periodic exposure to simulated altitude. Journal of Sports Medicine and Physical Fitness. 3:135–142, 1968.

NAFIS, IBN-AL (1208–1288 approx.)
Only in the last thirty years has the work of this great Egyptian physician been rediscovered, and even today his contributions to medicine are inadequately recognized. In his early thirties he planned a comprehensive 300 volume medical text of which 80 volumes were published. Primarily a surgeon, he defined three stages for each operation: diagnosis during which a patient entrusts the surgeon with his life; the operation; and finally postoperative care. His most extraordinary contribution was his description of the pulmonary circulation in 1242, centuries before Servetus, Colombo, and Harvey. He wrote *"This is the right cavity of the two cavities of the heart. When the blood in this cavity has become thin, it must be transferred into the left cavity, where the pneuma is generated. But there is no passage between these two cavities, the substance of the heart there being impermeable. It neither contains a visible passage, as some people have thought, nor does it contain an invisible passage which would permit the passage of blood, as Galen thought. The pores of the heart there are compact and the substance of the heart is thick. It must, therefore, be that when the blood has become thin, it is passed into the arterial vein (pulmonary artery) to the lung, in order to be dispersed inside the substance of the lung, and to mix with the air. The finest parts of the blood*

are then strained, passing into the venous artery (pulmonary vein) reaching the left of the two cavities of the heart, after mixing with the air and becoming fit for the generation of pneuma . . ." It is said that his religion and compassion prevented him from dissection, which might have led him to an accurate definition of the total circulation. How widely known his work was during his lifetime is unknown, and whether or not reports of his work reached and influenced his successors is hotly debated.

Nair, C. S., Gopinathan, P. M. and Dasgupta, A. Effect of mountaineering on the cardio-pulmonary response to submaximal exercise of women mountaineers. Indian Journal of Medical Research. 64(7):1081-1085, 1976.

PARACELSUS, THEOPHRASTUS (1493-1541)
The real name for this extraordinary man was von Hohenheim. Where or even whether he took formal medical training is unknown, but he did serve as a military surgeon, and he understood that most diseases were of external origin, describing silicosis and tuberculosis as occupational diseases, and recognizing for the first time that syphilis could be congenital. He understood and used the anesthetic and sedative qualities of certain volatile liquids similar to ether, and used mercury and other chemicals as medications. He was a great and pioneering physician, an able chemist, but uncompromisingly destructive toward tradition.

Pease, A. Mountain climbing in antiquity. Appalachia. 33: 289-298, June 1961.

Perkins, J. Introduction: Handbook of Physiology: Respiration. Volume 1, pp. 1-62. American Physiological Society, 1964.
A review of the evolution of knowledge in atmospherics, gas laws, respiration and ventilatory control from Aristotle to modern times. Many old illustrations and 200 references.

Perutz, M. Hemoglobin structure and respiratory transport. Scientific American. 239: 92-122, December 1979.

Phillipson, E. Regulation of breathing during sleep. American Review Respiratory Disease. 115: 217-224, 1977.

PRIESTLEY, JOSEPH (1733-1804)
Since he was educated for the ministry it is not surprising that Priestley's initial writings were theological discussions of the nature of matter. They aroused great controversy but throughout all of his work runs a vein of religious conviction which occasionally confuses or obscures his great original contributions. He began to study gases at the age of thirty-seven and became one of the outstanding gas chemists of the world, making many new gases such as ammonia and sulfur and nitrogen dioxides, and of course his work on oxygen. He seems to have cultivated the role of poor scientist in contrast to Lavoisier with whom his competitive rivalry sharpened with time. In 1770 he began publication of a series of six important books on gases which were widely studied and influential and which

show strong influence of Stephen Hales. Priestley's major clash with Lavoisier came over the latter's demonstration of the composition of water and claim for priority in discovering oxygen. Priestley clung to the phologiston theory even after his voluntary exile to Pennsylvania because of his support of the French Revolution, but his contribution to our knowledge of gases was enormous.

Pugh, G. Physiological and medical aspects of the Himalayan scientific and mountaineering expedition, 1960–61. British Medical Journal. 2: 621, September 8, 1962.
  Summary of observations made during five months at 19,000 feet including basal metabolism, muscular exercise, respiratory regulation, blood volume, hemoglobin, and renal function. The most complete set of studies of physiological changes during prolonged residence at great heights.

Ravenhill, T. Some experiences of mountain sickness in the Andes. Journal of Tropical Medicine and Hygiene. 20: 313, October 15, 1913.
  This appears to be the first definite description of acute mountain sickness, pulmonary edema, and cerebral edema due to altitude. The author describes his personal observations of numerous cases, and his puzzlement that some altitude residents do, while others do not, become ill on reascent to altitude after a brief stay at sea level. No references; a classic paper.

Reed, D. and Kellogg, R. Changes in respiratory response to CO_2 during natural sleep at sea level and at altitude. Journal Applied Physiology. 13: 325-330, 1958.

Reinhard, Johan. High altitude archaeology and Andean mountain gods. American Alpine Journal, 25, 54–67, 1983.
  A brief but fascinating description of what the Incas built, and how they used their structures, some as high as 22,000 feet, more than 400 years ago. Few articles on this subject are available in English, and they make us wonder whether the Incas were able to acclimatize more completely to higher elevations than we can today.

Reite, M., et al. Sleep physiology at high altitude. Electroencephalography and Clinical Neurophysiology. 38: 463-471, 1975.

Rennie, D., and Morrissey, J. Retinal changes in Himalayan climbers. Archives of Ophthalmology. 93: 395-400, 1975.

Rennie, B. D. See Nuptse and die. Lancet, 2:1177–9, 1976.

Robertson, J. D. The membrane of the living cell. Scientific American. April 1962.

Roy, S. Circulatory and ventilatory effects of high altitude acclimatization and deacclimatization of Indian soldiers—a prospective study 1964-1972. General Printing Company, Delhi, undated.
  A massive study of adaptations and mal-adaptations to altitude experienced during and after the Indian conflict with China. Very large amounts of data were collected and attempts made to analyze factors contributing

to health or illness on exposure to altitude. The report is marred by typographical errors in tables and in text.

Ryn, Zdzislaw. Nervous system and altitude syndrome of high altitude asthenia. Acta Medica Polska. 22:2-28. 1979.

This is a shortened version of a large manuscript describing the emotional and neurological condition of 40 Polish climbers before, during and after several expeditions to very high altitude. Though a little hard to follow, and though the effects of altitude were complicated by other severe privations, Ryn concluded that some damage does remain after exposure to extreme heights. All of the individuals had altitude illness.

SAUSSURE, HORACE BENEDICT DE (1740-1799)

Although de Saussure is best known for his interest in Mont Blanc, his degree in philosophy from Geneva was in physics, and he was a distinguished mathematician, botanist and geologist as well. He made studies of the transmission of heat and cold and electricity and magnetism on Mont Blanc as well as observing his own pulse and respirations on all his mountain ascents. His extensive studies of geology, meteorology and physiology were published in his four volume work *"Voyages Dans Les Alpes,"* a collectors' item until reprinted recently. In 1760 he made his first visit to Chamonix and became passionately interested in Mont Blanc, and the reward which he offered to the person who would reach the summit first undoubtedly hastened the ascent.

SCHEELE, CARL WILHELM (1742-1786)

Born, educated, and living his entire life in Sweden, Scheele was primarily a pharmacist and chemist whose ingenuity, curiosity, and persistence made him one of the most distinguished scientists of his time. While still under twenty he challenged the phlogiston theory and undertook a series of experiments on plants and animals which convinced him that life was supported by some element in air which was converted in the animal to a gas which would not support life. Although he took voluminous notes he was slow to publish, and his notebooks have only recently been deciphered. On September 30, 1774 he wrote to thank Lavoisier for one of the latter's books and in his letter gave detailed instructions how to prepare oxygen, together with basic information on its chemical and physiological properties—the earliest known written description of oxygen. Scheele knew that some English scientist was following similar studies, and sent to the printer in December 1775 a manuscript in which he described the preparation of oxygen which would support combustion, and of nitrogen which would not. Publication was delayed for various reasons, and by the time his book appeared in July 1777, others had published, and credit for Scheele's discoveries went to them. He did important work in both organic and inorganic chemistry, but is almost unknown for his most important contribution.

SCHEUCHZER, JOHANN JAKOB (1672-1733)

Born in Switzerland and dedicated to the natural sciences, he practiced medicine, studied mathematics, founded the science of paleontology, and from 1700 onward made many excursions throughout the Alps studying geology, botany and fossils. He wrote almost 300 books on the history and natural history of Switzerland. His detailed reports of dragons in the Alps, inspired undoubtedly by his interest in fossils, are very interesting but less important than most of his other accomplishments.

Schneider, E. Physiological effects of altitude. Physiological Reviews. 1: 631, 1921.
    A comprehensive summary of the acute and chronic effects of altitude on man with detailed discussion of the various contemporary theories of etiology. The author notes signs and symptoms of nausea, vomiting, headache, but makes no mention of pulmonary or cerebral edema. One hundred and four references.

Schoene, R. B. Control of ventilation in climbers to extreme altitude. Journal of Applied Physiology. 53:886–890. 1982.

Schumacher, G. and Petajan, J. High altitude stress and retinal hemorrhages: Relation to vascular headache mechanisms. Archives of Environmental Health. 30: 217-221, 1975.

SERVETUS, MICHAEL (1511–1553)
    Servetus was born and first educated in philosophy in Spain, where his religious studies raised in him doubts about the Holy Trinity which made him a fugitive and later led to his execution. He went to France and studied law, where he published his most heretical work for which he was most criticized. He became a proofreader for a publisher, and this aroused interest in medicine which he studied in Paris, later practicing medicine. His most important book was a theological text in which he described the circulation of the blood from the heart through the pulmonary artery to the lungs and back to the heart. Servetus understood that some "vital spirit" entered the lungs, passed into the blood, and was carried back to the heart and throughout the body. He was on the threshold of comprehending the circulation of the blood, but his text was primarily a religious one, and all but three copies were destroyed when he was burned at the stake for heresy, seventy-five years before Harvey's announcement. Thus Servetus, like Colombo and Ibn-al-Nafis, made basic contributions to Harvey of which few today are aware.

Sheldon, M. I. and Green, J. F. Evidence for CO_2 chemosensitivity: effects on ventilation. Journal of Applied Physiology. 52:1192–1197. 1982.

Shields, J. L. et al. Effects of altitude acclimatization on pulmonary function in women. Journal of Applied Physiology. 25:606–609, 1968.

Singh, I., Kapila, C., et al. High altitude pulmonary edema. Lancet. 229–34, January 30, 1965.
    Three hundred thirty-two Indian soldiers developed pulmonary edema at altitudes above 11,000 feet following rapid ascent. The condition occurred in 15.5% of persons reaching altitude for the first time, and in 13.0% of

those returning after a stay at low altitude. Pulmonary edema, cerebral edema and acute mountain sickness are suggested to be various reactions to the same underlying physiologic response to hypoxia, and mechanisms are proposed. Treatment with aminophylline, atropine, morphine and digoxin is discussed. Failure of oxygen to relieve hemoglobin desaturation is noted.

Singh, I., Khanna, P., et al. Acute mountain sickness. New England Journal of Medicine. 280: 175-84, 1969.
Clinical observations on 1,925 individuals with various forms of acute mountain sickness in the Himalayan Sino-Indian war. Relationships between acute mountain sickness, cerebral and pulmonary edema and antidiuresis are discussed. Various treatments are evaluated. The largest series thus far collected.

Spalter, H. and Bruce, G. Ocular changes in pulmonary insufficiency. Transactions of American Academy of Ophthalmology and Otolaryngology. 661-676, 1964.
Changes in the ocular fundi in patients with hypoxia due to chronic pulmonary disease are described. The retinopathy (which included increased diameter and tortuosity of vessels, papilledema and hemorrhages) was attributed to carbon dioxide retention and resulting acidosis. Literature is reviewed and photographs presented.

STAHL, GEORG ERNST (1660-1734)
Allegedly intolerant and narrow-minded, and undoubtedly controversial, Stahl was an outstanding and active physician and academician, a chemist, and a natural philosopher. He devoted much of his attention to distinguishing between the living and the non-living and the *anima* which separates them. He preached preventive medicine and felt that doctors had to deal with the entire body and mind rather than individual organs. Strongly influenced by Becher, Stahl apparently originated the name "phlogiston" to define combustibility. Although he recognized that phlogiston and air were related, he believed that phlogiston was an element rather than a quality, and considered carbon as almost pure phlogiston. Although the phlogiston theory was of course wrong, it stimulated much of the essential study which was to follow in the next century.

Staub, N. "State of the art review." Pathogenesis of pulmonary edema. American Review of Respiratory Disease. 109: 358, 1974.
A careful review of the development and pathology of various types of interstitial and alveolar edema, with extensive references and illustrations of the various causes, including hypoxia.

Stiles, Merritt H. The Mexico City Olympic games. Minnesota Medicine. 9 January 1971.

Sutton, J. R., Houston, C., et al. Effect of acetazolamide on hypoxemia during sleep at high altitude. New England Journal of Medicine. 301: 1329-31, 1979.

Sutton, J. R., Gray, G. W. et al. Effects of duration at altitude and acetazolamide on ventilation and oxygenation during sleep at altitude. Sleep 3: 455–464, 1980.

Sutton, John R. Hormonal response to altitude. In press. 1983.

Sutton, J. R., and Jones, N. L. Exercise at altitude. Annual Review of Physiology. 45:427–37, 1983.

Urrie, T. T. et al. Spironolactone and acute mountain sickness. Medical Journal of Australia, July 31, 1976.

Viault, F. Increase in circulating red blood cells. Comptes Rendues Academy of Science, Paris. 111, 917, 1890.

Viswanathan, R., Jain, S., et al. Pulmonary edema at high altitude. American Review of Respiratory Disease. 100: 342, 1969.
In a series of three papers the authors examine the production of edema in animals, the clinical and hemodynamic features, and the pathogenesis, and conclude that the condition is due to an abnormal hypoxic response in susceptible individuals who manifest a genetically determined condition by greater than normal pre-capillary vascular resistance in lungs, leading to pulmonary artery hypertension. The mechanism whereby edema results is not explained.

Vogel, J., Hartley, L., et al. Cardiac output during exercise in altitude natives at sea level and high altitude. Journal of Applied Physiology. 36: 173-176, 1974.

Wagner, Jeamis. Physiological adjustments of women to prolonged work during acute hypoxia. Journal of Applied Physiology. 49(3):367-373, 1980.

Ward, Michael. Exercise edema and mountain sickness. A field investigation. Alpine Journal (London) 85(129) 168–175. 1980.

Ward, M. Deterioration and effects of severe hypoxia on brain. Proceedings of the Royal Society. 143: 40, 1954.

Way, A. Exercise capacity of high altitude Peruvian Quechua Indians migrant to low altitude. Human Biology. 48(1): 175-191, February 1976.

West, J. B. State of the art; ventilation-perfusion relationships. American Review of Respiratory Disease. 116(5): 919-944, 1977.

West, J. B. Weight loss in chronic obstructive lung disease. Chest. 83:842, June 1983.

West, J. B. et al. Pulmonary gas exchange on the summit of Mt. Everest. Journal of Applied Physiology. In press.

West, J. B. Climbing Mt. Everest without oxygen: an analysis of maximal exer-exercise during extreme hypoxia. Respiration Physiology. 52:265-269. 1983.
In this new paper some projections and data are combined to show under what conditions a man can reach the top of Everest, and be able to go even higher — perhaps — breathing only ambient air. Does it remind us of the engineers' statement that a bumble bee cannot fly?

Woodworth, J. Brief notes and bibliography of the history of mountain medicine. Appalachia. June 1976.

   This brief paper has a short but excellent bibliography of unusual old studies.

APPENDIX ONE
ALTITUDE AND BAROMETRIC PRESSURE

When Perier made his tremendous discovery that atmospheric pressure decreased the higher his party climbed on the Puy-de-Dome he was measuring the true atmospheric pressure as shown by his mercury barometer, but this was not necessarily an indicator of the height above sea level, which at that time could not be measured. Today however we can make extremely accurate measurements, both of atmospheric pressure and of vertical elevation, which complicates and confuses the reporting of altitude studies. But it's not really as difficult as it seems.

By triangulation, surveyors can measure the vertical distance in feet or meters between mean sea level (average between tides) and the top of a mountain, and we call that its altitude or height above sea level. This is the figure shown on most maps for most mountains.

Atmospheric pressure has been measured very accurately on many mountains and in aircraft and balloons high in the atmosphere, and in very many parts of the world. From these measurements a "standard atmosphere" curve has been drawn which relates vertical distance above sea level to atmospheric pressure under "standard conditions."

However, on top of a mountain, as anywhere else, atmospheric pressure varies with temperature, weather, distance from the equator, and other factors. For example, on an 18,000 foot summit atmospheric pressure might vary from 405 torr to 370 torr depending on the temperature, season of the year, and latitude. As the atmospheric pressure varied, so of course would the partial pressure of oxygen since the composition of air is extraordinarily constant and unaffected by altitude, temperature or weather. Oxygen makes up 20.93% of air everywhere, and this percentage of the measured atmospheric pressure tells us the partial pressure of oxygen we breathe. So long as we think of altitude in terms of millimeters of mercury or torr of pressure we are accurately assessing the "physiological altitude" regardless of the number of linear feet or meters above sea level, as Bruce Dill has stated so succinctly. But we need a mercury barometer or we must correct an aircraft altimeter.

Altimeters used by climbers and in aircraft are generally of the aneroid type. In these the altitude is measured by changes in the atmospheric pressure exerted on a small sealed container whose expansion as pressure decreases moves a lever which moves hands indicating the altitude in feet or meters. However, the scale on aneroid barometers and altimeters is derived from the standard pressure/altitude curve, and applies only under "standard conditions." The altimeter may show the actual linear feet of elevation, but only under specific conditions and in certain places, and unless corrected it does not (usually) give "physiological altitude." An added complication comes from the fact that the layer of air surrounding the earth is not as thick over the poles as over the equator, and corrections for latitude as well as temperature must be made for reading aneroid barometers. Terris Moore has pointed out that a mountain 29,000 feet above sea level in linear altitude would have a "physiological altitude" equivalent to that of a 26,730 foot summit at 75 degrees north latitude in January, but that of a 30,620 foot summit at 30 degrees north latitude in July. He has suggested that the "physiological altitude" on Mount McKinley is considerably higher, and on Mount Everest considerably lower than their triangulated height if one measures it as pressure derived from applying the elevation to the standard atmospheric pressure/altitude curve.

Obviously this concerns climbers and pilots who measure their height with altimeters, but should not in any way disturb the conscientious physiologist who should think of altitude only in terms of millimeters of mercury or torr of atmospheric pressure. For an excellent discussion of this effect see: West, John B., Lahiri, S. et al. Barometric pressures at extreme altitudes on Mt. Everest: physiological significance. Journal of Applied Physiology. 54:1166–1194. 1983.

APPENDIX TWO
WHO SHOULD NOT GO HIGH?

In the parts of the world which might be described as 'over-developed' there is growing interest in maintenance of good health and avoidance of disease, inadequate though both seem in actual practice! And as more and more people take to work and play in mountainous areas, doctors are more often being asked "How high can I go? Is it safe for me to go skiing (or climbing – or trekking)?" Some who would never have thought of a trek to Everest Base Camp a few years ago, now consider it seriously. But not every doctor can appropriately answer such questions. In fact, health and risk factors are so much an individual matter that for many patients only approximate answers can be given.

But we as physicians owe it to our patients to give informed answers, and here I will outline how I myself respond to the many people, both strangers and friends, who ask whether or not they can go to a moderate altitude. The comments which follow are for persons with some kind of health problem who want to go to a mountain resort at 8–10,000 feet altitude; those considering a major climb or even a Himalayan trek above 12–14,000 feet need more detailed evaluation.

Quite properly doctors tend to be conservative when advising persons under their care about dangers, but I suggest that when we do talk with patients about going to the mountains we should be sure we are protecting them and not ourselves. A relaxing vacation in the mountains may do more than diet or medication for many, and may decrease some risks due to life style.

Obviously each patient is an individual and differs from other "cases", similar though they may seem. But in general the person who is reasonably active at sea level can go to 8–9,000 feet without much risk, providing he or she is informed about altitude, and is willing to limit activity for a few days. Knowing about altitude means knowing when to call for help or go down. . . .

Only a few problems can be considered "absolute" contraindications to going to moderate altitude (See Table) but even those should be tempered with individual considerations. Just as other frontiers of human performance are being pushed back, so do we find people climbing and skiing despite disabilities which a few years ago would have been thought totally incapacitating. I refer not so much to skeletal problems, where guts and patience overcome so many barriers, but to those involving heart and lungs which doctors often tend to regard too conservatively.

Although what little hard data is available indicates that angina is not made worse at moderate altitude, perhaps because hypoxia is such a powerful coronary vaso-dilator, it would be inadvisable for one with frequent angina or considerable damage to coronary blood vessels to go to altitude. A recent infarction ("heart attack"), or several old ones, is a contra-indication, except when recovery has been complete for several years. The patient with heart failure, unless well-controlled for some time, will be at greater risk, as may be one with severe hypertension which is poorly controlled at sea level.

Persons with recurrent clotting or bleeding problems may be taking unnecessary risks and should probably not go high; those taking anticoagulants should be carefully evaluated and warned about other drugs such as aspirin. Blacks with sickling disease should not go high unless they have already found that they can do so without trouble.

The unfortunates who have had "many" (i.e. four or more) episodes of altitude pulmonary or brain edema should probably take up low altitude sports — or if addicted to mountains, at least allow extra time to acclimatize and be certain to go down at the first sign of trouble because such susceptibles are likely to be affected again and again.

Patients so crippled with lung disease that they are short of breath on even mild exertion at sea level will be worse at altitude; advanced chronic pulmonary insufficiency is a strong contra-indication. Asthma, on the other hand, even when severe or chronic, may be improved.

The rare person with congenital or acquired absence of a pulmonary artery is likely to develop pulmonary edema at altitude (or when ill with a disease causing lack of oxygen), but one who has lost part of one lung, or even a whole lung may not be. A "floppy mitral valve" carries an unknown risk at altitude and we need more information, because such people can go into left-sided heart failure with pulmonary edema rather easily.

Arrhythmias may be made worse: fibrillation (totally irregular heartbeat) if well controlled by digitalis or other medication is not likely to be made worse, whereas frequent premature or extra beats, or other abnormal rhythms may be troublesome and even dangerous at altitude.

With so many open heart operations being done, we should be able to advise such patients with confidence, but I know of no data on which to take a position. A patient with a complete recovery three months after heart surgery would seem a reasonably safe risk for careful activity at moderate altitude.

Persons who have recently had chest or abdominal surgery within a week or ten days probably should delay their trip to altitude because of the possible damage caused by expanding gas, not because of hypoxia. Similarly, persons with severe recurrent ear or nasal sinus problems are likely to have difficulty with pressure changes.

I have commented elsewhere on risks in pregnancy and for the very young or very old. Persons with diabetes, thyroid, adrenal or pituitary glandular disorders, the very obsese or the very thin must be evaluated on an individual basis. Only a few diseases are more prevalent among altitude residents than at sea level, and in general those who live high tend to be healthier! Mountain travel in the less developed world carries risks other than those due to altitude — and these have to be considered carefully. For example, colitis, chronic peptic ulcer, hemorrhoids and ano-rectal or other gastro-intestinal problems may be dangerously worsened by the diarrheas so common in the third world. Such problems are not related to altitude.

The effects of medication may be altered by altitude, but we know very little about this. Anti-hypertensive dosage may need to be changed. Contraceptive tablets should be avoided above 12–13,000 feet, because the tendency for blood to clot is increased; they are probably not an added risk below 10,000 feet. Alcohol and altitude are additive: one drink does the work of two — or three — or four. Sedatives and tranquillizers are also more powerful and have led (at great altitude) to confusion, irrational or even fatal acts. Coffee and tea may aggravate the sleeping problems common above 8-10,000 feet.

From the preceding rough guide, three things should be emphasized:

There is not a great wealth of experience on which to evaluate risk for patients with specific diseases who go to altitude.

Patients should be well informed about altitude and the illnesses it may cause or worsen, and should be prepared to get help or to go down when warnings appear.

Doctors should base advice on what is best for the patient, not to protect themselves; if you don't know, find some one who does. The doctor who is thoroughly familiar with his patient is better able to judge risk than the specialist consultant.

WHO SHOULD NOT GO HIGH
Table One

Major Contra-indications
    Repeated episodes of pulmonary or brain edema
    Severe or frequent angina (heart pain)
    Severe arteriosclerosis of heart blood vessels
    Severe uncontrolled high blood pressure
    Congestive heart failure
    Severe, advanced, chronic lung disease
    History of sickle cell crisis
    Recurrent episodes of bleeding or clotting
    Congenital or acquired absence of pulmonary artery

Minor Contra-indications
    Mild, controllable angina
    Poorly controlled hypertension
    Mild to moderate arteriosclerosis
    History of well controlled congestive failure
    Various heart valve disorders
    Certain recurrent irregularities of rhythm
    Severe obesity and/or alveolar hypo-ventilation
    Poorly controlled endocrine or hormone disorders
    Sickle cell trait and sickle cell anemia

To be Avoided at Altitude
    Contraceptive tablets
    Sedatives and Tranquillizers
    Excess alcohol, stimulants, caffeine
    All addictive or habituating drugs

INDEX

Note: The appendices and bibliography have not been included in the indexing.